CW00419300

The Golden Book of
COOKING

The Golden Book of
COOKING

APPLE

First published in the UK in 2011 by
Apple Press
7 Greenland Street
London NW1 0ND
United Kingdom
www.apple-press.com

The Golden Book of Cooking
was created and produced by McRae Books Srl
McRae Books is an imprint of McRae Publishing Ltd, London
info@mcraebooks.com, mcraepublishing.co.uk

Project Director Anne McRae
Art Director Marco Nardi
Photography Brent Parker Jones (R&R Photostudio)
Texts Rachael Lane, Carla Bardi
Editing Carla Bardi, Anne McRae
Food Styling Rachael Lane
Stylist Lee Blaylock
Food Preparation Rebeca Quinn, Michelle Finn
Layouts Aurora Granata
Pre-press Filippo Delle Monache

ISBN 978-1-84543-418-2

Printed and bound in China

NOTE TO OUR READERS
Eating eggs or egg whites that are not completely cooked poses the possibility of salmonella
food poisoning. The risk is greater for pregnant women, the elderly, the very young,
and persons with impaired immune systems. If you are concerned about salmonella,
you can use reconstituted powdered egg whites or pasteurized eggs.

The level of difficulty for each recipe is given on a scale from
1 (easy) to 3 (complicated).

CONTENTS

INTRODUCTION

INTRODUCTION

The Golden Book of Cooking is a one-stop compendium of some of the best-loved and most interesting dishes from cuisines around the world. Our goal was to find the best version of each recipe and make it foolproof and perfect every time. The authors have adapted classic recipes, often adding new twists or simply making them streamlined and practical for busy home cooks. They have also developed new recipes based on or freely inspired by old favorites.

This has led to an exciting range of recipes in each chapter. For example, in the first Soups section you will find firm favorites like Leek and potato soup, Clam chowder, and Butternut squash soup, alongside a perfect Minestrone, two Tuscan bread soups, French onion soup, Goulash, Tom kha gai (Thai chicken soup), Laksa, and a simple, Japanese-inspired Fennel miso, among others. Each recipe is accompanied by a stunning photograph, showing you exactly how the finished dish will look. It's a modern, global vision, providing you with more than 280 recipes to create the delicious food we enjoy today, at home, in your own kitchen.

To ensure success every time, we have also provided 60 "cooking lessons" in the form of step-by-step photography sequences showing you exactly how to carry out a wide selection of basic cooking techniques, as well as how to execute the key steps in some of the more challenging recipes.

Getting the most out of this book:

All the recipes have been developed and edited in the same way to create simple, logical work flows. Before you begin to cook, always read the recipe through, making sure you have all the ingredients and equipment. Beneath the ingredients list on each page you will find a summary of how many people the recipe will serve, the time it will take you to prepare and cook the dish, and a guide to the level of difficulty. Level of difficulty ranges from 1 (simple), to 2 (medium), and 3 (challenging). Most recipes fall into the first and second categories.

Measurements: We have given all measurements in both the imperial and metric systems. Always follow either one or the other for each recipe as conversions may not always be exact. In converting pounds and ounces to metrics we have preferred in most cases to round them off, so that $1^1/2$ pounds has become 750 g, and so on. This works well for most recipes; in more scientific areas, such as baking, we have been more precise. You should also take extra care with these recipes, weighing and measuring ingredients accurately as even the smallest difference can lead to disaster!

Teaspoon and tablespoon measures should be level unless otherwise specified. When we refer to tablespoons, we mean a standard $1/2$ ounce (15 g) (dry weight) spoon.

Ingredients: The ingredients appear in each list according to the order of use in the recipe. It goes without saying that you should always choose the freshest and best ingredients for optimum results. Buy the best brands from reliable sources. Check use-by dates regularly and discard any food that is stale or has been incorrectly stored. Cooking and salad oils should always be as fresh as possible otherwise they will taint dishes and spoil them.

Wash all ingredients that will be eaten raw and rinse eggs before use (salmonella is more likely to be present on the shell than inside). Be aware that eating raw eggs does expose you to the (very limited) danger of contracting salmonella.

Equipment: Almost all the recipes in this book can be made with the equipment to be found in any reasonably well-stocked home kitchen. On the few occasions where we have suggested using specialist equipment, we have always given an everyday utensil that can be used instead. We have assumed that most people will have a food processor, blender, or electric mixer of some kind for grinding, chopping, mixing, and beating.

Getting down to it: Always weigh, measure, and prepare all the ingredients for each recipe before you begin the preparation. This may seem tedious, but it will streamline the process and allow you to focus on techniques, doneness cues, and any problems that might arise; it will make cooking less stressful and the end results will be better. You will also know at the beginning that you actually have all the ingredients!

Finishing up: Presentation of food is so important. Take the time to garnish and decorate your dishes, although do keep it simple. An artfully arranged sprig of flat-leaf parsley or a few cilantro leaves strewn across the dish is often enough. Keep color and flavor in mind when garnishing; fresh green parsley will look fabulous on an orange pumpkin soup while it will be invisible on a green salad. Remember too that certain taste combinations always work: mint and peas; raspberries and chocolate; orange and chocolate; apples and blue cheese; pineapple and pork; the list is endless. Look online and think about it when you cook.

SOUPS

FENNEL MISO

Heat the oil in a large soup pot over medium heat. Add the fennel, carrot, leeks, and potatoes and sauté until the vegetables are softened, 8–10 minutes. • Stir in the ginger, garlic, chiles, and fennel seeds. Season with salt and sauté over low heat for 10 minutes more. • Dissolve the miso in $1/2$ cup (125 ml) of the boiling water. Stir the miso mixture and remaining water into the soup. Simmer until the potatoes are tender, 15–20 minutes. • Add the watercress, snow peas, and lemon juice. Simmer for 3 minutes more. • Garnish with the extra watercress and serve hot.

2	tablespoons vegetable oil
1	pound (500 g) fennel bulbs, cut into wedges and finely sliced
1	carrot, cut into very thin strips
	Whites of 2 leeks, cut into $1/2$-inch (1-cm) rounds
2	potatoes, peeled and diced
1	(1-inch/2.5-cm) piece fresh ginger, peeled and finely chopped
1	clove garlic, finely chopped
$1/2$	small fresh green chile, seeded and finely chopped
1	small fresh red chile, seeded and finely chopped
1	teaspoon fennel seeds
	Salt
3	tablespoons barley miso
6	cups (1.5 liters) water, boiling
$1^1/2$	cups (150 g) watercress, coarsely chopped + extra leaves to garnish
5	snow peas (mangetout), halved
1	tablespoon freshly squeezed lemon juice

■ ■ ■ Miso, also known as bean paste, is a traditional Japanese seasoning made by fermenting soya bean paste with rice, barley, or rye. It is used for making miso soup, as well as in salad dressings, braised dishes, and in many sauces and pickles. It is readily available at Asian food stores or in the Asian foods section of well-stocked supermarkets.

Serves: 4–6
Preparation: 20 minutes
Cooking: 45 minutes
Level: 1

PAPPA AL POMODORO (TUSCAN BREAD SOUP)

Heat the oil in a large soup pot over low heat. Add the garlic and basil and sauté for 2 minutes. • Add the bread and cook over medium heat, stirring constantly, for 2 minutes. Add the tomatoes and 1 cup (250 ml) of the water. Simmer for 15 minutes, stirring often. • Season with salt and pepper and add more water if required. Traditionally, this soup is quite thick (like porridge); add more water to reach the desired consistency. How much water you need to add will also depend on how juicy the tomatoes are. • Drizzle with the extra oil, garnish with the extra basil, and serve hot.

5   tablespoons extra-virgin olive oil + extra to serve

3   cloves garlic, finely chopped

10   leaves fresh basil, torn + extra to garnish

14   ounces (400 g) firm-textured day-old white or brown bread, diced

2   pounds (1 kg) tomatoes, peeled, seeded, and finely chopped

1¼   cups (300 ml) water + extra as required

Salt and freshly ground black pepper

Serves: 4
Preparation: 15 minutes
Cooking: 20 minutes
Level: 1

■ ■ ■ *This delicious thick soup comes from Tuscany, where yesterday's bread is never wasted. For a spicy version, add a crumbled dry chile at the end of the cooking time. You can also make this soup using canned tomatoes; substitute the fresh tomatoes with 4 cups (800 g) canned tomatoes, with juice.*

LEEK, POTATO, AND PEARL BARLEY SOUP

Combine the leeks and vegetable stock in a large soup pot over medium heat. Bring to a boil and simmer for 10 minutes. • Add the potatoes and simmer for 15 minutes. • Add the barley, stirring constantly, and simmer until the barley is tender, about 45 minutes. • Stir in the butter. Sprinkle with the Parmesan, dust with the nutmeg, and garnish with the parsley. • Serve hot.

3   leeks, white parts only, finely chopped

8   cups (2 liters) Vegetable Stock (see page 94)

1   pound (500 g) potatoes, peeled and diced

½   cup (100 g) pearl barley

2   tablespoons butter

4   tablespoons freshly grated Parmesan cheese

¼   teaspoon freshly grated nutmeg

1   tablespoon finely chopped fresh parsley

Serves: 6
Preparation: 25 minutes
Cooking: 1 hour 10 minutes
Level: 1

CLAM CHOWDER

If using fresh clams, place them in a large pot with the water and 1 teaspoon of butter. Simmer until they have opened up, 8–10 minutes. • Strain the clams through a large sieve into a large bowl. Reserve the stock. Remove the clam meat from the shells. Discard any unopened shells. • Chop the larger clams and leave the small ones whole. • If using canned clams, drain the juices and add to the clam juice. • If using frozen clams, defrost them first. • Melt the butter in a large soup pot over medium heat. Add the onion, celery, garlic, and $1/2$ teaspoon salt and sauté over medium heat until softened, 3–4 minutes. • Mix in the flour and stir in the clam stock or juice and the wine. Add the potatoes, bay leaf, and allspice berries. Simmer until the potatoes are tender, about 10 minutes. • Add the corn and simmer for 5 minutes. • Remove from the heat and discard the bay leaf and allspice berries. Stir in the cream and clams. Simmer very gently for 2–3 minutes, but do not boil. Season with salt and pepper. • Serve hot.

■ ■ ■ *Allspice berries are the unripe berries of a small West Indian tree. They have a lovely flavor that brings to mind a combination of cloves, cinnamon, and nutmeg. If preferred, substitute with $1/2$ teaspoon of ground allspice or a tiny pinch each of ground cloves, cinnamon, nutmeg, and black pepper.*

28

3	pounds (1.5 kg) fresh clams, in shell or 1 (10-ounce/300-g) can clams or 12 ounces (350 g) frozen clam meat
$1^{1}/4$	cups (300 ml) water or bottled clam juice, if using canned clams
$1/4$	cup (60 g) butter
1	onion, finely chopped
1	stalk celery, finely chopped
2	cloves garlic, finely chopped
	Salt
2	tablespoons all-purpose (plain) flour
$2/3$	cup (150 ml) dry white wine
3	medium potatoes, peeled and diced
1	bay leaf
2	allspice berries
1	cup (150 g) frozen corn (sweetcorn)
$1^{1}/2$	cups (375 ml) heavy (double) cream
	Freshly ground black pepper

Serves: 4–6
Preparation: 30 minutes
Cooking: 30 minutes
Level: 2

LEEK AND POTATO SOUP

Heat the butter in a large soup pot over medium heat. Add the leeks, onion, garlic, carrot, celery, and parsley and sauté until the vegetables are almost tender, 10–15 minutes. • Add the potatoes and water. Season with salt and pepper. Simmer over medium heat until the potatoes are tender, about 15 minutes. • Remove the pan from the heat. Blend with a handheld blender until smooth. Return the pan to the heat and reheat gently. • Serve hot.

30

¼ cup (60 g) butter
6 leeks, trimmed and thinly sliced
1 large onion, finely chopped
1 clove garlic, finely chopped
1 carrot, finely chopped
1 stalk celery, finely chopped
1 small bunch fresh parsley, finely chopped
6 large potatoes, peeled and diced
4 cups (1 liter) water
  Salt and freshly ground black pepper

Serves: 4
Preparation: 20 minutes
Cooking: 25–30 minutes
Level: 1

MINESTRONE

Bring 8 cups (2 liters) of water to a boil in a large saucepan with the garbanzo beans. Skim off any foam. Reduce the heat and simmer until the beans are almost tender, 1–2 hours. Drain, reserving the stock. • Cook the lentils separately in a medium saucepan of cold water until tender, 30–40 minutes. Drain well. • Heat the oil in a large saucepan over medium heat. • Add the onion and pancetta and sauté until the onion is transparent, 3–4 minutes. • Add the herbs and tomato passato and simmer for 5 minutes. • Add the remaining 8 cups (2 liters) of water and the ham bone, if using, and bring to a boil. Season with salt and add all the mixed diced vegetables. • Simmer over low heat for 30 minutes. • Add the drained beans and lentils and about half of the reserved stock. • Chop the garlic and lard together and add to the pot. Simmer until the vegetables are tender, 30–40 minutes. • Add the pasta about 10 minutes before the vegetables are cooked and simmer until al dente. If there is not enough liquid, add more of the reserved stock. • Sprinkle with cheese and season with pepper. Serve hot.

■■■*There are as many versions of this classic Italian soup as there are Italian cooks! Feel free to vary the vegetables according to the season or your personal tastes. You can also substitute the pasta with the same quantity of rice or pearl barley. If you are short of time, use drained canned garbanzo beans (chickpeas) and lentils.*

4	quarts (4 liters) water
1	cup (150 g) dried garbanzo beans (chickpeas), soaked overnight and drained
1	cup (150 g) lentils
2	tablespoon extra-virgin olive oil
1	onion, finely chopped
1/2	cup (60 g) finely chopped pancetta
3	tablespoons finely chopped mixed fresh herbs (such as marjoram, thyme, parsley, and sage)
1	cup (250 ml) tomato passata (crushed tomatoes)
1	ham bone (optional)
	Salt
1	pound (500 g) mixed vegetables (carrots, celery, spinach, Swiss chard, potatoes, zucchini/courgettes), cut into cubes
2	cloves garlic
2	tablespoons lard (or butter), cut up
8	ounces (250 g) ditalini or other small soup pasta
1/4	cup (30 g) freshly grated Parmesan cheese
	Freshly ground black pepper

Serves: 4–6
Preparation: 1 hour
 + 12 hours to soak
Cooking: 2–3 hours
Level: 1

CHICKEN STOCK

Step 1: Place the chicken and water in a large stock pot over medium heat and bring to a boil. Add the onions, carrots, celery, parsley, bay leaves, and salt and bring to a boil. Reduce the heat and simmer for 3–4 hours. Never allow the water to boil; just keep it gently simmering. Add more boiling water as the stock evaporates, making sure that the chicken and vegetables are always covered with water. **Step 2:** Skim off and discard any scum that forms on the surface during cooking. • Turn off the heat, remove the chicken and vegetables, and let the stock cool. Strain through a sieve. • **Step 3:** Refrigerate the stock until the fat hardens on the surface. Skim off the fat and discard it. • Use the stock as directed in the recipes.

3 pounds (1.5 kg) chicken wings, backs and necks or one whole 4-pound (2-kg) boiling chicken

About 5 quarts (5 liters) cold water

2 medium onions, quartered

2 medium carrots, halved

2 stalks celery, cut into thirds

Small bunch fresh parsley

2 bay leaves

1 tablespoon sea salt

Makes: About 3 quarts (3 liters)
Preparation: 15 minutes
Cooking: 3–4 hours
Level: 1

▪ ▪ ▪ *Don't freeze excess stock in one large batch otherwise you will have to thaw it all even if you only need a small amount. To freeze, pour the cooled stock into ice cube trays, cup-size plastic containers, or silicone muffin pans and place in the freezer until solid. Once frozen, remove from the containers and pack into zip-lock freezer bags. If you leave the stock in the ice cube trays or open plastic containers it will pick the odors and flavors of the other foods in the freezer.*

PREPARING CHICKEN STOCK

Homemade stock is more aromatic and has less salt than canned or bouillon cube stocks. Chicken stock is easy to prepare and although it takes several hours to cook, it is well worth the effort. Stock freezes well, so prepare it in large quantities and freeze in individual portions for use in soups, risottos, and many other dishes.

1. PLACE the chicken and water in a large stock pot and bring to a boil. Add the onions, carrots, celery, parsley, bay leaves, and salt and return to a gentle simmer. Never allow the stock to boil, but keep at a gently simmer. Top up with more water as the stock evaporates, keeping it to the level of the chicken and vegetables. Simmer for 3–4 hours.

2. DURING COOKING, skim off and discard any foam or scum that forms on the surface off the stock.

3. REFRIGERATE the stock until the fat hardens on the surface. Skim off the fat and discard it.

BLACK-EYED PEA SOUP WITH CILANTRO

38

Heat the oil in a large soup pot over medium heat. Add the shallots, celery, garlic, and chile and sauté until softened, 5–7 minutes. • Pour in the chicken stock and add the black-eyed peas. Bring to a boil. Cover and simmer over low heat until the black-eyed peas are almost soft, 40–50 minutes. • Add the cayenne pepper and season with salt and black pepper. Add the tomatoes and simmer for 20 more minutes. • Stir in the lime juice and cilantro. Garnish with the remaining cilantro and serve hot.

2   tablespoons extra-virgin olive oil

4   shallots, finely chopped

4   stalks celery, coarsely chopped

4   cloves garlic, finely chopped

1   fresh red or green chile, seeded and finely chopped

8   cups (2 liters) Chicken Stock (see pages 34–35)

1¹⁄₂ cups (150 g) black-eyed peas, soaked overnight and drained

¹⁄₄ teaspoon cayenne pepper

   Salt and freshly ground black pepper

5   tomatoes, peeled and chopped

   Freshly squeezed juice of 2 limes

2   tablespoons finely chopped fresh cilantro (coriander) + extra to garnish

Serves: 6
Preparation: 15 minutes
   + 12 hours to soak beans
Cooking: 70–80 minutes
Level: 1

BUTTERNUT SQUASH SOUP

Melt the butter in a large soup pot over medium heat. Add the onions, garlic, salt, cumin, coriander, and mustard and sauté until the onions are tender, about 5 minutes. • Add the squash, potato, honey, chile, and ginger. Pour in 4 cups (1 liter) of the chicken stock and bring to a boil over low heat. Cover and simmer until the vegetables have softened, about 15 minutes. • Add the garbanzo beans, remaining 2 cups (500 ml) of chicken stock, and half the lemon juice. Simmer for 5 minutes. Remove from the heat. • Blend with a handheld blender until smooth. • Return the pan to the heat and reheat gently, adding the remaining lemon juice. Add a little boiling water if the soup is too thick. Season with salt, black pepper, and cayenne pepper. • Swirl in the yogurt and garnish with the bell pepper.

2 tablespoons butter

2 small onions, finely chopped

1 clove garlic, finely chopped

1 teaspoon salt

1/2 teaspoon ground cumin

1/2 teaspoon ground coriander

1/4 teaspoon dry mustard powder

2 medium butternut squash, peeled, seeded, and cut into 1-inch (2.5-cm) cubes

1 potato, cubed

1 teaspoon honey

1 green chile, seeded and finely chopped

1 (1-inch/2.5-cm) piece fresh ginger, peeled and finely chopped

6 cups (1.5 liters) Chicken Stock (see pages 34–35)

2 cups (400 g) canned garbanzo beans (chickpeas), drained

Freshly squeezed juice of 2 lemons

Salt and freshly ground black pepper

1/4 teaspoon cayenne pepper

1/2 cup (125 ml) plain yogurt

2 tablespoons diced red bell pepper (capsicum)

Serves: 6
Preparation: 20 minutes
Cooking: 30 minutes
Level: 1

BROCCOLI SOUP
WITH CHEESE CROUTONS

Separate the broccoli into florets. Chop the stalk into small dice and coarsely chop the leaves.
• Heat 2 tablespoons of the oil in a large soup pot over medium heat. Add the garlic and sauté until softened, 2–3 minutes. • Add the broccoli (leaves, florets, and stalks), potato, and chicken stock. Season with salt and white pepper. Partially cover and simmer over low heat until the broccoli is very tender, 15–20 minutes. • While the soup is cooking, toast the bread. • Remove the soup from the heat and blend with a handheld blender until smooth.
• Ladle the soup into preheated individual serving bowls. • Top the toasted bread with cheese and bell pepper. Float the croutons on the soup and drizzle with the remaining 2 tablespoons of oil. • Serve hot.

1	large head broccoli (about 2 pounds/1 kg)
4	tablespoons (60 ml) extra-virgin olive oil
2	cloves garlic, finely chopped
1	large potato, peeled and diced
6	cups (1.5 liters) Chicken Stock (see pages 34–35)
	Salt and freshly ground white pepper
1	small baguette (French loaf), sliced
1/2	cup (60 g) freshly grated Emmental cheese
2	tablespoons diced red bell pepper (capsicum)

Serves: 4
Preparation: 20 minutes
Cooking: 25 minutes
Level: 1

CHINESE CHICKEN AND CORN SOUP

Combine the chicken stock, rice wine, and ginger in a large soup pot and bring to a boil. Decrease the heat to medium-low, add the chicken and corn, and simmer until the chicken is cooked, about 10 minutes. • Remove the chicken and set aside to cool. Shred the chicken using your fingers and return to the pot. • Combine the water and cornstarch in a small bowl to make a smooth, thin paste. Add to the soup, stirring to combine. Simmer, stirring frequently until thickencd, 3–5 minutes. • **Step 1:** Beat the egg whites and sesame oil lightly in a small bowl. Gradually pour the egg white mixture into the soup in a thin steady stream, beating gently and constantly with a balloon whisk, to create thin threads of egg white. Season with salt. • Serve the soup hot, garnished with the scallion.

44

6 cups (1.5 liters) Chicken Stock (see pages 34–35)

3 tablespoons rice wine

2 teaspoons finely grated fresh ginger

1 boneless, skinless chicken breast

2 cups (400 g) canned creamed corn (sweetcorn)

3 tablespoons water

2 tablespoons cornstarch (cornflour)

2 large egg whites

2 teaspoons sesame oil

Salt

1 scallion (spring onion) finely sliccd, to garnish

Serves: 4–6
Preparation: 15 minutes
Cooking: 20 minutes
Level: 1

▩ ADDING EGG WHITES TO SOUP

Lightly beaten egg whites are often added to Chinese soups to create "ribbons." The egg whites cook in the hot stock and are separated into ribbons by gentle whisking. Always use fresh, organic eggs for this recipe.

1. POUR the egg white mixture into the soup in a thin steady stream, whisking gently in one direction only with a balloon whisk, wooden spoon, or chopsticks.

CHICKEN NOODLE SOUP

Mix the tamarind, chile oil, chiles, garlic, ginger, and soy and oyster sauces in a large wok. Warm the wok over medium heat. • Add the sugar and curry leaves, if using, and pour in the chicken stock. Bring to a boil, stirring constantly. Simmer for 5 minutes. • Add the chicken and simmer for 5 minutes, stirring often. • Stir in the carrots, bean sprouts, baby corn, bell peppers, and rice noodles and simmer until the chicken and vegetables are tender, about 10 minutes. • Garnish with the cilantro and serve hot.

2	tablespoons tamarind paste
1	tablespoon Asian chile oil
5	dried red chiles, crumbled
5	cloves garlic, finely chopped
1	tablespoon minced fresh ginger
¼	cup (60 ml) dark soy sauce
1	tablespoon oyster sauce
1	tablespoon sugar
6	curry leaves (optional)
6	cups (1.5 liters) Chicken Stock (see pages 34–35)
2	boneless skinless chicken breasts, cut into thin strips
2	carrots, finely chopped
1	cup (50 g) bean sprouts
8	baby corn (sweetcorn)
1	small green bell pepper (capsicum), chopped
1	red bell pepper (capsicum), chopped
6	ounces (180 g) rice vermicelli
2	tablespoons fresh cilantro (coriander), to garnish

■ ■ ■ *The tamarind tree, originally from tropical Africa, is cultivated throughout the tropical world. Its pods are harvested for the delicious sour-tasting pulp that forms around the seeds. The pulp is compressed and used in many Indian and Southeast Asian dishes. You can buy it in Asian food stores and markets.*

Serves: 4–6
Preparation: 30 minutes
Cooking: 25 minutes
Level: 1

TOM YAM KUNG (THAI SHRIMP SOUP)

Peel and devein the shrimp, leaving the tails on. Reserve the heads and shells. • Heat the oil in a large saucepan over medium-high heat. Add the shrimp heads and shells and cook, stirring constantly, until the shells are orange and highly fragrant, about 5 minutes. • Add the lemongrass, coriander roots, galangal, chiles, and lime leaves and stir to combine. Pour in the water or stock and bring to a boil. Decrease the heat to medium-low and gently simmer for 20 minutes. • Strain the shrimp stock through a fine-mesh sieve into a clean soup pot. Discard the shells and coriander root.
• Return the lemongrass, galangal, chiles, and lime leaves to the strained stock. Add the tomatoes, mushrooms, fish sauce, lime juice, and jaggery, and simmer for 5 minutes. • Add the shrimp and simmer until they change color, 2–3 minutes.
• Serve hot garnished with the cilantro.

1	pound (500 g) raw shrimp (green prawns)
1	tablespoon vegetable oil
2	stalks lemongrass, bruised
2	coriander roots, cleaned and bruised
1	(1$\frac{1}{2}$-inch/4-cm) piece galangal or fresh ginger, sliced
4	small red chiles
4	kaffir lime leaves
5	cups (1.25 liters) water or Chicken Stock (see pages 34–35)
3	tomatoes, cut into wedges
4	ounces (125 g) canned straw mushrooms, halved
2	tablespoons Thai fish sauce
3	tablespoons freshly squeezed lime juice
1	tablespoon coarsely grated jaggery (palm sugar) or brown sugar
$\frac{1}{2}$	cup (25 g) fresh cilantro (coriander) leaves

Serves: 4–6
Preparation: 30 minutes
Cooking: 35–40 minutes
Level: 2

▥ ▥ ▥ *The kaffir lime tree grows in many parts of Southeast Asia. Its leaves are used to flavor a variety of Asian dishes. They are avaliable fresh or dried in Asian food markets. If you are lucky enough to find fresh leaves, freeze them for later use.*
Jaggery is a form of unrefined sugar used in many parts of the world. Substitute with dark brown sugar.

CORN SOUP WITH CHICKEN AND CHILE

Heat the oil in a large soup pot over high heat. Add the chicken and sauté until white, 7–8 minutes. Set aside in a warm oven. • Pour the milk into the soup pot and add the onion and potatoes. Bring to a boil. Lower the heat and add the cilantro, chiles, and corn. Simmer over very low heat for 10 minutes, stirring often. Remove from the heat. • Blend with a handheld blender until smooth. Mix in the cornstarch paste. • Return the soup to the heat and simmer until thickened, 2–3 minutes. • Remove from the heat and season with salt and pepper. Stir in the cream and keep stirring for 2–3 minutes. Stir in the chicken. • Garnish with the chives and extra chiles and serve hot.

1 tablespoon extra-virgin olive oil

1 boneless skinless chicken breast, cut into small pieces

4 cups (1 liter) milk

1 large onion, finely chopped

12 ounces (350 g) potatoes, peeled and diced

2 tablespoons finely chopped fresh cilantro (coriander)

2 small red chiles, seeded and finely chopped + extra to garnish

1 pound (500 g) frozen or canned corn (sweet corn)

1 tablespoon cornstarch (cornflour) mixed with 3 tablespoons cold water

Salt and freshly ground black pepper

1/2 cup (125 ml) light (single) cream

2 tablespoons snipped fresh chives, to garnish

Serves: 4–6
Preparation: 15 minutes
Cooking: 25 minutes
Level: 1

TOM KHA GAI (THAI CHICKEN SOUP)

Spice Paste: Step 1: Place all the spice paste ingredients in a large mortar and pestle and pound until smooth. Alternatively, chop in a spice grinder or food processor until smooth.

Soup: Place the coconut milk in a large soup pot over medium heat and bring to a boil. Decrease the heat and simmer until the milk splits, 3–4 minutes. Add the spice paste and return to a boil. • Add the chicken stock, fish sauce, kaffir lime leaves, and jaggery and return to a boil. • Add the chicken and simmer until cooked, about 10 minutes. Remove the chicken using a slotted spoon and set aside to cool. Shred the chicken. • Strain the soup through a fine-mesh sieve, discarding the solids. Return the soup to the heat, add the lime juice, and bring back to a simmer. • Divide the chicken evenly among 4 heated serving bowls and ladle the soup over the top. Garnish with the cilantro and serve hot.

Spice Paste

3   shallots, chopped

3   stalks lemongrass, white part only, chopped

1   ($1\frac{1}{2}$-inch/4 cm) piece galangal or fresh ginger, chopped

4   small hot chiles, chopped

3   coriander roots

2   cloves garlic, sliced

Soup

4   cups (1 liter) coconut milk

4   cups (1 liter) Chicken Stock (see pages 34–35)

$\frac{1}{3}$ cup (90 ml) Thai fish sauce

8   kaffir lime leaves

1   tablespoon grated jaggery (palm sugar) or brown sugar

4   chicken thigh fillets

$\frac{1}{3}$ cup (90 ml) lime juice

$\frac{1}{3}$ cup cilantro (coriander)

Serves: 4–6
Preparation: 30 minutes
Cooking: 15–20 minutes
Level: 1

■ PREPARING SPICE PASTE

Many Asian or North African dishes are flavored with spice pastes that are made by pounding or grinding herbs, spices, and other seasonings. They are simple to prepare and taste so much fresher than store-bought pastes.

1. PLACE all the spice paste ingredients in a mortar and pestle and pound until smooth and fragrant. Alternatively, grind in a spice grinder or chop in a food processor until smooth.

AVGOLEMONO (GREEK CHICKEN, EGG AND LEMON SOUP)

54

Combine the chicken stock, rice, and bay leaves in a large soup pot over medium heat and bring to a boil. Decrease the heat and simmer until rice is half cooked, about 8 minutes. • Add the chicken and simmer until it is cooked, about 10 minutes. • Remove the chicken and set aside on a plate to cool slightly. Shred the chicken using your fingers and return to the pot. • Combine the eggs and lemon juice in a medium bowl. • Whisking constantly, gradually pour 1 cup (250 ml) of the hot stock into the egg mixture. Remove the stock from the heat and add the egg mixture, stirring to combine. Season with salt and pepper. • Garnish with the parsley and serve hot.

6	cups (1.5 liters) Chicken Stock (see pages 34–35)
$1/2$	cup (100 g) short- or medium-grain rice
2	bay leaves
2	boneless skinless chicken breasts
2	large eggs, lightly beaten
	Freshly squeezed juice of 1 lemon
	Salt and freshly ground black pepper
2	tablespoons coarsely chopped fresh parsley to garnish

Serves: 4–6
Preparation: 15 minutes
Cooking: 20–25 minutes
Level: 2

■ ■ ■ *This is a classic Greek soup made with chicken stock, eggs, and lemon juice that are cooked together until they thicken (but before they curdle). Avgolemono can be translated as "egg-lemon," and is a sauce or flavoring used in many Eastern Mediterranean dishes.*

RED LENTIL SOUP WITH LIME

Heat the oil in a large soup pot over medium heat. Add the onion, celery, and carrot and sauté until softened, 3–4 minutes. • Stir in the garlic, marjoram, thyme, and cumin. Add the lentils, chicken stock, lime zest, and bay leaf and bring to a boil. • Cover and simmer over low heat until the lentils are soft, 25–30 minutes. • Discard the bay leaf and add 1 tablespoon of the lime juice. Remove from the heat. Blend with a handheld blender until smooth. • Return the pot to the heat and reheat gently. If the soup is too thick, add a little boiling water. Season with salt and pepper and add the remaining 1 tablespoon of lime juice. • Garnish with the parsley and serve hot.

3	tablespoons sunflower oil
1	large onion, finely chopped
1	stalk celery, finely chopped
1	carrot, finely chopped
1	clove garlic, finely chopped
½	teaspoon dried marjoram
2	soft stems lemon thyme, or ½ teaspoon dried thyme
1	teaspoon cumin seeds, toasted and ground
1¼	cups (350 g) red lentils
8	cups (2 liters) Chicken Stock (see pages 34–35)
	Finely grated zest of ¼ lime
1	bay leaf
2	tablespoons freshly squeezed lime juice
	Water (optional)
	Salt and freshly ground black pepper
2	tablespoons finely chopped fresh parsley

Serves: 6
Preparation: 20 minutes
Cooking: 35–40 minutes
Level: 1

LAKSA (MALAYSIAN COCONUT AND CURRY SOUP)

58

Laksa Paste: Place all of the laksa paste ingredients in a large mortar and pestle or food processor and blend until smooth.

Soup: Place the hokkein and vermicelli noodles in a medium bowl, cover with boiling water, and set aside for 10 minutes to soften. • Heat the peanut oil in a large saucepan over medium-low heat. Add the laksa paste and cook, stirring constantly, until fragrant, about 30 seconds. • Add the coconut milk and kaffir lime leaves, if using, and bring to a boil. Decrease the heat to low and simmer until the cream splits, about 5 minutes. • Add the chicken stock and bring to a boil. Decrease the heat and simmer for 10 minutes. • Add the fish sauce, lime juice, and jaggery, and stir to combine. • Add the fish balls, tofu, and shrimp and simmer until the shrimp change color, 2–3 minutes.

■ ■ ■ *If you are not familiar with Asian food you may be worried about some of the ingredients in this soup; don't be, they are all quite easy to find in Asian food stores or online. Alternatively, they can be substituted with local products or simply omitted.*
Dried shrimp are small shrimp that have been sun-dried. They are available whole and in the form of powder or paste. They add a wonderful flavor to soups, curries, and other dishes.
Galangal, also known as blue ginger, is a root that is widely used to flavor Asian dishes. Substitute with ordinary fresh ginger.

Laksa Paste

2   stalks lemongrass, white part only, coarsely chopped

4   small dried red chiles, crumbled

1/2 teaspoon dried shrimp

2   teaspoons dried coriander

8   cloves garlic, coarsely chopped

2   shallots, coarsely chopped

1   (1-inch/2.5-cm) piece turmeric root or 1 teaspoon ground turmeric

1   tablespoon coarsely chopped galangal or fresh ginger

2   ounces (60 g) candlenuts or raw cashews, chopped

2   tablespoons cilantro (coriander) leaves

Soup

8   ounces (200 g) hokkein noodles

8   ounces (200 g) vermicelli rice noodles

1/4 cup (60 ml) peanut oil

4   cups (1 liter) coconut milk

4   kaffir lime leaves (optional)

2 cups (500 ml) Chicken Stock (see pages 34–35)

2 tablespoons Thai fish sauce

2 tablespoons freshly squeezed lime juice

1 teaspoon coarsely grated jaggery (palm sugar) or brown sugar

8 small fish balls

4 cubes fried tofu, cut into quarters

12 raw shrimp (green prawns), shelled and deveined, tails left on

2 cups (100 g) bean sprouts

2 tablespoons fresh cilantro (coriander) leaves

2 tablespoons Vietnamese or normal mint leaves

2 scallions (spring onions) finely sliced

2 hard boiled eggs, sliced, to garnish

3 teaspoons sambal oelek (chilli paste), to garnish

Serves: 4–6
Preparation: 45 minutes
Cooking: 45–50 minutes
Level: 3

Meanwhile, divide the noodles among 4–6 large heated serving bowls and top with bean sprouts, cilantro, mint, and scallions. Ladle the laksa stock over the top and divide the fish balls, tofu, and shrimp evenly among the bowls. • Garnish each bowl with slices of egg and sambal oelek. Serve hot.

59

Fish balls are a common food in the southern regions of China and in many other Asian cuisines. They are made from finely chopped or ground fish meat shaped into small round balls. They are available fresh or frozen from Asian markets and food stores.

The kaffir lime tree grows in many parts of Southeast Asia. Its leaves are used to flavor many Asian dishes. They are available fresh or dried in Asian food markets. If you are lucky enough to find fresh leaves, freeze them for later use.

Jaggery is a form of unrefined sugar used in many parts of the world. Substitute with dark brown sugar.

BEEF STOCK

Rinse and peel or scrape the vegetables. Stick the onion quarters with the cloves. • **Step 1:** Place all the ingredients in a large soup pot and cover with the water. Place over medium heat and bring to a boil. • **Step 2:** Simmer over low heat for 3 hours. Skim the stock during cooking to remove the scum that will rise to the surface, at first abundantly but then tapering off. • **Step 3:** Strain the stock through a fine-mesh sieve into a large bowl, discarding the vegetables, meat, and bones. • When the stock is completely cool, chill in the refrigerator. • If you wish to remove the fat, it will solidify on the top and can be skimmed off and discarded. • Use the stock as directed in the recipes.

1	large onion, quartered
2	cloves
1	large carrot, halved
1	leek
2	stalks celery, including leaves
4	whole cloves (optional)
	Small bunch fresh parsley
2	bay leaves
2	cloves garlic, peeled
2	very ripe tomatoes
1	tablespoon coarse sea salt
3	pounds (1.5 kg) boiling beef
2	pounds (1 kg) beef bones
	About 5 quarts (5 liters) cold water

Makes: About 3 quarts (3 liters)
Preparation: 15 minutes
Cooking: 3–4 hours
Level: 1

■ ■ ■ Depending on the type of meat and bones you use to make the stock, it will contain a certain amount of fat. If you wish to remove this, simply chill it in the refrigerator until it solidifies them skim off. Many people prefer to leave at least some of the fat in the stock as it increases flavor.
If liked, slice the meat (which will be very tender) and serve as a main course.

PREPARING BEEF STOCK

Beef stock is a basic ingredient in so many recipes—from soups and sauces, to risottos and meat and vegetable dishes—that it really is worth taking the time to make it at home. It freezes well and can be made in large quantities and frozen for later use.

1. PLACE all the ingredients in a large soup pot and pour in the water. Place over medium heat and bring to a boil.

2. DECREASE the heat to low and simmer for 3 hours. Skim off the scum that will rise to the top of the stock during cooking.

3. STRAIN the stock through a fine-mesh sieve into a large bowl, discarding the vegetables, meat, and bones. Let cool, then chill.

4. WHEN COLD, the fat will solidify on top of the stock. If you wish to remove it, just skim it off the top.

HARIRA (NORTH AFRICAN LAMB SOUP)

Heat the oil in a soup pot over medium heat. Add the onions, carrots, celery (reserving a few leaves to garnish), turmeric, pepper, cinnamon, and ginger and sauté until softened and fragrant, about 5 minutes. • Add the lamb and bones and cook, stirring often, until browned, 10–15 minutes. • Add the tomato passata, garbanzo beans, and tomato paste and stir to combine. Pour in 6 cups (1.5 liters) of water and bring to a boil. Decrease the heat to low and simmer until the garbanzo beans are tender, about 1 hour. • **Step 1:** Stir the flour with the remaining 1/2 cup (125 ml) of water in a small bowl until smooth. Gradually pour the flour mixture into the soup, stirring constantly. Decrease the heat to low and simmer until thickened, 4–5 minutes. • Add the rice, cilantro, and parsley and return to a boil. Simmer until the rice is cooked, about 15 minutes. • Add the lemon juice and season with salt. Serve hot garnished with the celery leaves.

3	tablespoons extra-virgin olive oil
2	large onions, chopped
1	carrot, diced
5	stalks celery, including leaves, finely chopped
1	teaspoon turmeric
1	teaspoon freshly ground black pepper
1	teaspoon ground cinnamon
1	teaspoon ground ginger
1	pound (500 g) lamb shoulder chops, boned and cut into small chunks, bones reserved
2	cups (500 ml) tomato passata (crushed, sieved tomatoes)
1	cup (100 g) dried garbanzo beans (chickpeas), soaked overnight
2	tablespoons tomato paste
6	cups (1.5 liters) water + 1/2 cup (125 ml) extra
2	tablespoons all-purpose (plain) flour
1/4	cup (50 g) long-grain rice
1/2	cup (25 g) finely chopped fresh cilantro (coriander)
1/4	cup finely chopped fresh parsley leaves
	Freshly squeezed juice of 1 lemon
	Salt

Serves: 8
Preparation: 30 minutes + 12 hours to soak
Cooking: 1 hour 35 minutes
Level: 1

■ THICKENING SOUP

1. COMBINE the flour and water in a small bowl. Pour the flour mixture into the soup in a thin, steady stream, stirring constantly. Simmer, stirring often, over low heat until thickened, 4–5 minutes.

PHO BO (VIETNAMESE BEEF NOODLE SOUP)

Place the oxtail and stewing beef in a large soup pot. Cover with water and bring to a boil. Drain and discard the water. Rinse the meat and return to a large, clean soup pot. Set aside. • Dry-fry the cinnamon, cardamom, star anise, cloves, and coriander seeds in a small frying pan over medium heat until fragrant, about 30 seconds. • Add the onion and ginger and dry-fry for 3–4 minutes. • Add the spiced onion mixture and water to the reserved meat and bring to a boil. Reduce the heat and simmer for 2 hours, skimming the surface as required. Remove the stewing beef and set aside to cool. • Add the fish sauce and sugar to the stock in the pot and simmer for 45 minutes. • Strain the stock through a fine-mesh sieve into a large clean soup pot. • Remove the oxtail meat from the bones and cut into small dice. Set aside. Discard the remaining solids. • Return the stock to the heat and keep warm until required. • Soak the noodles in boiling water until softened, about 3 minutes. • Thinly slice the cooled stewing beef. • To assemble the soup, divide the noodles, beef fillet, stewing beef, and oxtail among six to eight heated soup bowls. Top with bean sprouts, scallions, cilantro, and basil. Ladle the boiling stock over the top. • Serve hot, with the chiles, lime wedges, and fish sauce added as desired.

1¹/₂	pounds (750 g) oxtail, chopped
1¹/₄	pounds (600 g) stewing beef
1	cinnamon stick
2	cardamom pods, bruised
2	star anise
2	whole cloves
¹/₂	teaspoon coriander seeds
1	onion, unpeeled, halved
1	(¹/₂-inch/1-cm) piece ginger, bruised
10	cups (2.5 liters) water
3	tablespoons Thai fish sauce + extra to serve
2	tablespoons sugar
8	ounces (250 g) fresh vermicelli rice noodles
6	ounces (180 g) beef fillet, thinly sliced
1¹/₂	cups (60 g) bean sprouts
3	scallions (spring onions), finely sliced
¹/₂	cup (25 g) chopped fresh cilantro (coriander) leaves
¹/₂	cup (25 g) chopped fresh Thai basil leaves
8	small fresh red chiles to garnish
	Lime wedges, to serve

Serves: 6–8
Preparation: 45 minutes
Cooking: About 3 hours
Level: 2

SPICY BEEF SOUP

Heat the oil in a large soup pot over medium heat. Add the onion, garlic, carrot, celery, chile, and parsley and sauté until the onion is softened, 3–4 minutes. • Add the beef and sauté until nicely browned, about 5 minutes. • Add the tomatoes, potatoes, beef stock, salt, and pepper. Partially cover the pan and simmer over low heat until the potatoes are tender, about 20 minutes. • Garnish with the cilantro and serve hot.

2	tablespoons extra-virgin olive oil
1	large white onion, finely chopped
2	cloves garlic, finely chopped
1	carrot, finely chopped
1	stalk celery, finely chopped
1	fresh red chile, finely sliced
2	tablespoons finely chopped fresh parsley
12	ounces (350 g) ground (minced) beef
4	cup (800 g) canned tomatoes, with juice
3	large potatoes, peeled and diced
4	cups (1 liter) Beef Stock (see pages 62–63)
	Salt and freshly ground black pepper
2	tablespoons finely chopped cilantro (coriander), to garnish,

Serves: 4–6
Preparation: 15 minutes
Cooking: 30 minutes
Level: 1

CALDO GALLEGO

Heat the oil in a large soup pot over medium heat. Add the onions and garlic and season with salt. Sauté until the onions and garlic are softened, 3–4 minutes. • Stir in the paprika, chorizo, and ham. Sauté until lightly browned, about 5 minutes. • Add the potatoes, bell peppers, garbanzo beans, and tomatoes. Season with salt and pepper. Pour in the water and add the bay leaves and sage. Bring to a boil. • Simmer over low heat until the potatoes are tender, about 30 minutes. • Remove the bay leaves. Sprinkle with the parsley and serve hot.

72

⅓ cup (90 ml) extra-virgin olive oil

2 large Spanish onions, finely chopped

4 cloves garlic, sliced

Salt and freshly ground black pepper

1½ teaspoons hot paprika

8 ounces (250 g) chorizo sausage, thinly sliced

8 ounces (250 g) smoked ham, cut into cubes

2 potatoes, peeled and cut into small cubes

1 red bell pepper (capsicum), diced

1 green bell pepper (capsicum), diced

1 (14-ounce/400-g) can garbanzo beans (chickpeas), drained

10 medium tomatoes, peeled and chopped

6 cups (1.5 liters) cold water

2 bay leaves

2 teaspoons finely chopped fresh sage

3 tablespoons finely chopped fresh parsley

■ ■ ■ *This spicy soup comes from the Galician region of Spain. There are many different versions, but they all include chorizo, garbanzo beans, and tomatoes.*

Serves: 4–6
Preparation: 15 minutes
Cooking: 40–45 minutes
Level: 2

RIBOLLITA

Put the beans in a large soup pot with the cherry tomatoes, garlic, and sage. Cover with cold water. Bring slowly to a boil, cover, and simmer until tender, about 1 hour. • Season with salt. Discard the garlic and sage. Drain the beans and set aside. • Clean the pot and heat 4 tablespoons of the oil over medium heat. Add the onions, leeks, carrots, kale, cabbage, tomatoes, zucchini, peas, parsley, and thyme and sauté until softened, about 10 minutes. • Add the beans, followed by the beef stock and season lightly with salt and pepper. Cover and simmer over very low heat for about 1 hour, adding more stock if the soup becomes too thick. • Remove the soup from the heat and let sit for at least 2 hours. Leave overnight, if liked. • Preheat the oven to 325°F (160°C/gas 3). • Place a layer of toast in the bottom of an earthenware baking dish or ovenproof pot. Ladle some of the soup over the top. Season generously with freshly ground black pepper and repeat this layering process until all the soup and toast are in the dish. • Bake for about 20 minutes, until heated through. • Drizzle with the remaining 3 tablespoons of oil and serve hot.

■ ■ ■ *This thick Tuscan soup is often made by adding bread to the leftovers of a minestrone and baking in the oven until heated through. Drizzle with plenty of good Tuscan oil before serving.*

1¼ cups (200 g) dried cannellini beans, soaked overnight

3   cherry tomatoes

2   cloves garlic

6   leaves fresh sage

     Water

     Salt

7   tablespoons (100 ml) extra-virgin olive oil

2   onions, thinly sliced

2   leeks, thinly sliced

2   carrots, sliced

8   ounces (250 g) Tuscan kale or Swiss chard (silver beet), shredded

½   small savoy cabbage, shredded

2   cups (400 g) canned tomatoes, with juice

2   zucchini (courgettes), sliced

1   cup (150 g) frozen peas

2   tablespoons finely chopped fresh parsley

     Small sprig of thyme

6   cups (1.5 liters) Beef Stock + extra as needed (see pages 62–63)

12   ounces (350 g) day-old firm-textured bread, toasted

     Freshly ground black pepper

Serves: 6–8
Preparation: 45 minutes
    + 12 hours to soak
    + 2 hours to rest
Cooking: 2 hours 20 minutes
Level: 2

MIDDLE EASTERN MEATBALL SOUP

76

Meatballs: Place all the ingredients for the meatballs in a bowl and mix well. • Dampen your hands and shape the mixture into meatballs the size of walnuts. Set aside.

Soup: Heat the butter in a large soup pot over medium heat. Add the onion and sauté until softened, 3–4 minutes. • Add the tomatoes, celery, bell pepper, chiles, coriander, paprika, salt, and turmeric. Stir well. Sauté until all the moisture has evaporated and the oil has begun to seep to the top, 15–20 minutes. • Remove the pot from the heat and blend with a handheld blender until smooth. • Add the meatballs and return to the heat. Cook over low heat, stirring occasionally, for 10 minutes. • Pour in beef stock. Simmer until the soup has thickened slightly, about 15 minutes. • Add the parsley, lime juice, and the garbanzo beans. Simmer until heated through, 3–4 minutes. • Serve hot.

Meatballs

1   pound (500 g) ground (minced) lamb
2   teaspoons minced ginger
2   cloves garlic, finely chopped
1   teaspoon ground turmeric
    Juice of ½ lemon
½   teaspoon salt
2   tablespoons ground coriander
2   tablespoons finely chopped fresh cilantro (coriander)
½   teaspoon hot paprika

Soup

3   tablespoons butter
1   onion, finely chopped
1   cup (250 ml) tomato passata (crushed tomatoes)
1   large stalk celery, diced
1   red bell pepper (capsicum), seeded and diced
2   small fresh red chiles, seeded and finely chopped
1   tablespoon ground coriander
1   teaspoon sweet paprika
½   teaspoon salt
¼   teaspoon ground turmeric
4   cups (1 liter) Beef Stock (see pages 62–63)
2   tablespoons finely chopped fresh parsley
    Freshly squeezed juice of ½ lime
2   cups (400 g) canned garbanzo beans (chickpeas), drained

Serves: 4–6
Preparation: 15 minutes
Cooking: 50 minutes
Level: 2

GOULASH SOUP

Melt the butter in a large soup pot over high heat. Add the beef in small batches and cook until seared, 1–2 minutes. Set aside. • Add the onions and sauté until softened, 3–4 minutes. • Add the garlic, thyme, and caraway seeds and sauté for 2 minutes. • Add the paprika and ½ teaspoon of salt. Sauté over medium heat until all the paprika has been incorporated, about 5 minutes. • Mix in the flour. Pour in 1 cup (250 ml) of beef stock. Cook over low heat for 1 minute, stirring constantly. • Stir in the tomato paste, bell pepper, and tomatoes, then pour in the remaining 7 cups (1.75 liters) of beef stock. • Return the meat to the pan and bring to a boil. Cover and simmer over low heat until the meat is tender, about 1 hour 30 minutes. Add more stock if the soup thickens too much. • Stir in the cream and wine and cook for 1 minute. Season with salt and pepper. • Serve the soup hot, garnished with the sour cream.

■ ■ ■ *Goulash is a traditional Hungarian soup or stew. Its name comes from* gulyás, *the Hungarian word for "herdsman." Versions that include a variety of vegetables, such as carrots, bell peppers, and tomatoes, are considered by Hungarians to be goulash soup* (gulyásleves). *Paprika, the ground spice made from a variety of sweet red peppers, gives this dish its characteristic red color and fragrance.*

¼ cup (60 g) butter

1¾ pounds (750 g) lean beef (stew beef), cut into small chunks

3 onions, finely chopped

3 cloves garlic, finely chopped

1 teaspoon dried thyme, or 1 tablespoon finely chopped fresh thyme

½ teaspoon caraway seeds, crushed

2 tablespoons hot paprika

Salt

1½ tablespoons all-purpose (plain) flour

8 cups (2 liters) Beef Stock + extra as needed (see pages 62–63)

1 tablespoon tomato paste (concentrate)

1 green bell pepper (capsicum), thinly sliced

3 tomatoes, peeled and quartered

¼ cup (60 ml) light (single) cream

¼ cup (60 ml) dry red wine

Freshly ground black pepper

½ cup (125 ml) sour cream, to serve

Serves: 6–8
Preparation: 20 minutes
Cooking: 1 hour 45 minutes
Level: 1

FRENCH ONION SOUP

80

Heat the butter in a soup pot over low heat. Add the onions and let sweat without stirring for 15–20 minutes. Continue cooking, stirring occasionally until the onions are deep golden brown and caramelized, another 15–20 minutes. • Sprinkle with the flour and cook, stirring often, for 5 minutes. • Pour in the beef stock and season with salt and pepper. Bring to a boil then decrease the heat to low and simmer for 20 minutes. • Cut the bread into rounds so that each slice will perfectly cover the top of the soup bowls. • Preheat a broiler (grill) and toast the bread lightly on both sides. • Divide the soup evenly among four ovenproof soup bowls and place a slice of toasted bread on each. Sprinkle with the cheese. • Place under the broiler until the cheese is bubbling and golden brown, about 5 minutes. • Serve hot.

¼ cup (60 ml) butter

4 large white onions, finely chopped

2 tablespoons all-purpose (plain) flour

6 cups (1.5 liters) Beef Stock (see pages 62–63)

Salt and freshly ground black pepper

4 large slices firm-textured bread

1 cup (125 g) freshly grated cheese (Gruyère, Cheddar, Emmental)

Serves: 4
Preparation: 15 minutes
Cooking: About 1 hour
Level: 1

▦ ▦ ▦ *This traditional French soup is a wonderful, warming dish for cold winter days. If you are short of time, you can just sauté the onions over medium heat until golden, about 5 minutes. However, if you take the time to caramelize them slowly over very low heat the flavor of the soup will be so much better.*

RICE
AND OTHER
GRAINS

1 ARBORIO RICE

2 BASMATI RICE

3 THAI JASMINE RICE

1. An Italian rice. Its plump, starchy grain is ideal for risottos, but also good in soups and paella. Less suitable for sweet rice dishes. Does not require rinsing or soaking.

2. Fragrant, long-grain rice from India and Pakistan. Not starchy; the grains stay separate. Ideal for steaming, boiling, pilafs, biryani, fried dishes. Soak for 30 minutes before cooking.

3. Very fragrant, long-grain Thai rice. Ideal for steaming, boiling, fried dishes, and to accompany Thai dishes. Rinse before cooking.

TYPES OF RICE

4 BLACK RICE

5 RED RICE

6 THAI PURPLE RICE

4. There are many varieties; other than color, they don't have much in common. Famous black rices include non-sticky Chinese Forbidden rice and Italian Black Venus rice.

5. There are several varieties, including Bhutanese red rice, Thai red cargo rice, and Camargue red rice. Soak and rinse before cooking. Another type, Red yeast rice is believed to lower cholesterol.

6. A sticky Thai rice, also known as Thai or Indonesian black rice. Naturally sweet, it is ideal for puddings and desserts. Soak and rinse before cooking.

7 LONG-GRAIN BROWN RICE

8 SHORT-GRAIN BROWN RICE

9 PARBOILED RICE

7. Both long- and short-grain brown rice have more flavor, fiber, and nutritional value than white rice. Unmilled or partly milled, brown rice retains the bran and germ in the outer husk of the grain.

8. Both long- and short-grain brown rice take longer to cook and go rancid more quickly than white rice. Store in a dark, cool place for not more than 3 months. Ideal for boiling and salads.

9. This rice is boiled in the husk which forces nutrients into the grain. When milled, the nutrients remain. Firm and non-sticky, it is quicker to cook than brown rice. Ideal for salads and sides.

Rice is a staple food for more than half of humanity and over 8,000 varieties are cultivated around the world. There are many different ways of classifying rice: by the shape or size of the grain (usually summarized as short-, medium-, and long-grain); by its degree of "stickiness" (determined by the amount of starch contained in the grains); or by color (red, black, brown, etc) or aroma. Here we have chosen 12 of the more common types and explained how they are best used in the kitchen.

10 LONG-GRAIN STICKY RICE

11 SHORT-GRAIN STICKY RICE

12 WILD RICE

10. Also known as glutinous or sweet rice. Used for snacks and sweets in Asian cuisines, but also to accompany savory dishes. Soak for two hours before cooking, Better steamed than boiled.

11. Short-grain sticky rice is ideal for sushi, rice balls, puddings, desserts, sweet snacks. Rinse well and soak for 15–30 minutes before cooking.

12. Wild rice is a cereal rather than a true rice. Native to North America and China, it is never milled so is nutrient-rich. Strongly flavored, it is ideal for soups, stuffings, salads, casseroles.

MILANESE RISOTTO

Step 1: Melt 4 tablespoons (60 g) of butter in a large saucepan over medium heat. Add the onion and sauté until softened, 3–4 minutes. • **Step 2:** Add the rice and stir for 2 minutes, until the grains are well coated and becoming translucent. • Pour in the wine and stir until the alcohol has evaporated, 2–3 minutes. • **Step 3:** Begin stirring in the stock, a ladleful at a time. Cook and stir until each addition has been absorbed. After 7–8 minutes, stir in 4–5 tablespoons of Parmesan. About 3 minutes before the rice is tender, stir in the saffron. Keep adding stock and stirring until the rice is tender. The total cooking time from when you begin adding the stock will be 15–18 minutes. • **Step 4:** Stir in the remaining Parmesan and butter. Let stand for 2–3 minutes, then serve hot.

■ ■ ■ *This is a classic Italian risotto. The original recipe uses 5 tablespoons of fat leftover from a roast instead of butter (and 2–3 tablespoons of bone marrow too). Many claim that the wine is not traditional, so leave it out if you prefer. As with all risottos, it is important to learn that the stock should be added very gradually during cooking and the rice should be stirred almost continuously. This releases the starches in the rice, giving the risotto its characteristic creamy consistency. It is very important to use a high-quality risotto rice that will soften without becoming soggy or sticky. Arborio, Carnaroli, or Vialone nano are the top three Italian rices used to make risottos.*

6 **tablespoons (90 g) butter**

1 **small onion, finely chopped**

2 **cups (400 g) risotto rice, such as Arborio or Carnaroli**

$1/3$ **cup (90 ml) dry white wine**

4 **cups (1 liter) Beef Stock, boiling (see pages 62–63)**

$1/2$ **cup (60 g) freshly grated Parmesan cheese**

$1/4$ **teaspoon saffron or $1/2$ teaspoon saffron threads**

Freshly ground white pepper

Serves: 4–6
Preparation: 15 minutes
   + 2–3 minutes to rest
Cooking: 20–25 minutes
Level: 1

■ PREPARING RISOTTO

It is not difficult to make a good, creamy risotto, but it does require constant attention and a little experience. There are a few basic steps common to most risottos: firstly, butter is melted and an onion lightly sautéed. Then wine is added and simmered until evaporated. At that point stock is added, a ladleful at a time, and the dish is stirred and simmered until the rice is creamy and tender.

1. MELT 4 tablespoons (60 g) of butter in a large saucepan over medium heat. Add the onion and sauté until softened, 3–4 minutes.

2. ADD the rice and stir for 2 minutes, until the grains are coated and almost translucent. Add the wine and stir until the alcohol has evaporated, 2–3 minutes.

3. STIR IN the stock, one ladleful at a time. Cook and stir until each addition has been absorbed and the rice is tender but still *al dente*, 15–18 minutes.

4. STIR IN the remaining butter and the cheese. Let the risotto stand for 2–3 minutes before serving.

PROSCIUTTO AND PARMESAN RISOTTO

Melt 1 tablespoon of butter in a small frying pan over medium heat. Add the prosciutto and sauté until golden brown, 3–4 minutes. Remove from the heat and set aside. • Melt the remaining 4 tablespoons (60 g) of butter in a large saucepan over medium heat. Add the onion and sauté until softened, 3–4 minutes. • Add the rice and stir until the grains are well coated and almost translucent, about 2 minutes. • Pour in the wine and stir until the alcohol evaporates, 2–3 minutes. • Begin stirring in the stock, a ladleful at a time. Cook and stir until each addition has been absorbed and the rice is tender but still al dente, 15–18 minutes. • Stir in the prosciutto and mascarpone. Season with salt and pepper. • Let rest for 2–3 minutes. • Serve hot sprinkled with the Parmesan.

5	tablespoons (75 g) butter
1	cup (120 g) diced prosciutto (Parma ham)
1	small white onion, finely chopped
2	cups (400 g) risotto rice, such as Arborio or Carnaroli
1/2	cup (125 ml) dry white wine
4	cups (1 liter) Beef Stock, boiling (see pages 62–63)
1/2	cup (125 g) mascarpone cheese
1/2	cup (60 g) Parmesan cheese, flaked
	Salt and freshly ground black pepper

Serves: 4–6
Preparation: 15 minutes
+ 2–3 minutes to rest
Cooking: 30–35 minutes
Level: 1

RISOTTO WITH GRAPES AND PANCETTA

92

Melt the butter in a large frying pan over medium heat. Add the onion and pancetta and sauté until the onion is softened and the pancetta is lightly browned, about 5 minutes. • Add the rice and stir until well coated and almost translucent, about 2 minutes. • Pour in the wine and cook until the alcohol has evaporated, 2–3 minutes. • Begin stirring in the stock, a ladleful at a time. Cook and stir until each addition has been absorbed and the rice is tender but still al dente, 15–18 minutes. • Add the grapes, chives, and parsley. Season with salt and white pepper. • Let rest for 2–3 minutes. • Serve hot sprinkled with the Parmesan.

1/4 cup (60 g) butter

1 onion, finely chopped

1 cup (125 g) diced pancetta

2 cups (400 g) risotto rice, such as Arborio or Carnaroli

1 cup (250 ml) dry white wine

4 cups (1 liter) Chicken Stock, boiling (see pages 34–35)

12 ounces (350 g) seedless white or green grapes, peeled

Small bunch fresh chives, snipped

2 tablespoons finely chopped fresh parsley

Salt and freshly ground white pepper

1 cup (125 g) freshly grated Parmesan cheese

Serves: 4–6
Preparation: 20 minutes
  + 2–3 minutes to rest
Cooking: 25–30 minutes
Level: 1

ASPARAGUS RISOTTO WITH MINT

94

Vegetable Stock: This recipe will make about twice as much stock as you will need for the risotto. Freeze the rest for later use. • Heat the oil in a large stock pot over medium heat. Add the onions, carrots, celery, tomatoes, parsley, peppercorns, bay leaves, and salt and sauté for 5 minutes. • Pour in the water, partially cover the pan, and bring to a boil. Simmer over low heat for 1 hour. • Strain through a fine-mesh sieve, discarding the vegetables.

Risotto: Melt 2 tablespoons of butter in a large frying pan over medium heat. Add the chopped asparagus stems and sauté for 3 minutes. • Pour in 1 cup (250 ml) of the stock and bring to a boil. Reduce the heat and simmer until the asparagus is very tender, 10–15 minutes. • Transfer to a bowl and blend with a handheld blender until smooth. Set aside. • Wipe the pan clean. Melt the remaining 2 tablespoons of butter in the frying pan over medium heat. Add the onion and sauté until softened, 3–4 minutes. • Add the rice and stir until coated and almost translucent, about 2 minutes. • Stir in the wine and cook until the alcohol has evaporated, 2–3 minutes. • Begin adding the remaining stock, a ladleful at a time. Cook and stir until each addition is absorbed. • After about 10 minutes, add the asparagus purée and the reserved tips. Add more stock and cook and stir until the rice is tender, 5–8 minutes. • Add the cream and season with white pepper. • Let rest for 2–3 minutes. • Serve hot sprinkled with the Parmesan and mint.

Vegetable Stock

2	tablespoons extra-virgin olive oil
2	white onions, studded with 2 cloves
2	carrots, chopped, 2 stalks celery, with leaves, 2 small tomatoes, small bunch fresh parsley, 8 black peppercorns, 2 bay leaves
1	teaspoon sea salt
10	cups (2.5 liters) cold water

Risotto

4	tablespoons (60 g) butter
1¹/₄	pounds (600 g) asparagus, stems cut into short lengths and tips reserved
1	onion, finely chopped
2	cups (400 g) risotto rice, such as Arborio or Carnaroli
¹/₃	cup (90 ml) dry white wine
¹/₄	cup (60 ml) heavy (double) cream
	Freshly ground white pepper
¹/₂	cup (60 g) Parmesan cheese, in flakes
1	small bunch mint, finely chopped

Serves: 4–6
Preparation: 30 minutes + 2–3 minutes to rest
Cooking: 1 hour 45–50 minutes
Level: 2

SEAFOOD PAELLA

Heat the oil in a paella pan or large frying pan over medium-high heat. Add the onion and garlic and sauté until softened, 3–4 minutes. • Add the bell peppers and tomatoes and sauté until softened, about 5 minutes. • Add the rice, saffron mixture, and paprika and stir to coat. Pour in the wine and stir until evaporated, 2–3 minutes. • Pour in the hot stock, decrease the heat to low, and simmer for 25 minutes, stirring occasionally to ensure even cooking of the rice. • Add the mussels, shrimp, squid, fish, and peas and simmer, stirring occasionally, until the fish and shrimp begin to change color. • Remove from the heat, cover, and set aside for 10 minutes to rest. • Stir in the parsley and discard any unopened mussels. Season with salt and pepper. • Serve hot garnished with the wedges of lemon.

■ ■ ■ *Paella is a traditional rice dish from the Valencia region of Spain. It is cooked in a large pan measuring about 18 inches (45 cm) in diameter. There are many different versions. If possible, use imported Spanish rice which is available in gourmet food stores and online. If you can't get Spanish rice, substitute with the much more widely available Arborio rice instead.*

3	tablespoons extra-virgin olive oil
2	white onions, diced
3	cloves, garlic finely chopped
2	red bell peppers (capsicums), seeded and sliced
6	tomatoes, diced
2	cups (400 g) Spanish paella rice, such as Cassparra or Bomba
1	teaspoon saffron threads infused in 3 tablespoons hot water
1	tablespoon smoked sweet paprika
$1/2$	cup (125 ml) dry white wine
4	cups (1 liter) Fish Stock, boiling (see page 102)
12	mussels, in shell, scrubbed
8	ounces (250 g) shrimp (prawns), peeled and deveined, with tails
8	ounces (250 g) cleaned fresh squid, cut into $1^{1}/2$ inch (4 cm) pieces
1	pound (500 g) firm white fish fillet, cut into $1^{1}/2$ inch (4 cm) pieces
$1/2$	cup (75 g) frozen peas
4	tablespoons finely chopped fresh parsley
	Salt and freshly ground black pepper
2	lemons, cut into wedges, to serve

Serves: 6
Preparation: 30 minutes
   + 10 minutes to rest
Cooking: 50 minutes
Level: 2

SPICY LAMB AND PORK PAELLA

Season the lamb with salt and pepper. • Heat the oil in a paella pan or large frying pan over medium heat. Add the lamb and sauté until browned, about 5 minutes. Remove the lamb from the pan and keep warm. • Brown the pork in the same oil, 5–8 minutes. Remove from the pan and keep warm. • Sauté the bell pepper and green beans in the same pan for 3 minutes. • Increase the heat and add the chorizo, cayenne pepper, and chile. Sauté for 30 seconds. • Add the rice and cook for 3 minutes, stirring constantly. • Stir in the tomatoes and cook for 3 minutes. • Add the pork, lamb, saffron mixture, chicken stock, salt, pepper, and rosemary and bring to a boil. Cover and simmer over low heat for 20 minutes without stirring, shaking the pan every so often to keep the rice from sticking. • When the rice is tender, remove from the heat and let rest for 5–10 minutes before serving.

1	pound (500 g) boned lamb, cut into thin strips
	Salt and freshly ground black pepper
1/4	cup (60 ml) extra-virgin olive oil
8	ounces (250 g) pork loin, cut into thin strips
1	red bell pepper (capsicum), seeded and sliced
8	ounces (250 g) green beans, sliced
4	ounces (125 g) chorizo or spicy salami, thinly sliced
1	tablespoon cayenne
1	teaspoon finely chopped fresh red chile
2	cups (400 g) Spanish paella rice, such as Cassparra or Bomba
4	large tomatoes, peeled and chopped
6	saffron threads, crumbled dissolved in 1 tablespoon hot water
4	cups (1 liter) Chicken Stock, boiling (see pages 34–35)
1	tablespoon finely chopped fresh rosemary

Serves: 6
Preparation: 20 minutes
Cooking: 40 minutes
+ 5–10 minutes to rest
Level: 1

EASY CARIBBEAN RICE

Put the rice in a bowl and cover with cold water. Let soak for 30 minutes. • Drain the rice and rinse under cold running water until the water almost runs clear. • Bring the 3 cups (750 ml) of water to a boil in a large saucepan. Add the rice and salt. Mix well. Cover and simmer over low heat until the rice is tender, 12–15 minutes. • Stir in the beans, pineapple, nuts, onion, garlic, and chile sauce. • Place in a large frying pan and toss over high heat until heated through and well mixed, 1–2 minutes. • Serve hot.

1½	cups (300 g) basmati rice
3	cups (750 ml) water
½	teaspoon salt
2	cups (400 g) canned red kidney beans, drained
1	cup (100 g) canned pineapple chunks, drained
½	cup (60 g) slivered almonds or other nuts
1	sweet onion, finely chopped
2	cloves garlic, finely chopped
1	teaspoon hot chile sauce

■ ■ ■ This is a simple rice dish you can whip up in a jiffy for a quick lunch or supper. Add some finely chopped cilantro (coriander) or basil for extra color.

Serves: 4–6
Preparation: 5 minutes
+ 30 minutes to soak
Cooking: 15–20 minutes
Level: 1

■ RINSING AND SOAKING RICE

1. SOAKING basmati rice improves flavor. Put the rice in a bowl and cover with cold water. Let soak for 30 minutes. Drain.
2. RINSE under cold running water until the water almost runs clear. If short of time, just rinse the rice before cooking.

CAMBODIAN RICE

Fish Stock: Soak the fish heads and bones in a large bowl of cold water for one hour. This will remove any traces of blood. • Drain and place in a large stock pot with the water over medium heat. Bring to a boil. Add all the other ingredients and return to a gentle simmer. Lower the heat and simmer for about 1¹/2 hours. • Strain the stock through a fine-mesh sieve, discarding the solids.

Cambodian Rice: Soak the rice for 30 minutes. • Drain and rinse well. • Heat 4 tablespoons (60 ml) of oil in a large frying pan over medium heat. Add the onion and garlic and sauté until pale gold, 3–4 minutes. • Add the pork and chicken and sauté until browned all over, 8–10 minutes. • Add the shrimp and sauté for 2 minutes. • Add the rice and cook for 3 minutes, stirring constantly. • Pour in 4 cups (1 liter) of fish stock, vinegar, aniseed, ginger, and cinnamon. Season with salt and pepper. Cover and simmer over low heat until the rice is tender, about 20 minutes. • Beat the eggs with a pinch of salt in a small bowl. • Heat the remaining 1 tablespoon of oil in a small frying pan over medium heat and fry the eggs until firm. Cut into strips. • Gently mix the fried eggs into the rice. Garnish with chiles and serve hot.

■ ■ ■ You can use a fish stock cube to make this dish, but homemade stock is always better. The fish stock recipe will make about 8 cups (2 liters), twice what you need. Fish stock will keep in the refrigerator for 3–4 days and can be frozen for up to 3 months.

Fish Stock

1	pound (500 g) mixed fish heads and bones
3	quarts (3 liters) water
1	carrot, chopped
1	stalk celery, chopped
1	onion, chopped
1	small bunch fresh parsley
1	bay leaf
4	black peppercorns
¹/2	cup (125 ml) white wine
1	clove garlic
1	sprig fresh thyme
1	tablespoon sea salt

Cambodian Rice

1¹/4	cups (250 g) basmati rice
5	tablespoons peanut oil
1	onion, finely chopped
2	cloves garlic, sliced
12	ounces (350 g) pork, diced
1	boneless skinless chicken breast, diced
4	ounces (125 g) shrimp (prawns), peeled
2	tablespoons white wine vinegar
	Pinch of aniseed
1	teaspoon grated ginger
¹/2	teaspoon cinnamon
	Salt and freshly ground black pepper
2	large eggs
2	fresh green chiles, seeded and finely sliced

Serves: 4–6
Preparation: 20 minutes
   + 1¹/2 hours to soak
Cooking: 30 minutes
Level: 2

BIRYANI

Put the rice in a bowl and cover with cold water. Let soak for 30 minutes. • Drain the rice and rinse under cold running water until the water almost runs clear. • Heat 2 tablespoons of ghee in a large frying pan over medium heat. Add the onions and garlic and sauté until softened, 3–4 minutes. Set aside. • Heat the remaining 2 tablespoons of ghee in a large saucepan over medium heat. Add the chile, cardamom, garam masala, coriander, cumin, and turmeric, and cook until fragrant, about 30 seconds. • Add the rice and stir to coat. Add the tomatoes, golden raisins, and water and bring to a boil. Decrease the heat and simmer, without stirring, for 3 minutes. • Stir in the onion mixture, cover, and simmer for 2 more minutes. • Turn off the heat and set the rice aside to finishing cooking, 10–15 minutes. • Stir in the cashews and cilantro. Season with salt and pepper. • Garnish with the extra cilantro and serve hot.

■ ■ ■ A Biryani can be any one of a number of spiced rice dishes. The word itself, of Persian origin, means "fried." Biryanis are very popular in Indian cuisine.

1¹⁄₂	cups (300 g) basmati rice
4	tablespoons (60 g) ghee or vegetable oil
2	large onions, thinly sliced
2	cloves garlic, finely chopped
1	large green chile, seeded and sliced
6	cardamom pods, bruised
2	teaspoons garam masala
¹⁄₂	teaspoon ground coriander
¹⁄₂	teaspoon cumin seeds
¹⁄₄	teaspoon ground turmeric
2	tomatoes, diced
3	tablespoons golden raisins (sultanas)
2	cups (500 ml) water
¹⁄₃	cup (50 g) cashews, lightly toasted
3	tablespoons finely chopped cilantro (coriander) + extra leaves to garnish
	Salt and freshly ground pepper

Serves: 4–6
Preparation: 20 minutes
  + 30 minutes to soak
Cooking: 20–25 minutes
Level: 1

SALMON SUSHI ROLLS

Sushi Rice: Wash the rice in a colander under cold running water until the water runs clear. • Place the rice and 3 cups (750 ml) of water in a medium saucepan, cover and bring to a boil over medium heat. • Reduce the heat to low and simmer for 5 minutes. Remove from the heat, cover, and let stand for 15 minutes. • Meanwhile, place the vinegar, sugar, and salt in a small saucepan and gently heat, stirring occasionally until the sugar has dissolved. Remove from the heat and let cool. • Transfer the rice to a large bowl and stir in vinegar mixture to combine. Let cool slightly. **Sushi Rolls:** Lay a nori sheet on a bamboo sushi mat. • Dip your hands in cold water to prevent the rice from sticking, then spread about one-fifth of the rice evenly over the nori sheet, leaving a 1/2-inch (1-cm) border on one long side. • Lay strips of salmon, avocado, and cucumber lengthwise down the center of the rice. • Lightly moisten the exposed nori sheet with a little water. Using the sushi mat, firmly roll up the sushi roll to enclose the filling. Repeat the process with the remaining ingredients. • Place the rolls, seam side down on a chopping board. Trim the edges with a sharp knife and slice into rounds 1 inch (2.5 cm) thick. • Serve with the soy sauce, pickled ginger, and wasabi.

▦▦▦ *Sushi rolls are not hard to make, but you will need a bamboo sushi mat to help you roll them up. Sushi mats and nori sheets (made from seaweed) are available online and in Asian food markets.*

Sushi Rice

2 1/2 cups (500 g) short-grain sticky rice (Japanese sushi rice)

3 cups (750 ml) water

1/4 cup (60 ml) rice wine vinegar

2 tablespoons sugar

1 teaspoon salt

Sushi Rolls

5 nori sheets

4 ounces (125 g) smoked or raw salmon, sliced into 1/2-inch (1-cm) thick, long strips

1 avocado, halved, pitted, and sliced into 1/2-inch (1-cm) thick, long strips

1 small cucumber, peeled, seeded, and sliced lengthwise into 1/2-inch (1-cm) thick strips

1/3 cup (90 ml) soy sauce, to serve

2 tablespoons pickled ginger, drained, to serve

2 teaspoons wasabi paste, to serve

Serves: 4–6
Preparation: 45 minutes
Cooking: 5 minutes + 15 minutes to stand
Level: 2

CALIFORNIA SUSHI ROLLS

Prepare the sushi rice following the instructions on page 106.

Sushi Rolls: Lay a nori sheet on a clean work surface. Dip your hands in cold water to prevent the rice from sticking, and spread about one-fifth of the rice evenly over the nori sheet, leaving a $1/2$-inch (1-cm) border on one long side. Sprinkle with $1/2$ tablespoon of the sesame seeds. • Quickly turn the nori sheet over and place on a bamboo sushi mat. Spread $1/2$ tablespoon of mayonnaise over the nori. Lay strips of tuna, avocado, and bell pepper lengthwise down the center of the nori sheet. • Use the sushi mat to firmly roll up the sushi roll to enclose the filling. • Repeat the process with the remaining ingredients. Refrigerate until ready to serve. • Using a sharp, wet knife, slice the sushi into rounds about 1 inch (2.5 cm) thick. • Serve with soy sauce, pickled ginger, and wasabi.

■ ■ ■ *A California sushi roll is really just an inside-out sushi roll. Once you have spread the rice on the nori, you flip it, and lay the filling along the center of the nori. When you roll it up, the rice is on the outside.*

1   recipe Sushi Rice (see page 106)

Sushi Rolls

5   nori sheets

4   ounces (125 g) very fresh tuna, sliced into $1/2$-inch (1-cm)-thick, long strips

1   avocado, halved, pitted, and sliced into $1/2$-inch (1-cm) thick, long strips

$1/2$ red bell pepper (capsicum) seeded and sliced lengthwise into $1/2$-inch (1-cm) thick strips

$2^1/2$ tablespoons mayonnaise

$2^1/2$ tablespoons sesame seeds, toasted

$1/3$ cup (90 ml) soy sauce, to serve

2   tablespoons pickled ginger, drained, to serve

2   teaspoons wasabi paste, to serve

Serves: 4–6
Preparation: 45 minutes
Cooking: 5 minutes
   + 15 minutes to stand
Level: 3

TURKISH PILAF

Put the rice in a bowl and cover with cold water. Let soak for 30 minutes. • Drain the rice and rinse under cold running water until the water almost runs clear. • Place the eggplant in a colander, sprinkle with coarse sea salt and let drain for 30 minutes. • Shake off the excess salt and pat dry with paper towels. • Heat the oil in a large frying pan over medium-high heat. Add the eggplant and sauté until tender, 5–10 minutes. Drain on paper towels. • Melt the butter in a large heavy-based saucepan over medium heat. Add the onion and garlic and sauté until softened, 3–4 minutes. • Add the cinnamon, allspice, and rice and stir until the rice turns from opaque to white, about 2 minutes. • Add the eggplant and currants and stir to combine. Pour in the chicken stock and bring to a boil. Decrease the heat to low, cover, and simmer until the rice is tender and the liquid is absorbed, 15–20 minutes. • Remove from the heat and stir in the pine nuts and parsley. Season with salt and pepper. Fluff the rice with a fork. • Serve hot, with the yogurt passed separately.

2	cups (400 g) basmati rice
1	large eggplant (aubergine), cut into $3/4$-inch (2-cm) cubes
	Coarse sea salt
$1/4$	cup (60 ml) extra-virgin olive oil
3	tablespoons butter
1	large onion, finely sliced
1	clove garlic, finely chopped
1	cinnamon stick
$1/2$	teaspoon allspice or pumpkin pie spice
$1/3$	cup (60 g) currants
$2^{1}/4$	cups (550 ml) Chicken Stock (see pages 34–35)
$1/3$	cup (60 g) pine nuts, lightly toasted
3	tablespoons finely chopped fresh parsley
	Salt and freshly ground pepper
	Plain yogurt, to serve

Serves: 6
Preparation: 30 minutes + 30 minutes to soak and drain
Cooking: 30–40 minutes
Level: 1

▪ ▪ ▪ *A pilaf, also known as a pilav, plov, pilau, or pulao, is a Central Asian or Indian dish in which rice (or sometimes cracked wheat) is first browned in butter or oil, then simmered—along with spices, vegetables, and meat—in stock until tender.*

LAMB PILAU

112

Put the rice in a bowl and cover with cold water. Let soak for 30 minutes. • Drain the rice and rinse under cold running water until the water almost runs clear. • Heat the butter and oil in a large saucepan over medium heat. Add the onion and sauté until softened, 3-4 minutes. • Add the lamb and cinnamon and sauté until browned, about 5 minutes. • Add the rice and stir for 1 minute. • Pour in the chicken stock, add the tomatoes and dates, and bring to a boil. Decrease the heat to low, cover, and simmer until the rice is tender and all of the liquid is absorbed, 15–20 minutes. • Remove from the heat and stir in the almonds, mint, and parsley. • Season with salt and pepper and serve hot.

$1^{1}/_{2}$ cups (300 g) basmati rice

2 tablespoons butter

1 tablespoon extra-virgin olive oil

1 large white onion, finely sliced

1 pound (500 g) lamb fillet, trimmed and cut into 1-inch (2.5-cm) cubes

1 cinnamon stick

$2^{1}/_{4}$ cups (550 ml) Chicken Stock (see pages 34–35)

3 medium tomatoes, diced

$^{1}/_{2}$ cup (90 g) dates, pitted and sliced

$^{3}/_{4}$ cup (120 g) flaked almonds, lightly toasted

2 tablespoons finely chopped fresh mint

2 tablespoons finely chopped fresh parsley

Salt and freshly ground black pepper

Serves: 6
Preparation: 30 minutes
  + 30 minutes to soak
Cooking: 25–30 minutes
Level: 1

COCONUT RICE WITH THAI BEEF

114

Coconut Rice: Rinse the rice under cold running water until the water almost runs clear. • Combine the rice, coconut milk, water, and salt in a medium saucepan. Cover and bring to a boil. Decrease the heat to low and simmer until the rice is tender and the liquid has been absorbed, 15–20 minutes.

Thai Beef: When the rice is almost done, combine the fish sauce, soy sauce, and sugar in a small bowl; set aside. • Heat a wok over high heat. Add the oil and garlic and half the chiles. Stir-fry for 15 seconds. Add the beef and stir-fry, breaking up the meat with a wooden spoon, until browned and cooked through, 4–5 minutes. • Add the soy mixture and stir-fry for 30 seconds. • Add the basil and remaining chiles and stir to combine. • Serve the beef over the coconut rice, garnished with the wedges of lime.

Coconut Rice

1^1/2 cups (300 g) jasmine rice

2 cups (500 ml) canned coconut milk

^{3}/4 cup (180 ml) water

^{1}/2 teaspoon salt

Thai Beef

2 tablespoons Thai fish sauce

2 tablespoons soy sauce

1 teaspoon sugar

1 tablespoon vegetable oil

3 cloves garlic, sliced

3 long hot chiles or red jalapeno chiles, seeded and sliced into 2-inch (5-cm) matchsticks

1^1/4 pounds (600 g) ground (minced) beef sirloin

1 cup (50 g) loosely packed fresh basil leaves, torn

Lime wedges to garnish

Serves: 4–6
Preparation: 30 minutes + 30 minutes to soak
Cooking: 20 minutes
Level: 1

■ ■ ■ *Coconut rice is simple to prepare and can be served with many Thai or Indian curries or topped with vegetarian, seafood, or meat sauces.*

COUSCOUS WITH SEVEN VEGETABLES

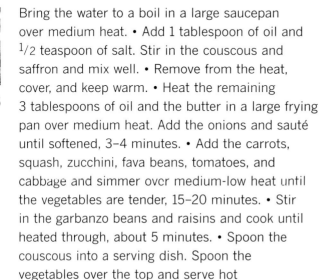

Bring the water to a boil in a large saucepan over medium heat. • Add 1 tablespoon of oil and $1/2$ teaspoon of salt. Stir in the couscous and saffron and mix well. • Remove from the heat, cover, and keep warm. • Heat the remaining 3 tablespoons of oil and the butter in a large frying pan over medium heat. Add the onions and sauté until softened, 3–4 minutes. • Add the carrots, squash, zucchini, fava beans, tomatoes, and cabbage and simmer over medium-low heat until the vegetables are tender, 15–20 minutes. • Stir in the garbanzo beans and raisins and cook until heated through, about 5 minutes. • Spoon the couscous into a serving dish. Spoon the vegetables over the top and serve hot garnished with cilantro leaves.

■ ■ ■ *We have included this delicious vegetarian recipe for couscous in the grains chapter, although technically couscous is a type of pasta made from semolina. Couscous is a staple food across North Africa, where it is cooked by prolonged steaming in a couscoussier. In Europe and North America it is available in handy precooked packages which only require a little boiling water and salt and are ready in minutes.*

$1^{1}/3$	cups (350 ml) water
4	tablespoons (60 ml) extra-virgin olive oil
	Salt
2	cups (350 g) couscous
$1/8$	teaspoon saffron threads
2	tablespoons butter
2	large onions, finely chopped
3	carrots, thinly sliced
1	yellow summer squash, thinly sliced
3	zucchini (courgette), thinly sliced
1	cup (60 g) fresh fava (broad) beans
3	large tomatoes, peeled and chopped
$1/2$	medium green or white cabbage, finely shredded
2	cups (400 g) canned garbanzo beans (chickpeas), drained
$1/4$	cup (45 g) raisins
	Fresh cilantro (coriander) to garnish

Serves: 6
Preparation: 30 minutes
Cooking: 25–30 minutes
Level: 1

BULGUR WITH LAMB AND GARBANZO BEANS

118

Heat the oil in a large frying pan over medium heat. Add the onions and sauté until softened, 3–4 minutes. • Add the lamb and sauté until browned, 8–10 minutes. • Add the bulgur and water. Season with salt, pepper, and cinnamon. Partially cover the pan and simmer over low heat until the lamb and bulgur are both tender, about 30 minutes. Stir often during cooking, adding more water if it has all been absorbed and the bulgur begins to stick to the pan. • Stir in the garbanzo beans and cook until heated through. Sprinkle with the cilantro and serve hot.

$1/4$ cup (60 ml) extra-virgin olive oil

2 medium onions, finely chopped

12 ounces (350 g) lamb, cut into small cubes

2 cups (300 g) medium grind bulgur

2 cups (500 ml) water + more as needed

Salt and freshly ground black pepper

$1/2$ teaspoon ground cinnamon

2 cups (400 g) canned garbanzo beans (chickpeas), drained

2 tablespoons finely chopped fresh cilantro (coriander)

Serves: 4
Preparation: 15 minutes
Cooking: 50 minutes
Level: 1

■ ■ ■ *Bulgur is made by steaming wheat berries whole, then drying them, and cracking them into grits. The steaming process means that the wheat is precooked and thus very quick to prepare. It is available in three grind sizes: fine, medium, and large.*

PEARL BARLEY RISOTTO

Heat the oil in a large frying pan over medium heat. Add the onion and garlic and sauté until softened, 3–4 minutes. • Turn the heat up to high and add the pearl barley. Stir rapidly for 1–2 minutes to coat the grains. • Add half the wine and cook until almost absorbed. Add the rest of the wine and cook and stir until absorbed. • Add 2 cups (500 ml) of the stock, cover the pan, and cook until almost all absorbed. • Uncover and begin adding the vegctable stock, a ladleful at a time, stirring until each addition is absorbed. Cook and stir, adding more stock, until the barley is tender, about 40 minutes. • Add the butter and cheese and season with salt and pepper. Stir in the parsley, basil, cilantro, and lemon juice and serve hot.

3	tablespoons extra-virgin olive oil
1	small onion, finely chopped
2	cloves garlic, finely chopped
$1^{1}/_{2}$	cups (300 g) pearl barley
1	cup (250 ml) dry white wine
6	cups (1.5 liters) Vegetable Stock (see page 94)
2	tablespoons butter
$^{1}/_{2}$	cup (60 g) freshly grated Parmesan cheese
	Salt and freshly ground black pepper
1	tablespoon finely chopped fresh parsley
1	tablespoon finely chopped fresh basil
1	tablespoon finely chopped fresh cilantro (coriander)
2	tablespoons freshly squeezed lemon juice

■ ■ ■ *Barley can be cooked in the same way as risotto rice. If cooked slowly while being gently stirred, barley releases starches that create a wonderful creamy consistency just like risotto.*

Serves: 4–6
Preparation: 20 minutes
Cooking: 50–60 minutes
Level: 2

WHEAT BERRIES WITH ZUCCHINI AND PARMESAN

122

Soak the wheat berries in cold water for 12 hours.
• Drain and transfer to a large saucepan. Pour in
enough hot water to generously cover the wheat.
• Bring to a boil and simmer until tender, about
1 hour. • Grill the zucchini in a hot grill pan until
tender. • Transfer to a bowl, season with salt and
pepper, and drizzle with 2 tablespoons of oil.
Sprinkle with the parsley and mint. • Drain the
wheat berries thoroughly and set aside to cool.
• Place the zucchini on a large serving dish and
spoon the wheat over the top. Drizzle with the
remaining oil and the lemon juice. • Top with the
walnuts, Parmesan, and a few more leaves of fresh
mint to garnish and serve.

2	cups (350 g) wheat berries
4	zucchini (courgettes), thinly sliced lengthwise
	Salt and freshly ground black pepper
6	tablespoons (90 ml) extra-virgin olive oil
2	tablespoons finely chopped fresh parsley
1	tablespoon finely chopped fresh mint + extra leaves to garnish
1	tablespoon freshly squeezed lemon juice
20	walnuts, toasted and coarsely chopped
3¹⁄₂	ounces (100 g) Parmesan cheese, shaved

 *Wheat is an important staple food in many parts
of the world and provides nourishment for millions of
people every day in the forms of bread, pasta, and
other baked goods. In its unprocessed form, wheat is a
highly nutritious food, a good source of B vitamins and
many other nutrients. Unfortunately it is usually eaten
in highly processed products such as white bread and
refined pasta. The unrefined whole wheat berries in this
recipe need 12 hours soaking before cooking, but they
are bursting with dietary fiber and goodness and have
a delicious nutty flavor.*

Serves: 4–6
Preparation: 30 minutes
  + 12 hours to soak
Cooking: 1 hour
Level: 1

POLENTA WITH MEAT SAUCE

Meat Sauce: Heat the oil in a medium saucepan over low heat. Add the onions, carrots, and celery. Cover and sweat over low heat for 20 minutes.
• Add the garlic and sausage, turn up the heat to high, and add the beef. Sauté until cooked through and browned. • Stir in the flour. Pour in the wine and cook until it has evaporated, 2–3 minutes.
• Add the tomatoes, parsley, nutmeg, rosemary, sage, bay leaf, lemon zest, salt, and pepper.
• Simmer over low heat for at least 4 hours, adding a little water to keep it moist. • Prepare the polenta while the sauce is cooking.

Basic Polenta: Step 1: Bring the water and salt to a boil in a saucepan large enough to hold at least 4 quarts (4 liters) of liquid. • Add the cornmeal gradually, stirring constantly so that no lumps form. Polenta should always be perfectly smooth.

Step 2: Stir the polenta over low heat by moving a long, wooden spoon in a circular motion. Stir constantly for the 40–45 minutes. When the polenta is ready it will begin to draw away from the sides of the pot on which a thin crust will form.

Step 3: Pour the cooked polenta onto a serving board or platter.

To Serve: Spoon the meat sauce over the hot polenta and sprinkle with Parmesan. Serve hot.

 *This is a spectacular meat sauce which is also good spooned over freshly cooked rice and with all kinds of pasta.*

Meat Sauce

2	tablespoons extra-virgin olive oil
2	onions, finely chopped
2	carrots, finely chopped
2	stalks celery, finely chopped
2	cloves garlic, finely chopped
8	ounces (250 g) Italian sausage, peeled
1	pound (500 g) ground (minced) beef
1	tablespoon all-purpose (plain) flour
1/2	cup (125 ml) red wine
1	pound (500 g) tomatoes, peeled and chopped
1	tablespoon finely chopped fresh parsley
1/4	teaspoon freshly grated nutmeg
	Sprig of fresh rosemary
	Sprig of fresh sage
1	bay leaf
1	small piece lemon zest
	Salt and freshly ground black pepper
	Freshly grated Parmesan cheese

Basic Polenta

2	quarts (2 liters) cold water
1	tablespoon sea salt
3 1/2	cups (500 g) polenta (coarse-grain yellow cornmeal)

Serves: 8
Preparation: 30 minutes
Cooking: 4 hours
Level: 2

PREPARING POLENTA

Polenta is made from stoneground yellow cornmeal. Although corn is a native American grain, this delicious dish comes from northern Italy where it was the staple food of the poor for centuries. By the end of the 20th century, this traditional Italian peasant food had become a star in the culinary sky in many parts of the world and rightly so, since it tastes so good!

1. BRING the water and salt to a boil in a large pot. Add the cornmeal gradually, stirring constantly so that no lumps form.

2. STIR the polenta over low heat with a long wooden spoon. After 40–45 minutes the polenta will begin to pull away from the sides of the pot.

3. POUR the cooked polenta onto a serving board or large platter. Serve hot with a sauce or let cool.

4. COOL POLENTA can be sliced and fried (serve topped with tomato, mushroom, or meat sauce) or baked.

BAKED POLENTA WITH TOMATO AND CHEESE

Prepare the polenta. • Drizzle a clean work surface with cold water and turn the hot polenta out onto it. Spread to about $1/2$ inch (1 cm) thick and let cool, about 1 hour. • Preheat the oven to 400°F (200°C/gas 6). • Lightly oil eight individual ovenproof baking dishes. • Heat the oil in a large frying pan over medium heat. Add the garlic and sauté until pale gold. • Add the tomatoes and simmer until reduced a little, about 20 minutes. Season with salt and pepper. • Use a glass or cookie cutter to cut out disks of polenta about 2 inches (5 cm) in diameter. • Arrange the polenta disks in the baking dishes, overlapping them slightly, roof-tile fashion. • Spoon the hot tomato sauce over the top and sprinkle with the cheese. • Bake for 10–15 minutes, or until the cheese is bubbling and golden brown. • Serve hot.

1	**quantity Basic Polenta (see pages 124–125)**
$1/4$	**cup (60 ml) extra-virgin olive oil**
2	**cloves garlic, finely chopped**
4	**cups (800 g) canned tomatoes, with juice**
	Salt and freshly ground black pepper
2	**cups (250 g) freshly grated Emmental (or Cheddar) cheese**

Serves: 8
Preparation: 30 minutes
  + 1 hour to cool
Cooking: $1^1/2$ hours
Level: 2

BAKED SEMOLINA GNOCCHI WITH GORGONZOLA

Semolina Gnocchi: Bring the milk to a boil in a medium saucepan. • Gradually pour the semolina into the milk, stirring all the time. Cook, stirring constantly, until the mixture comes away from the sides of the pan, 10–15 minutes. • Remove from the heat and stir the egg yolks in one at a time, followed by the butter. The mixture should be thick, but still soft. Season with salt. • Pour the gnocchi mixture out onto a lightly oiled work surface and spread to about 1/2 inch (1 cm) thick. Let cool, 1–2 hours.
Sauce: Melt the butter in a medium saucepan and stir in the flour. • Gradually add the milk and cook over low heat, stirring constantly, for 5 minutes. Season with salt and white pepper. Remove from the heat. • Preheat the oven to 450°F (225°C/gas 7). • Oil six to eight individual ovenproof dishes. • Use a glass or cookie cutter to cut out the gnocchi in rounds about 2 inches (5 cm) in diameter. • Arrange the gnocchi in the prepared dishes, overlapping them a little, roof-tile style. • Sprinkle the Gorgonzola over the gnocchi and pour the sauce over the top. Sprinkle with Parmesan. • Bake for 15 minutes, or until nicely browned and bubbling. • Serve hot.

Semolina Gnocchi
6   cups (1.5 liters) milk
2¼ cups (400 g) semolina
5   large egg yolks
¼   cup (60 g) butter
    Salt

Sauce
3   tablespoons butter
3   tablespoons all-purpose (plain) flour
2   cups (500 ml) hot milk
    Salt and freshly ground white pepper
8   ounces (250 g) Gorgonzola cheese, cut into small cubes
½   cup (60 g) freshly grated Parmesan cheese

Serves: 6–8
Preparation: 15 minutes
  + 1–2 hours to cool
Cooking: 30–35 minutes
Level: 1

■ ■ ■ *This is a traditional Italian dish usually known as* Gnocchi alla romana.

PASTA

1 PENNE

2 FARFALLE

3 FUSILLI

1. Penne are the most popular type of short, dried pasta. They come in two types, *lisce* (smooth) and *rigato* (ridged). The ridged variety is good with smooth, oil-based sauces because the ridges trap the sauce.

2. Farfalle, also known as bow-ties, are another common short pasta shape. They are good with smooth and chunky sauces and also in pasta salads. Small farfalle are used in soups.

3. Fusilli are one of two spiral-shaped short pasta types. The other type is called eliche. They are good with smooth and chunky sauces, which get trapped in their spirals.

TYPES OF PASTA

4 SPAGHETTI

5 BUCATINI

6 ZITI

4. Spaghetti is the most popular and best known pasta type. Versatile and always delicious, spaghetti is good with smooth, not-too-chunky sauces.

5. There are several types of thick spaghetti-shaped pasta. These include bucatini, which have a hole down the center, and linguine (also known as bavette), which are slightly flattened.

6. Ziti are a large, hollow spaghetti-shaped pasta from Naples. They are usually snapped into 2–3 pieces before cooking, otherwise they are impossible to wrap around a fork to eat.

7 TAGLIATELLE

8 PAPPARDELLE

9 LASAGNA

7. Tagliatelle are the most common type of fresh ribbon pasta. Indistinguishable from fettuccine, they are made from soft wheat flour and eggs. Spinach tagliatelle are also very popular.

8. Pappardelle are wider than tagliatelle and are traditionally served with flavorsome sauces made from duck, hare, boar, or other wild game.

9. Lasagna is made from fresh pasta cut into wide strips that are blanched and then baked with meat, seafood, cheese, or vegetable sauces.

135

The huge variety of pasta types can be broken down into two basic groups: dried pasta and fresh pasta. Almost all dried pasta is made from hard, durum wheat flour and is produced industrially. About 90 percent of all pasta is dried and it includes favorites such as spaghetti and penne. Fresh pasta is made from soft wheat flour and is either prepared at home or bought in gourmet food stores. It includes simple ribbon types such as tagliatelle, as well as stuffed shapes like ravioli and tortellini.

10 RAVIOLI

11 TORTELLI

12 TORTELLINI

10. Stuffed pasta, made from fresh pasta which is rolled and filled. Square, round, or half-moon shaped ravioli are always popular. Fillings include meat, cheese, spinach, and pumpkin.

11. Half-moon shaped stuffed pasta is often called tortelli (but also ravioli, depending on which region of Italy it comes from). Classic Tuscan tortelli are filled with potato.

12. Tortellini come from Emilia in central Italy and are filled with ground mixtures of famous local products, such as Parma ham, mortadella, Parmesan, and pork loin, and with spices such as nutmeg.

BASIC TOMATO SAUCE

Cook the tomatoes with ¼ teaspoon of salt in a covered saucepan over medium heat for 5 minutes. • Transfer to a colander with large holes and let drain for 1 hour. • Return to the saucepan and add the onion, garlic, basil, oil, and sugar. season with salt. Cover and bring to a boil over medium heat. Simmer over low heat until the sauce has thickened and reduced, about 40 minutes. • Remove from the heat and run through a food mill or process in a food processor until smooth.

3 pounds (1.5 kg) firm-ripe tomatoes, preferably San Marzano, peeled and coarsely chopped

Salt

1 red onion, thinly sliced

2 cloves garlic, finely chopped

Leaves from 1 small bunch fresh basil, torn

2 tablespoons extra-virgin olive oil

⅛ teaspoon sugar

Serves: 4–6
Preparation: 20 minutes
  + 1 hour to drain
Cooking: 50 minutes
Level: 1

■ ■ ■ *This is a versatile tomato sauce that can be served with all types of pasta—short, long, dried, fresh, filled, or baked—and with many other dishes too. It is a traditional recipe from the Campania region around Naples, in southern Italy, where it is made with the local San Marzano tomatoes. These oval shaped "meaty" tomatoes have few seeds and a strong, sweet flavor, making them ideal for sauces.*

PENNE WITH SPICY TOMATO SAUCE

Heat the oil in a large frying pan over medium heat. Add the pancetta and sauté until golden and crisp, about 5 minutes. Using a slotted spoon, transfer the pancetta to a heated plate. • In the same oil, sauté the chiles and garlic until the garlic is pale gold, 3–4 minutes. • Stir in the tomatoes and season with salt. Add the parsley and simmer until the tomatoes have broken down and the sauce is reduced, 15–20 minutes. • Add the pancetta and simmer for 2–3 minutes. • Meanwhile, cook the pasta in a large pot of salted boiling water until al dente. Drain and add to the sauce. Toss well. • Sprinkle with the pecorino and serve hot.

⅓ cup (90 ml) extra-virgin olive oil

5 ounces (150 g) pancetta, cut into thin strips

2 fresh red chiles, seeded and finely chopped

5 cloves garlic, finely chopped

2 pounds (1 kg) tomatoes, peeled and coarsely chopped

Salt

2 tablespoons finely chopped fresh parsley

1 pound (500 g) penne

½ cup (60 g) freshly grated pecorino cheese

Serves: 4–6
Preparation: 15 minutes
Cooking: 30 minutes
Level: 1

■ ■ ■ *This is a classic spicy sauce. Its Italian name is arrabbiata, which means "angry." This sauce goes well with dried pasta shapes both long and short. It is especially good with those that are ridged or folded so that they can trap and hold the chunky pieces of pancetta. Remember that not everyone loves a really fiery sauce; you can always serve extra dried chile or chile oil at the table.*

FARFALLE WITH PEAS AND HAM

Heat the butter in a large frying pan over medium-low heat. Add the peas and ham and sauté until the peas are tender, 5–10 minutes. • Stir in 4 tablespoons (60 ml) of the cream and simmer until the sauce thickens. Season with salt and pepper. • Meanwhile, cook the farfalle in a large pot of salted boiling water until al dente. • Drain well and transfer to the pan with the sauce. Add the remaining 2 tablespoons of cream, parsley, and Parmesan. Toss well and serve hot.

140

¼   cup (60 g) butter

2   cups (300 g) fresh or frozen peas

8   ounces (250 g) thinly sliced ham, cut in small squares

6   tablespoons (90 ml) heavy (double) cream

1   pound (500 g) farfalle (bow-ties)

2   tablespoons finely chopped fresh parsley

    Salt and freshly ground black pepper

½   cup (60 g) freshly grated Parmesan cheese

Serves: 4–6
Preparation: 10 minutes
Cooking: 15 minutes
Level: 1

■■■ *This is a simple pasta sauce that you can prepare in the time it takes the pasta to cook. It goes well with other short pasta types too, such as penne, fusilli, or spirals. Try it with whole-wheat (wholemeal) penne.*

FUSILLI WITH RICOTTA AND SUN-DRIED TOMATOES

142

Combine the ricotta, mint, and parsley in a medium bowl and beat with a fork to make a smooth cream. Season with salt and pepper. • Put the sun-dried tomatoes in a bowl and add the garlic, capers, and oil. Mix well. • Chop the arugula and tomato mixture in a food processor to make a smooth paste. • Meanwhile, cook the pasta in a large pot of salted boiling water until al dente. Drain well, reserving 2 tablespoons of the cooking liquid. • Transfer the pasta to a heated serving bowl. Stir the reserved cooking liquid into the pesto. Add the ricotta and pesto to the pasta and toss well. • Garnish with the arugula leaves and serve hot.

2	cups (500 g) fresh ricotta cheese, drained
1	tablespoon finely chopped fresh mint
1	tablespoon finely chopped fresh parsley
	Salt and freshly ground black pepper
4	ounces (125 g) sun-dried tomatoes, soaked in warm water for 15 minutes, drained, and chopped
1	clove garlic, chopped
1	tablespoon salt-cured capers, rinsed
1/3	cup (90 ml) extra-virgin olive oil
3	cups (150 g) arugula (rocket), chopped + extra leaves to garnish
1	pound (500 g) fusilli

Serves: 4–6
Preparation: 15 minutes
Cooking: 15 minutes
Level: 1

■■■ *If you like spicy sauces, garnish this dish with a finely chopped fresh red or green chile.*

BUCATINI WITH AMATRICIANA SAUCE

Sauté the pancetta in a large non-stick frying pan over medium heat until lightly browned, about 5 minutes. • Add the onion and sauté until softened, 3–4 minutes. • Add the tomatoes and chile. Mix well and season with salt and pepper. Partially cover the pan and simmer over low heat until the tomatoes are well reduced, about 30 minutes. • Meanwhile, cook the pasta in a large pot of salted boiling water until al dente. Drain well and add to the sauce. • Toss over high heat for 1 minute. Serve hot.

8　ounces (250 g) guanciale or pancetta, cut into thin strips

1　medium onion, finely chopped

2　pounds (1 kg) ripe tomatoes, peeled and chopped

1　small red fresh chile, seeded and chopped

　Salt and freshly ground black pepper

1　pound (500 g) bucatini

Serves: 4–6
Preparation: 15 minutes
Cooking: 40 minutes
Level: 1

■■■ This pasta sauce comes from the small town of Amatrice which nestles in the rolling hills of Lazio. Every summer a festival is held both in Amatrice and in the beautiful Piazza Campo de' Fiori in Rome to celebrate this special dish which has become a modern classic. Guanciale is a type of pancetta cut from the jowl and chest of the pig. It is highly prized in central Italy and also used in the well-known Carbonara Sauce (see page 148).

LINGUINE WITH PESTO, POTATOES AND BEANS

Pesto: Combine the garlic, pine nuts, basil, and Parmesan in a food processor and process until coarsely chopped. • With the motor running, gradually add the oil, processing until smooth and finely chopped.

Pasta: Cook the green beans in a large pot of salted boiling water until just tender, 4–6 minutes. Drain well. • Cook the linguine in a large pot of salted boiling water for 5 minutes. Add the potatoes and cook until the pasta is al dente and the potatoes are tender, about 5–7 minutes more. • Drain well, reserving 1–2 tablespoons of the cooking water, and transfer to a large serving bowl with the beans. • If the pesto is very thick (or if it has been stored in the refrigerator), add enough of the reserved cooking water to make the sauce liquid. • Spoon the pesto over the pasta mixture and toss well. • Season with pepper. Sprinkle with the Parmesan, garnish with the basil and serve hot.

Pesto

2 cloves garlic
2 tablespoons pine nuts
1 large bunch fresh basil
4 tablespoons freshly grated Parmesan cheese
½ cup (125 ml) extra-virgin olive oil

Pasta

14 ounces (400 g) green beans, chopped
1 pound (500 g) linguine
8 new potatoes, cut into ½-inch (1-cm) cubes
   Freshly ground black pepper
¼ cup (30 g) Parmesan cheese, flaked
   Sprigs of basil to garnish

Serves: 4–6
Preparation: 15 minutes
Cooking: 15 minutes
Level: 2

■■■ *This is a classic dish from the city of Genoa, in northeast Italy, the hometown of pesto.*

SPAGHETTI WITH CARBONARA SAUCE

148

Heat the oil in a small saucepan over medium heat. Add the onion and sauté until softened, 3–4 minutes. • Add the guanciale and sauté until crisp, about 5 minutes. Remove from the heat and set aside. • **Step 1:** Beat the eggs, cheese, and cream in a large heatproof bowl. • **Step 2:** Cook the pasta in a large pot of salted boiling water until al dente. • Drain and add to the guanciale in the pan. Return to medium-high heat and toss until the pasta is coated with the guanciale-flavored oil and very hot. **Step 3:** Pour the pasta mixture into the bowl with the egg mixture and toss briskly so that the eggs cook lightly but are still creamy. • Season with plenty of freshly ground black pepper. • Serve immediately.

2	tablespoons extra-virgin olive oil
1	small onion, finely chopped
5	ounces (150 g) diced guanciale or pancetta (or bacon)
4	large eggs
3/4	cup (90 g) freshly grated pecorino or Parmesan cheese
1/3	cup (90 ml) heavy (double) cream
	Salt and freshly ground black pepper
1	pound (500 g) spaghetti

Serves: 4–6
Preparation: 15 minutes
Cooking: 15 minutes
Level: 2

■■■ *Carbonara is another classic Roman sauce. In Italy, it is made with* guanciale *(a type of pancetta), but it can also be made with bacon. Some food historians have traced the origins of the dish to the end of World War II when Allied servicemen arrived in Rome with plenty of bacon and powdered eggs which local cooks were happy to make into this delicious pasta dish.*

■ PREPARING CARBONARA SAUCE

The trick with Carbonara sauce is to make sure that the eggs are cooked but still creamy and not full of little lumps of cooked egg. The best way to achieve this is to pour the very hot pasta and guanciale mixture into the bowl of eggs (rather than the other way around), and toss briskly. It is traditional to season the finished dish generously with freshly ground black pepper.

1. WHISK the eggs, cheese, and cream in a large heatproof bowl until well mixed.

2. COOK the pasta in a large pot of salted boiling water until al dente. Drained and add to the pan with the guanciale and toss well until the pasta is coated with the guanciale-flavored oil and very hot.

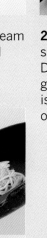

3. POUR the pasta into the egg mixture and toss briskly so that the eggs cook lightly but are still creamy.

SPAGHETTI WITH MEDITERRANEAN SAUCE

Heat the oil in a large frying pan over medium heat. Add the pancetta and sauté until lightly browned, 3–5 minutes • Add the onion, garlic, parsley, basil, and bell peppers. Sauté until the bell peppers and onions are almost tender, 10–15 minutes. • Stir in the tomatoes, chile, and oregano, and season with salt. Mix well, cover, and simmer over low heat until the tomatoes have broken down, about 15 minutes. Add the capers and olives. • Meanwhile, cook the pasta in a large pot of salted boiling water until al dente. • Drain and add to the pan. Toss over high heat for 1 minute. • Sprinkle with the cheese, garnish with the extra basil, and serve hot.

1/3 cup (90 ml) extra-virgin olive oil

3 ounces (90 g) pancetta, chopped

1 large white onion, finely chopped

1 clove garlic, finely chopped

2 tablespoons finely chopped fresh parsley

6 fresh basil leaves + extra to garnish

2 red bell peppers (capsicums), seeded and finely sliced

2 yellow bell peppers (capsicums), seeded and finely sliced

2 cups (400 g) canned tomatoes, with juice

1/2 fresh red chile, seeded and chopped

1/2 teaspoon dried oregano

Salt

2 tablespoons brined-cured capers, drained

Handful green olives, pitted and coarsely chopped

1 pound (500 g) spaghetti

1/2 cup (60 g) freshly grated pecorino or Parmesan cheese

Serves: 4–6
Preparation: 15 minutes
Cooking: 30 minutes
Level: 1

SPAGHETTI WITH PUTTANESCA SAUCE

Heat the oil in a large frying pan over medium heat. Add the garlic and chiles and sauté until the garlic is pale gold, 2–3 minutes. • Add the anchovies (if using) and stir gently until they dissolve into the oil. • Add the olives, capers, and tomatoes. Season with salt and pepper (the anchovies and olives are both quite salty, so be sure to taste the sauce before seasoning). Simmer over medium-low heat until the sauce reduces, 15–20 minutes. • Meanwhile, cook the spaghetti in a large pot of salted boiling water until al dente. • Drain well and transfer to a large heated serving dish. Pour the sauce over the top, toss well, and serve hot with the cheese.

¼ cup (60 ml) extra-virgin olive oil

3 cloves garlic, finely chopped

1–2 small dried red chiles, crumbled

6 anchovy fillets (optional)

2 cups (200 g) black olives, pitted

2 tablespoons brine-cured capers, drained

2 pounds (1 kg) ripe tomatoes, peeled and coarsely chopped

Salt and freshly ground black pepper

1 pound (500 g) spaghetti

Coarsely grated pecorino romano cheese to serve

Serves: 4–6
Preparation: 10 minutes
Cooking: 25–30 minutes
Level: 1

■ ■ ■ *This is a classic Neapolitan sauce. Its Italian name "puttanesca," comes from the Italian word* puttana *(whore), presumably because it is so hot and spicy!*

SPAGHETTI WITH SEAFOOD SAUCE

156

Soak the mussels and clams in cold water for 1 hour. • Clean the squid. Chop the bodies into rounds and the tentacles into short pieces. • Do not peel the shrimp tails. • Pour 2 tablespoons of the oil into a large frying pan, add the mussels and clams, and steam open over medium heat, 5–10 minutes. Discard any shells that do not open. • Heat the remaining 6 tablespoons (90 ml) of oil in a large frying pan and sauté the garlic, parsley, and chiles for 2 minutes over medium heat, taking care not to brown. Add the tomatoes and sauté for 3–4 minutes. • Add the squid and sauté over high heat for 3–4 minutes. Season with salt and pepper. Add the shrimp, clams, and mussels (if preferred, extract the clams and mussels from their shells, leaving just a few in the shell to make the finished dish look more attractive). Mix well and cook for 2 minutes more. Turn off the heat, cover, and set aside. Don't let it simmer or the calamari will turn to rubber. • Meanwhile, cook the spaghetti in a large pot of salted, boiling water until al dente. Drain well and add to the pan with the seafood sauce. Toss over medium-high heat for 1–2 minutes. • Transfer to a heated dish and serve hot.

12 ounces (350 g) clams, in shell

12 ounces (350 g) mussels, in shell

12 ounces (350 g) squid (calamari)

12 ounces (300 g) shrimp (prawns), heads removed

8 tablespoons (125 ml) extra-virgin olive oil

2 cloves garlic, fincly chopped

3 tablespoons finely chopped fresh parsley

1–2 small dried red chiles, crumbled

3 tomatoes, peeled and coarsely chopped

Salt and freshly ground black pepper

1 pound (500 g) spaghetti

Serves: 4–6
Preparation: 30 minutes
   + time to soak
Cooking: 20–25 minutes
Level: 2

■ PREPARING FRESH PASTA DOUGH

Plain fresh pasta is made of a simple mixture of flour and eggs. For 4 people, you will need 2⅔ cups (400 g) of all-purpose (plain) flour and four very fresh large eggs. Fresh pasta can also be colored or flavored with spinach or tomato purée, cocoa, herbs, or chiles, or can be made with whole-wheat (wholemeal), buckwheat, or other flours.

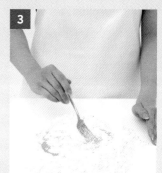

1. SIFT the flour onto a clean work surface and shape into a mound. Make a hollow in the center.

2. USE a fork to beat the eggs lightly in a small bowl. Pour the beaten eggs into the center of the mound of flour.

3. USE the fork to incorporate the eggs into the flour. Take care not to break the wall of flour or the eggs will run.

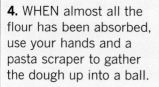

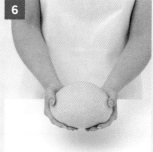

4. WHEN almost all the flour has been absorbed, use your hands and a pasta scraper to gather the dough up into a ball.

5. KNEAD by pushing down and forward on the pasta with the heel of your palm. Fold in half, give a quarter-turn, and repeat.

6. AFTER 10–15 minutes, it will be smooth and silky, with tiny air bubbles on the surface. Let rest for 30 minutes.

If making simple ribbon pasta, such as tagliatelle, run all the sheets of pasta through the machine one notch at a time. This will give them time to dry a little before being rolled to the next thickness. If making stuffed pasta, such as ravioli, roll the pasta one sheet at a time to the thinnest setting before rolling the next sheet. This will prevent them drying out.

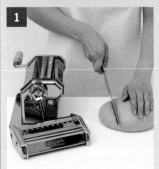

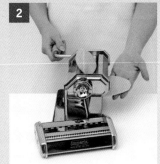

1. DIVIDE the dough into six pieces (for 14 ounces /400 g of pasta, enough for four people).

2. ROLL a piece of dough at the thickest setting. Continue rolling, reducing the thickness one notch at a time.

3. THE SHEETS should be evenly shaped. Long sheets are hard to manage; keep at about 12–14 inches (30–35 cm).

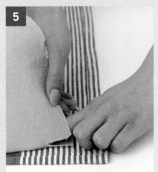

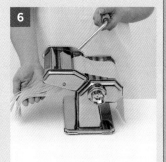

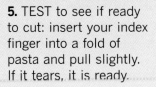

4. SPRINKLE the sheets with semolina and cover with a clean dry cloth. Let dry a little before you begin to cut them.

5. TEST to see if ready to cut: insert your index finger into a fold of pasta and pull slightly. If it tears, it is ready.

6. SET the machine to the width required and run each sheet through. Gather the pasta up and shape into "nests."

PAPPARDELLE WITH MEAT SAUCE

Fresh Pasta Dough (see the step-by-step instructions on pages 158–159): Sift the flour onto a clean work surface and make a well in the center. Break the eggs into the well and mix in to make a smooth dough. Knead for 10–15 minutes until smooth and elastic. Shape the dough into a ball, wrap in a clean kitchen towel, and let rest at room temperature for 30 minutes. • Roll out the pasta and cut into pappardelle, about 1 inch (2.5 cm) wide.
Meat Sauce: Heat the oil and butter in a large saucepan over medium heat. Add the pancetta, onion, carrot, celery, and garlic and sauté until the vegetables have softened, about 5 minutes. • Add the beef and sauté until browned, about 5 minutes. Pour in the wine and simmer until evaporated, 2–3 minutes. • Mix in the tomato paste, and beef stock. Season with salt and pepper. Return to a boil, then cover and simmer over very low heat for about 2 1/2 hours, stirring from time to time. Add more stock if the sauce starts to dry out. • Cook the pasta in a large pot of salted boiling water until al dente, 3–4 minutes. • Drain and transfer to a warmed serving bowl. Add the sauce and toss well. • Serve hot with the Parmesan cheese.

■ ■ ■ *This is a very good, basic meat sauce. You can serve it with all kinds of pasta, including long, short, fresh, and filled. The important thing is to simmer the sauce for at least two hours; the longer the better.*

Fresh Pasta Dough

2²⁄₃ cups (400 g) all-purpose (plain) flour

4   large eggs

Meat Sauce

3   tablespoons extra-virgin olive oil

2   tablespoons butter

4   ounces (125 g) pancetta, coarsely chopped

1   onion, finely chopped

1   carrot, finely chopped

1   stalk celery, finely chopped

1   clove garlic, finely chopped

1   pound (500 g) ground (minced) beef

¹⁄₂   cup (125 ml) dry white wine

2   tablespoons tomato paste (concentrate)

¹⁄₂   cup (125 ml) Beef Stock + extra as required (see pages 62–63)

     Salt and freshly ground black pepper

     Freshly grated Parmesan cheese to serve

Serves: 4
Preparation: 20 minutes + 1 hour for the pasta
Cooking: 2 hours 45 minutes
Level: 2

PAPPARDELLE WITH BELL PEPPER SAUCE

If using homemade pasta, prepare the pappardelle following the instructions on pages 158–160.

Bell Pepper Sauce: Heat the oil in a medium saucepan over medium heat. Add the onion, celery, and carrot and sauté until softened, 3–4 minutes. • Add the pancetta and sauté until golden brown, about 5 minutes. • Add the bell peppers, cover, and simmer over medium-low heat until tender, 10–15 minutes. Season with salt and pepper. • Cook the pasta in a large pot of salted boiling water until al dente, 3–4 minutes. • Drain and transfer to the pan with the sauce. Add the butter and half the Parmesan and toss gently. • Serve hot, sprinkled with the remaining Parmesan and the parsley.

1   recipe pappardelle (see pages 158–160) or 14 ounces (400 g) fresh store-bought pappardelle

Bell Pepper Sauce

¼   cup (60 ml) extra-virgin olive oil

1   onion, finely chopped

1   stalk celery, finely chopped

1   carrot, finely chopped

4   ounces (125 g) pancetta, finely chopped

1   pound (500 g) yellow bell peppers (capsicums), seeded and cut into thin strips

     Salt and freshly ground black pepper

2   tablespoons butter

1   cup (125 g) freshly grated Parmesan cheese

1   tablespoon finely chopped fresh parsley

Serves: 4
Preparation: 30 minutes
  + time for the pasta
Cooking: 25–30 minutes
Level: 2

PAPPARDELLE WITH DUCK SAUCE

If using homemade pasta, prepare the pappardelle following the instructions on pages 158–160. If liked, cut the pappardelle by hand using a fluted pastry cutter to create fluted borders.

Duck Sauce: Heat the oil in a large heavy saucepan over medium heat. Add the onion, bay leaf, sage, carrot, parsley, celery leaves, and ham and sauté until the vegetables are softened, 5–7 minutes. • Add the duck and sauté over medium-high heat until browned, 8–10 minutes. • Pour in the wine and simmer for 15 minutes. • Stir in the tomatoes and season with salt and pepper. Pour in the beef stock, cover, and simmer over low heat until the duck meat is very tender and coming away from the bone, about 1 hour. • Bone the duck and cut the meat into small chunks. Return the meat to the sauce and simmer for 15 minutes. • Meanwhile, cook the pasta in a large pot of salted boiling water until al dente, 3–4 minutes. • Drain and add to the sauce. Sprinkle with Parmesan and serve hot.

■ ■ ■ *This is a rich sauce from Tuscany and Umbria in central Italy where it is made on special occasions. Serve with a glass of very good, full-bodied red wine, such as a Brunello di Montalcino or a Vino Nobile di Montepulciano.*

1	recipe pappardelle (see pages 158–160) or 14 ounces (400 g) fresh store-bought pappardelle

Duck Sauce

4	tablespoons (60 ml) extra-virgin olive oil
1	onion, finely chopped
1	bay leaf
1	small bunch fresh sage, finely chopped
1	small carrot, finely chopped
1	tablespoon finely chopped fresh parsley
2	celery leaves, finely chopped
1	cup (100 g) ham, chopped
1	duck (about 3 pounds/ 1.5 kg), cleaned and cut into quarters
2/3	cup (150 ml) red wine
1	pound (500 g) tomatoes, peeled and chopped
	Salt and freshly ground black pepper
1	cup (250 ml) Beef Stock (see pages 62–63)
1	cup (125 g) freshly grated Parmesan cheese

Serves: 4
Preparation: 30 minutes + time for the pasta
Cooking: About 2 hours
Level: 3

TAGLIATELLE WITH EGGPLANT SAUCE

If using homemade pasta, prepare the tagliatelle following the instructions on pages 158–160. The tagliatelle should be cut about $1/2$ inch (1 cm) wide. **Eggplant Sauce:** Bring a large pan of lightly salted water to a boil. Add the eggplant and simmer for 4 minutes. Drain well, squeezing out any excess moisture. • Heat the oil in a large frying pan over medium heat. Add the garlic and thyme and sauté for 2 minutes. Add the eggplant and cook for 6–7 minutes, mashing gently with a fork. • Remove from the heat, add 1 tablespoon of the basil, and season with salt and pepper. • Transfer to a food processor and chop until smooth. • Return the eggplant sauce to the pan and add the tomatoes. Cook until the tomatoes have broken down and the sauce is creamy, 5–10 minutes. • Meanwhile, cook the pasta in a large pot of salted boiling water until al dente, 3–4 minutes. • Drain well, reserving 1–2 tablespoons of cooking water. Add the pasta and reserved water to the pan with the sauce. Sprinkle with the cheese and remaining basil, and toss gently. • Serve hot.

1   recipe tagliatelle (see pages 158–160) or 14 ounces (400 g) fresh store-bought tagliatelle

Eggplant Sauce

3   medium eggplant (aubergines) peeled and chopped into small cubes

$1/3$ cup (90 ml) extra-virgin olive oil

2   cloves garlic, finely chopped

1   tablespoon finely chopped fresh thyme

2   tablespoons finely chopped fresh basil

    Salt and freshly ground white pepper

3   large tomatoes, peeled and chopped

$1/2$ cup (60 g) freshly grated pecorino cheese

Serves: 4
Preparation: 20 minutes
    + time for the pasta
Cooking: 20–25 minutes
Level: 2

AGNOLOTTI WITH BEEF FILLING

Filling: Put the beef in a bowl with the wine. Cover and marinate in the refrigerator for 12 hours.
Pasta: Prepare the pasta dough. Let rest for 30 minutes at room temperature. • Drain the beef, reserving the marinade. • Heat 2 tablespoons of butter in a medium saucepan over high heat. Add the beef and sauté until browned, about 5 minutes. • Add the marinade and bring to a simmer. Season with salt. Cover and simmer over low heat, turning occasionally, for 1 hour. Add the stock if it starts to dry. • Remove from the heat. Reserve the cooking juices. • Chop the beef and ham finely in a food processor. • Stir in the Parmesan, eggs, and nutmeg. • Bring the milk to a boil. Add the rice and simmer until tender, 15–20 minutes. Drain and add to the meat. • Melt 2 tablespoons of butter over medium heat. Sauté the sausage, cabbage, garlic, and parsley for 5 minutes. Add to the meat. • Divide the pasta into 6 equal pieces. • **Step 1:** Roll through a pasta machine down to the thinnest setting. Alternatively, roll out by hand on a floured work surface to paper thin. • **Step 2:** Cut into 5-inch (10-cm) wide strips and put heaped teaspoons of filling along one edge, about 2 inches (5 cm) apart. Fold the pasta over and seal. Press down between the blobs of filling with your fingers to remove pockets of air. • **Step 3:** Use a fluted pastry wheel to cut out the agnolotti. • Cook in batches in a large pot of salted boiling water until al dente, 3–4 minutes. • Use a slotted spoon to transfer to a serving dish. • Melt the remaining 8 tablespoons (120 g) of butter with the cooking juices and rosemary. • Drizzle over the pasta. Sprinkle with Parmesan and serve hot.

Filling

12 ounces (350 g) stew beef, cut into chunks

1½ cups (375 ml) dry red wine

12 tablespoons (180 g) butter

Salt

1 cup (250 ml) Beef Stock (see page 62–63)

5 ounces (150 g) ham

½ cup (60 g) freshly grated Parmesan cheese + extra to serve

2 large eggs

⅛ teaspoon nutmeg

1 cup (250 ml) milk

½ cup (100 g) rice

4 ounces (120 g) Italian sausage meat, crumbled

2 cups (100 g) Savoy cabbage, shredded

1 clove garlic, finely chopped

1 tablespoon finely chopped fresh parsley

1 recipe Fresh Pasta Dough (see pages 158–160)

Handful fresh rosemary sprigs, to serve

Serves: 4–6
Preparation: 2 hours + 30 minutes to rest
Cooking: 2 hours + 12 hours to marinate
Level: 3

■ ASSEMBLING AGNOLOTTI AND RAVIOLI

Agnolotti are a type of square stuffed pasta from the northern Italian region of Piedmont. They usually have meat fillings (traditionally what was leftover from roasts). Most ravioli are square, although they can also be half-moon shaped or round, depending on where they come from. Ravioli can have meat, seafood, spinach, cheese, pumpkin, or herb fillings.

1. ROLL each piece of dough through the pasta machine to the thinnest setting. Alternatively, roll the dough out on a lightly floured work surface until paper thin.

2. CUT the dough in 5-inch (10-cm) wide strips. Put heaped teaspoons of filling along one edge, about 2 inches (5 cm) apart. Fold the pasta over and seal the edge. Press down between the blobs of filling with your fingers to remove pockets of air.

3. USE a fluted pastry wheel to cut out the agnolotti. Place on a floured clean cloth in a single layer until ready to cook.

RAVIOLI WITH OLIVE PESTO

If using homemade pasta, prepare the pasta and ravioli first following the instructions on page 174. **Olive Pesto:** Mix the olive paste with 3 tablespoons of the oil in a large bowl. • Cook the pasta in a large pot of salted boiling water until al dente, 3–4 minutes. • Drain and add to the olive paste mixture, tossing gently. Drizzle with the remaining 3 tablespoons of oil. • Add the tomatoes, capers, anchovies, and basil. Season with salt and pepper then toss again. • Serve at once.

■ ■ ■ *This simple sauce goes beautifully with ravioli that have cheese or mixed spinach and cheese fillings. It is also very good on spaghetti or penne.*
If you want to make your own spinach and cheese-filled ravioli, prepare 1 recipe of Fresh Pasta Dough (see pages 158–160) and 1 recipe of Spinach Gnocchi (for the filling; see page 194). Roll out the pasta dough and prepare the ravioli following the instructions for Assembling Agnolotti and Ravioli on page 169. They will take 3–4 minutes to cook.

1   recipe Ricotta Ravioli (see page 174) or 14 ounces (400 g) fresh store-bought ravioli with ricotta filling

Olive Pesto

1   cup (250 g) black olive paste

6   tablespoons (90 ml) extra-virgin olive oil

6   medium tomatoes, peeled and cut into small cubes

1   tablespoon salt-cured capers, rinsed

2   anchovy fillets preserved in oil, drained and finely chopped

10   leaves fresh basil, torn

Salt and freshly ground black pepper

Serves: 4
Preparation: 10 minutes
   + time for the pasta
Cooking: 3–4 minutes
Level: 2

RICOTTA RAVIOLI WITH MEAT SAUCE

Sauce: Use a meat pounder to tenderize the beef.
• Sprinkle with the pecorino, garlic, and parsley.
Roll up and tie with kitchen string. • Heat the oil
in a large frying pan over medium heat. Add the
pancetta and sauté until golden and crisp, about
5 minutes. • Carefully place the roll of beef in the
pan and sauté over high heat on all sides for about
5 minutes. • Pour in the wine and let it evaporate.
• Stir in the tomatoes and basil. Season with salt
and pepper. Cover the pan and simmer over low
heat until the meat is tender, about 2 hours.

Pasta: Prepare the pasta dough. Shape into a ball,
wrap in a clean kitchen towel and let rest for
30 minutes at room temperature.

Filling: Mix the ricotta, eggs, pecorino, parsley,
salt, and pepper in a large bowl and chill in the
refrigerator for 30 minutes. • Roll out the pasta
dough and prepare the ravioli following the
instructions for Assembling Agnolotti and Ravioli
on page 169. • Cook the ravioli in small batches in
a large pot of salted boiling water until al dente,
3–4 minutes. • Transfer to a serving dish with a
slotted spoon. Spoon the sauce over the top and
serve hot. • Slice the meat and serve after the
pasta as a main course.

*■■■This elaborate dish comes from southern Italy. The
meat flavors the sauce during the long slow cooking time
and is then sliced and served separately after the pasta.*

Sauce

1	pound (500 g) beef, in a single flat cut
3	tablespoons freshly grated pecorino cheese
1	clove garlic, finely chopped
1	tablespoon finely chopped fresh parsley
1/4	cup (60 ml) extra-virgin olive oil
2	slices of pancetta or bacon, cut into short lengths
1/3	cup (90 ml) dry white wine
1	pound (500 g) peeled tomatoes, pressed through a fine mesh strainer (passata)
	Leaves from 1 small bunch fresh basil, torn
	Salt and freshly ground black pepper
1	recipe Fresh Pasta Dough (see pages 158–160)

Filling

2	cups (500 g) fresh ricotta cheese, drained
2	large eggs
1/2	cup (60 g) freshly grated pecorino cheese
2	tablespoons finely chopped fresh parsley

Serves: 4–6
Prep: 1 hour + 30 minutes to rest and chill
Cooking: 2 1/2 hours
Level: 3

TORTELLINI IN BEEF STOCK

Filling: Dry-fry the pork in a nonstick frying pan: begin by cooking over high heat, then turn them once to seal. Reduce the heat and simmer for 4–5 minutes until cooked through. Season with salt and remove from heat. • Chop the pork with the mortadella and prosciutto in a food processor until finely ground. • Add half the egg (reserve the remaining portion for another use) and the Parmesan. Season with salt, pepper, and nutmeg. Transfer to a bowl and refrigerate for 2 hours.
Pasta: Prepare the pasta dough. Shape into a ball, wrap in a clean kitchen towel and let rest for 30 minutes. • Divide the pasta in 6 equal pieces.
Step 1: Roll the pasta dough through the pasta machine down to the thinnest setting. Alternatively, roll the pasta out on a lightly floured work surface to paper-thin. • **Step 2:** Use a smooth-edged 2-inch (5-cm) cookie cutter to cut out disks of pasta. • Shape small pieces of filling into balls about the size of marbles. Place a ball of filling at the center of each disk. • **Step 3:** Pick each one up and fold the pasta over to seal in a half-moon shape. • Fold each half-moon in half horizontally. • **Step 4:** Finish by twisting the pasta around your index finger and sealing the ends. • Lay the tortellini on a lightly floured clean cloth to dry until ready to cook. • Bring the stock to a boil in a large pot. • Cook the pasta in the boiling stock until al dente, 2–3 minutes. • Ladle the stock and tortellini into heated soup bowls and serve hot.

Filling

5	ounces (150 g) lean sliced pork
	Salt
4	ounces (125 g) mortadella
4	ounces (125 g) prosciutto (Parma ham)
1	large egg, lightly beaten
3	tablespoons freshly grated Parmesan cheese
	Freshly ground black pepper
1/8	teaspoon freshly grated nutmeg
1	recipe Fresh Pasta Dough (see pages 158–160)
6	cups (1.5 liters) Beef Stock (see pages 62–63)

Serves: 4–6
Preparation: 1 hour
  + 2 hours to chill
Cooking: 20 minutes
Level: 3

Exquisite little tortellini come from Emilia in central Italy. They usually have a meat-based filling made with a mixture of famous local products such as ground pork, mortadella, prosciutto, Parmesan, and spices. Tortellini served in boiling stock is a classic, but they can also be served with Meat Sauce (see page 160) and Basic Tomato Sauce (see page 136).

177

1. ROLL the pasta dough through the pasta machine down to the thinnest setting. Alternatively, roll the pasta out on a floured work surface to paper-thin.

2. USE a cookie cutter to cut out disks of pasta. Shape small pieces of filling into balls the size of marbles. Place one at the center of each disk of pastry.

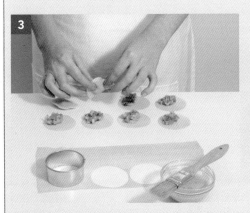

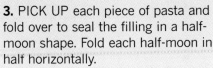

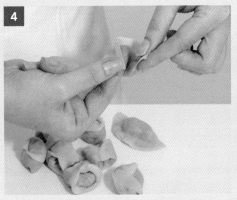

3. PICK UP each piece of pasta and fold over to seal the filling in a half-moon shape. Fold each half-moon in half horizontally.

4. FINISH by twisting the pasta around your index finger and sealing the ends.

TORTELLINI WITH PANCETTA AND LEEKS

If using homemade pasta, prepare the tortellini following the instructions on page 176–177.
Sauce: Melt the butter in a large frying pan over medium heat. Add the sliced leeks and sauté for 1 minute. Add the vermouth and let evaporate for 1 minute. • Lower the heat and simmer until the leeks are very tender, about 10 minutes. • Sauté the pancetta in another frying pan over medium heat for 1 minute. Add the cream and simmer until the mixture has reduced slightly, 3–4 minutes. • Add the pistachios and cooked leeks. Mix well. Add the chopped leek leaves and mix again. Season with salt and pepper. • Meanwhile, cook the tortellini in a large pot of salted boiling water until al dente, 3–4 minutes. Drain and add to the pan with the sauce. • Add the Parmesan and saffron and toss gently over low heat. Add the provolone and toss again. • Season with a little more freshly ground pepper and serve hot.

1 recipe tortellini (see page 176) or 14 ounces (400 g) fresh store-bought tortellini (with meat filling)

Sauce

⅓ cup (90 g) butter

2 large leeks, white parts thinly sliced, green leaves chopped

⅓ cup (90 ml) dry vermouth

8 ounces (250 g) pancetta

¾ cup (180 ml) heavy (double) cream

½ cup (75 g) blanched pistachios, coarsely chopped

Salt and freshly ground black pepper

4 tablespoons freshly grated Parmesan cheese

Pinch of saffron threads

1 cup (125 g) smoked provolone or other firm smoked cheese, cut into small cubes

Serves: 6
Preparation: 30 minutes + 2 hours to chill and for the pasta
Cooking: 20–25 minutes
Level: 3

LASAGNA

Pasta: Prepare the pasta dough. Shape into a ball, wrap in a clean kitchen towel and let rest for 30 minutes. • Divide the pasta into 6 equal pieces. **Step 1:** Roll the pasta dough through a pasta machine down to the second thinnest setting. Alternatively, roll out on a lightly floured work surface to fairly thin. • Cut into 6 x 8-inch (15 x 20-cm) rectangles. • **Step 2:** Bring a large pot of water to a boil. Add 1 tablespoon of sea salt and 1 tablespoon of oil. Add the lasagna sheets carefully one at a time and blanch for 3–5 seconds. • Scoop the sheets of pasta out using a large slotted spoon. • **Step 3:** Transfer to a large bowl of cold water with the remaining 1 tablespoon of salt and 1 tablespoon of oil. Dip into the cold water then remove with the slotted spoon. If the water warms up, add a few ice cubes. • Squeeze the excess water from each sheet. Lay the sheets out on a clean damp cloth. Make sure they do not overlap as they will stick together. **Béchamel Sauce:** Melt the butter in a medium saucepan over medium heat. Stir in the flour, salt, and nutmeg. Simmer over low heat, stirring constantly, for 1–2 minutes. • Remove from the heat and add the milk all at once. Stir well and return to the heat. Bring to a boil, then simmer over low heat, stirring constantly, until thickened, about 5 minutes. • Preheat the oven to 400°F (200°C/gas 6). • Butter a large baking dish. • Arrange four layers of pasta in the prepared dish, alternating with meat sauce, Béchamel, and Parmesan. • Bake for 20–25 minutes, until bubbling and golden. • Serve hot.

1   recipe Fresh Pasta Dough (see pages 158–160)

2   tablespoons coarse sea salt

2   tablespoons olive oil

Béchamel Sauce

3   tablespoons butter

3   tablespoons all-purpose (plain) flour

$1/4$ teaspoon salt

$1/4$ teaspoon ground nutmeg

2   cups (500 ml) milk

1   recipe Meat Sauce (see page 160)

1   cup (120 g) freshly grated Parmesan cheese

Serves: 6
Preparation: 1 hour + time for the pasta and meat sauce
Cooking: 1 hour
Level: 3

■ PREPARING LASAGNA SHEETS

The sheets of pasta for lasagna have to be blanched for a few seconds in boiling water, then cooled in cold water and gently squeezed. This partial cooking process is necessary for the success of your finished dish. Blanch the sheets in 3 quarts (3 liters) of boiling water with 1 tablespoon of coarse sea salt and 1 tablespoon of olive oil. Cool in the same quantity of cold water, salt, and oil.

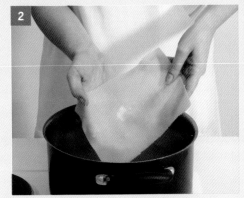

1. ROLL each piece of dough through the pasta machine down to the second thinnest setting. Cut into 6 x 8-inch (15 x 20-cm) rectangles.

2. BRING a large pot of water to a boil. Add 1 tablespoon of sea salt and oil. Blanch the sheets one at a time for 3–5 seconds. Remove with a slotted spoon.

3. TRANSFER to a large bowl of cold water with the remaining oil and sea salt. Dip into the cold water, then remove.

4. SQUEEZE the excess water gently from each sheet. Lay the sheets out in a single layer on a damp cloth.

CANNELLONI

Pasta: Prepare the pasta dough. Shape into a ball, wrap in a clean kitchen towel and let rest for 30 minutes. • Preheat the oven to 400°F (200°C/gas 6). • Butter a baking dish. • Divide the pasta into 6 equal pieces. • Roll the pasta dough through a pasta machine down to the second thinnest setting. Alternatively, roll out on a lightly floured work surface to fairly thin. • Cut into 4 x 5-inch (10 x 12-cm) rectangles. • Blanch the dough in a large pot of salted boiling water for 1 minute. Drain and lay it out on a damp cloth. Follow the same blanching procedure as for lasagna (see pages 182–183.) **Filling:** Finely chop the veal, spinach, and prosciutto in a food processor and transfer to a bowl. • Mix in the eggs and Parmesan. Season with salt, pepper, and nutmeg. • Spread some filling onto each piece of dough, leaving a border at the edges. • Roll up and arrange in the prepared baking dish, no more than two layers deep. Cover with meat sauce and top with Béchamel. Dot with the butter and sprinkle with the Parmesan. • Bake for 15–20 minutes, or until golden and bubbling. • Serve hot.

1	recipe Fresh Pasta Dough (see pages 158–160)

Filling

14	ounces (400 g) roast veal or beef
1/2	cup (100 g) cooked, drained spinach
5	ounces (150 g) prosciutto (Parma ham)
2	large eggs
1/4	cup (30 g) freshly grated Parmesan cheese
	Salt and freshly ground black pepper
1/4	teaspoon nutmeg

1	recipe Meat Sauce (see page 160)
1	recipe Béchamel Sauce (see page 184)
1	tablespoon butter
1/2	cup (60 g) freshly grated Parmesan cheese

Serves: 6
Preparation: 1 hour + time for the pasta and meat sauce
Cooking: 15–20 minutes
Level: 3

POTATO GNOCCHI WITH SUN-DRIED TOMATO SAUCE

Potato Gnocchi: Cook the potatoes whole in their skins in salted boiling water until tender, 25–30 minutes. • **Step 1:** Drain the potatoes and scrape off their skins while they are still warm. Mash until smooth in a bowl. • **Step 2:** Mix in the flour, salt, egg, and Parmesan and stir with a wooden spoon until smooth and well mixed. • **Step 3:** Shape the dough into a ball. Break off pieces and roll into cylinders just slightly thicker than your index finger. Cut into short lengths about 1 inch (2.5 cm) long. **Step 4:** If liked, you can make ridges in the gnocchi (to hold sauces better), by rolling the gnocchi one by one down the tines of a fork. • Place the gnocchi on a lightly floured clean cloth and let dry for 1–2 hours. Make sure the gnocchi are not touching each other or they may stick together.

Sun-Dried Tomato Sauce: Combine the pecorino with $1/2$ cup (125 ml) of milk in a small saucepan over low heat. • Stir the cornstarch in a small bowl with the remaining $1/4$ cup (60 ml) milk until smooth. Add to the pecorino mixture, stirring constantly, and bring to a gentle simmer. Remove from the heat and stir in all the herbs and sun-dried tomatoes. Season with salt and pepper. • **Step 5:** Cook the gnocchi in small batches in a large pot of salted boiling water until they rise to the surface, 2–3 minutes each batch. Scoop out with a slotted spoon and place in a heated serving dish. • Pour the sauce over the top. Toss gently, and serve hot.

Potato Gnocchi

- 2 pounds (1 kg) baking (floury) potatoes, with peel
- $1^2/3$ cups (250 g) all-purpose (plain) flour
- $1/2$ teaspoon salt
- 1 large egg, lightly beaten
- 3 tablespoons freshly grated Parmesan cheese

Sun-Dried Tomato Sauce

- 1 cup (120 g) freshly grated pecorino cheese
- $3/4$ cup (180 ml) milk
- 1 tablespoon cornstarch (cornflour)
- 4 tablespoons finely chopped fresh parsley
- 1 small bunch fresh chives, snipped
- 1 tablespoon finely chopped fresh thyme
- 1 tablespoon finely chopped fresh mint

  Salt and freshly ground black pepper
- 16 sun-dried tomatoes packed in oil, drained and finely chopped

Serves: 4–6
Preparation: 1 hour
 + 1–2 hours to rest
Cooking: 40–50 minutes
Level: 2

■ PREPARING POTATO GNOCCHI

Potato gnocchi are an Italian invention based on boiled mashed potato, flour, salt, and egg. They are delicious with this sun-dried tomato sauce, but do also try them with the Basic Tomato Sauce (see page 136), Pesto (see page 146), or Meat Sauce (see page 160).

1. SCRAPE the skins off the potatoes while still warm. Mash until smooth in a bowl.

2. MIX IN the flour, salt, egg, and Parmesan and stir with a wooden spoon until well mixed.

3. SHAPE the gnocchi dough into a ball. Break off pieces and roll them into cylinders just slightly thicker than your index finger. Cut into short pieces, about 1 inch (2.5 cm) long.

4. TO MAKE ridged gnocchi (which hold sauces better), roll the gnocchi one by one down the tines of a fork.

5. COOK the gnocchi in a large pot of salted boiling water until they rise to the surface, 2–3 minutes. Scoop out with a slotted spoon.

BAKED POTATO GNOCCHI

If using homemade potato gnocchi, prepare them following the instructions on pages 188–189. • Preheat the oven to 400°F (200°C/gas 6). • Melt the butter in a medium saucepan over medium heat. Add the tomatoes, garlic, onion, and salt. • Cover and simmer until the tomatoes have broken down, 10–15 minutes. Uncover and let reduce for 2–3 minutes. • Remove from the heat and process in a food processor until smooth. • Cook the gnocchi in small batches in a large pot of salted boiling water until they rise to the surface, 2–3 minutes each batch. Use a slotted spoon to transfer them to a baking dish. • Cover with half the sauce and sprinkle with half the Parmesan. Make a second layer with the gnocchi, sauce, and Parmesan. • Bake for 12–15 minutes, or until the cheese is golden brown and bubbling. • Serve hot.

1   recipe Potato Gnocchi (see pages 188-189) or 1 pound (500 g) fresh store-bought potato gnocchi

2   tablespoons butter

1   pound (500 g) tomatoes, peeled and coarsely chopped

1   clove garlic, lightly crushed but whole

1/2   red onion, thinly sliced

    Salt

3/4   cup (90 g) freshly grated Parmesan cheese

Serves: 4–6
Preparation: 30 minutes
    + time to make the gnocchi
Cooking: 30–40 minutes
Level: 3

SPINACH GNOCCHI
WITH TOMATO SAUCE

Spinach Gnocchi: Cook the spinach in a large pot with just a little salted water until wilted, 3–4 minutes. Drain well and set aside to cool. • When cool enough to handle, squeeze out the excess moisture and chop finely. • Mix the ricotta and spinach in a large bowl. • Add the eggs, 1 cup (125 g) of Parmesan, and $1/2$ cup (75 g) of flour. Season with salt and pepper and add the lemon zest. • Dip your hands in the extra flour until well coated and form the spinach mixture into 2-inch (5-cm) balls. • Cook the gnocchi in small batches a large pot of salted boiling water until they rise to the surface, 3–4 minutes per batch. • Remove with a slotted spoon and transfer to individual serving dishes. • Spoon the tomato sauce over the top of each serving and sprinkle with the extra Parmesan cheese. • Serve hot.

Spinach Gnocchi

1   pound (500 g) fresh spinach leaves, tough stalks removed

2   cups (500 g) fresh ricotta cheese, strained through a fine-mesh sieve

2   large eggs

1   cup (125 g) freshly grated Parmesan cheese + extra to serve

$1/2$ cup (75 g) all-purpose (plain) flour + extra to roll the gnocchi

Salt and freshly ground black pepper

Finely grated zest of $1/2$ lemon

1   recipe Basic Tomato Sauce (see page 136)

Serves: 6
Preparation: 30 minutes + time for the sauce
Cooking: 20 minutes
Level: 2

NOODLES

1 UDON NOODLES

2 SOBA NOODLES

3 RAMEN NOODLES

1. A popular Japanese noodle made from wheat flour. They are usually eaten hot in soups during the winter, and chilled with shredded nori or other toppings and dipping sauce during the summer.

2. A Japanese noodle made from buckwheat flour. They are usually served chilled with a dipping sauce, or in hot stock as a soup. For cold dishes, be sure to rinse the noodles in cold water after cooking.

3. A Japanese wheat noodle. They come in many shapes and sizes. They are often cooked and served in meat stock. Outside of Japan, instant or quick-cooking ramen noodles are better known.

TYPES OF NOODLES

4 FRESH EGG NOODLES

5 DRIED EGG NOODLES

6 CHINESE WHEAT NOODLES

4. These noodles come in every shape and size imaginable: flat, round, thick, thin, fresh, or dried. Made of wheat flour and egg, the fresh noodles are cooked for 2–3 minutes in boiling water.

5. Dried egg noodles are made of wheat flour and egg and are available in many shapes and sizes. Cook in boiling water for 4–5 minutes. Often flavored with shrimp.

6. Some Chinese noodles are made of wheat flour, salt, and water, without eggs. They are more delicate than egg noodles. Cook in boiling water for 5–10 minutes. They keep well.

7 HOKKIEN NOODLES

8 SINGAPORE EGG NOODLES

9 RICE STICK NOODLES

7. Yellow wheat and egg noodles originally from southern China but now very popular in Singapore, Malaysia, and Indonesia. Sold fresh or vacuum-packed and chilled.

8. Thin egg noodles made of wheat flour and egg. They are available fresh or dried.

9. Rice stick noodles are flat dried noodles. They come in various widths and are used in everything from spring rolls, salads, and soups to stir-fries and braised dishes.

A huge variety of different noodles are eaten all over Asia, but especially in China, Japan, Korea, and Southeast Asian countries such as Singapore, Malaysia, Thailand, and Indonesia. Generally speaking, wheat flour noodles come from northern China and Japan while rice noodles are from southern China and Southeast Asia. Given the variety of noodles available, it is usually best to follow the cooking instructions on the package.

10 FRESH RICE NOODLES

11 DRIED RICE VERMICELLI

12 CELLOPHANE NOODLES

10. Available in varying thicknesses. These noodles are steamed and lightly oiled then sealed into packages. They have a silky, slippery texture and are used in soups and stir-fries.

11. Thin translucent white noodles made from rice flour and packaged in blocks. Soak in boiling water before use. They expand when fried and are often used as a garnish

12. Also known as glass or bean thread noodles, these very thin noodles are made from mung bean starch. They become almost transparent when cooked by soaking in hot water.

PICKLED DAIKON NOODLE SALAD WITH SHRIMP

Soak the noodles in hot water according to the instructions on the package. • Drain well and transfer to a large bowl. • Add the shrimp, daikon, snow peas, and sesame oil. • Toss well and serve.

14 ounces (400 g) dried cellophane noodles

12 ounces (350 g) cooked shrimp (prawns), peeled and deveined

1/2 pickled daikon, cut into short lengths

5 ounces (150 g) snow peas (mangetout), very thinly sliced

2 tablespoons sesame oil

Serves: 4
Preparation: 15 minutes
Cooking: 5 minutes
Level: 1

■ ■ ■ *In summer and in the hot tropical parts of Asia, noodles are often served at room temperature or chilled. Cellophane noodles, also known as glass noodles and bean thread noodles, are often served in salads. Daikon is a large, mild-flavored radish used in Japanese cooking. Pickled daikon is available in Asian food stores and from online suppliers.*

THAI NOODLE SALAD

Salad: Cook the rice noodles following the instructions on the package. Drain well and place in a salad bowl. • Chill in the refrigerator for 30 minutes. • Add the cucumber, scallions, carrot, bean sprouts, and cilantro to the noodles in the bowl and toss gently.

Dressing: Mix the lime juice, fish sauce, soy sauce, shallot, garlic, chile, and jaggery in a small bowl until the sugar is dissolved. • Drizzle the dressing over the salad and toss well. Cover and refrigerate for at least 1 hour. • Serve chilled.

Salad

12 ounces (350 g) dried rice vermicelli noodles

1 small cucumber, very thinly sliced

8 scallions (spring onions), finely chopped

2 carrots, cut into matchsticks

2 cups (100 g) bean sprouts

3 tablespoons finely chopped fresh cilantro (coriander)

Dressing

5 tablespoons freshly squeezed lime juice

2 tablespoons Thai fish sauce

1 tablespoon light soy sauce

1 shallot, thinly sliced

2 cloves garlic, finely chopped

1 small red chile, seeded and finely chopped

2 tablespoons grated jaggery (palm sugar) or brown sugar

Serves: 4
Preparation: 15 minutes + 1^1/2 hours to chill
Cooking: 15 minutes
Level: 1

RICE NOODLE SALAD

204

Cook the rice noodles following the instructions on the package. Drain well and place in a salad bowl. • Heat the oil in a wok or frying pan over medium heat. Add the ginger and chiles and stir-fry for 2 minutes. • Add the bell pepper, raise the heat to medium-high, and stir-fry until softened, 2–3 minutes. Add the scallions and sauté for 2 minutes. • Place the bell pepper mixture in the salad bowl with the noodles. Add the cilantro and toss well. • Whisk the vegetable stock, lime juice, rice vinegar, soy sauce, and lemon zest in a small bowl. Drizzle over the noodles. • Sprinkle with the sesame seeds and chill for 30 minutes before serving.

8	ounces (250 g) long flat rice noodles
1	tablespoon sesame oil
1	(1-inch/2.5-cm) piece ginger, finely grated
2	small red chiles, seeded and thinly sliced
1	red bell pepper (capsicum), cut in small pieces
6	scallions (spring onions), sliced on the diagonal
1	bunch fresh cilantro (coriander) leaves
1/3	cup (90 ml) Vegetable Stock (see page 94)
	Freshly squeezed juice of 2 limes
2	tablespoons Japanese rice vinegar
2	tablespoons light soy sauce
1	teaspoon finely chopped lemon zest
3	tablespoons sesame seeds

Serves: 2–4
Preparation: 20 minutes
  + 30 minutes to chill
Cooking: 10 minutes
Level: 1

PAD THAI (THAI FRIED NOODLES)

Sauce: Combine the tamarind paste, oyster sauce, fish sauce, vinegar, jaggery, and sambal oelek in a small bowl and set aside.

Noodles: Place the rice stick noodles in a medium bowl and soak in hot water until softened, 5–10 minutes. • Drain well and set aside. • Heat the oil in a large wok over medium-high heat. Add the noodles and stir-fry for 1 minute, tossing to coat. • Add the eggs and tofu and cook for 1 minute, stirring frequently, until the eggs begin to scramble. • Add the onion, garlic, and shrimp paste and stir to combine. • Add the prepared sauce and bring to a boil. • Add the bean sprouts and chives and toss to combine. • Top with cilantro and peanuts. Garnish with cucumber and sambal oelek and a lime wedge on the side and serve.

■ ■ ■ *Pad Thai, which means "fried Thai style," is a favorite dish all over Thailand. It consists of stir-fried rice noodles with eggs, Thai fish sauce, tamarind, chiles, together with any combination of bean sprouts, chicken, shrimp, or tofu. The dish is usually garnished with peanuts, cilantro, and fresh lime juice.*

Sauce

3 tablespoons tamarind paste

3 tablespoons oyster sauce

2 tablespoons Thai fish sauce

2 tablespoons Chinese white wine vinegar

2 tablespoons coarsely grated jaggery (palm sugar) or brown sugar

1 teaspoon sambal oelek (chile paste) + extra to serve

Noodles

12 ounces (350 g) dried rice stick noodles

2 tablespoons peanut oil

4 large eggs, lightly beaten

8 ounces (250 g) puffed tofu, quartered

1 small onion, finely sliced

2 cloves garlic, finely chopped

2 tablespoons dried shrimp, finely chopped

1 cup (50 g) bean sprouts

1 small bunch fresh chives

½ cup (25 g) cilantro (coriander) leaves

¼ cup (40 g) roasted peanuts, chopped

Sliced cucumber

Lime wedges

Serves: 4
Preparation: 15 minutes
Cooking: 10 minutes
Level: 1

MEE GORENG (INDONESIAN FRIED NOODLES)

Bring a large saucepan of water to a boil over high heat. Add the noodles and cook until tender, about 3 minutes. • Drain and rinse under cold running water. Drain and set aside. • **Step 1:** Heat 1 tablespoon of oil in a medium frying pan over medium heat. Add the eggs and roll the pan to create a thin omelet. Cook until set, 1–2 minutes each side. • **Step 2:** Transfer to a work surface, roll up loosely, and slice into thin strips. Set aside. • Heat the remaining 2 tablespoons of oil in a wok or large frying pan over medium heat. Add the onion, garlic, chiles, and carrot and stir-fry until softened, 3–4 minutes. • Add the ketchup, oyster sauce, soy sauce, and sambal oelek and stir to combine. • Add the wom bok, spinach, bean sprouts, and pork and stir-fry for 2 minutes. • Add the noodles and sliced omelet and cook, tossing occasionally, until almost all the liquid has evaporated. • Serve hot with the scallions.

1	pound (500 g) dried egg noodles
3	tablespoons vegetable oil
2	large eggs, beaten
1	onion, thinly sliced
4	cloves garlic, finely chopped
2	large red chiles, seeded and finely sliced
1	carrot, thinly sliced into matchstick lengths
2	tablespoons ketchup
2	tablespoons oyster sauce
1	tablespoon soy sauce
1	teaspoon sambal oelek (chile paste)
¼	small wom bok (Chinese cabbage), finely shredded
1½	cups (125 g) spinach
1	cup (50 g) bean sprouts
5	ounces (150 g) barbecue pork, thinly sliced
2	scallions (spring onions), finely sliced

Serves: 4–6
Preparation: 15 minutes
Cooking: 10–15 minutes
Level: 1

▮ PREPARING EGG OMELET FOR GARNISH

1. HEAT 1 tablespoon oil in a medium frying pan over medium heat. Add the eggs, tilting the pan to spread evenly. Cook until set, 1–2 minutes each side.
2. TRANSFER to a work surface, roll up loosely, and slice into thin strips.

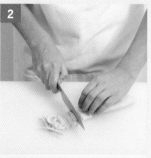

COOL SOBA NOODLES WITH DIPPING SAUCE

210

Dipping Sauce: Combine the dashi stock, rice wine, soy sauce, sesame oil, garlic, and ginger in a small saucepan over medium heat and bring to a boil. Remove from the heat and set aside to cool.
Noodles: Bring a medium saucepan of water to a boil over high heat. Unlike Italian pasta, you don't need to add salt to the water. Add the noodles and cook until tender, 3–6 minutes depending on the thickness of the noodles (or according to the instructions on the package). • Drain and rinse well under cold running water. Drain again. • Combine the noodles, carrot, and bell pepper in a large bowl and toss to combine. • Place the nori and white and black sesame seeds in a small frying pan and toast over medium-low heat until the white sesame seeds are golden and the nori is crisp, about 1 minute. • To serve, divide the noodles evenly among four serving bowls and sprinkle with the toasted nori and sesame seed mixture. Top with the scallions and pickled ginger. • Serve cold or chilled with the dipping sauce.

■ ■ ■ *Soba noodles are served cold with a dipping sauce during the hot, humid summer months in Japan. They are very refreshing. Dashi is a stock made by boiling dried seaweed. It is available in granulated or liquid forms in Asian Food stores.*

Dipping Sauce
1½ cups (375 ml) dashi stock
¼ cup (60 ml) rice wine
¼ cup (60 ml) soy sauce
1 teaspoon sesame oil
1 clove garlic, finely chopped
1 teaspoon finely grated fresh ginger

Noodles
8 ounces (250 g) dried soba (buckwheat) noodles
1 medium carrot, cut into thin matchsticks
1 red bell pepper (capsicum), seeded and thinly sliced
1 nori sheet, thinly sliced
1 teaspoon white sesame seeds
1 teaspoon black sesame seeds
3 scallions (spring onions), thinly sliced
¼ cup (20 g) pickled ginger

Serves: 4
Preparation: 20 minutes
Cooking: 10 minutes
Level: 2

CHINESE PORK CHOW MEIN

Sauce: Combine the cornstarch and water together in a small bowl. Add the oyster sauce, soy sauce and chicken stock and stir to combine. Set aside.
Noodles: Bring a medium saucepan of water to a boil over high heat. Add the noodles and simmer until tender, 4–5 minutes. • Drain and refresh under cold running water. Drain and set aside. • Heat the oil in a large wok or frying pan over medium heat. Add the onion, garlic, and ginger and stir-fry until softened, 3–4 minutes. • Add the pork and stir fry until it begins to brown, about 5 minutes. • Add the celery, bell pepper, and mushrooms and stir-fry until softened and browned, about 5 more minutes. • Pour in the sauce and bring to a boil. Add the noodles, bean sprouts, and scallions and toss to combine. • Serve hot.

■ ■ ■ Chow mein is a Chinese dish based on stir-fried noodles. It is very popular, especially in North America and there are many variations on the basic recipe.

Sauce

1 tablespoon cornstarch (cornflour)

3 tablespoons cold water

2 tablespoons oyster sauce

1 tablespoon soy sauce

1/3 cup (90 ml) Chicken Stock (see pages 34–35)

Noodles

8 ounces (250 g) dried wheat noodles

2 tablespoons vegetable oil

1 small onion, thinly sliced

2 cloves garlic, finely chopped

1 teaspoon finely grated fresh ginger

12 ounces (350 g) ground (minced) pork

2 stalks celery, thinly sliced

1 red bell pepper (capsicum), seeded and thinly sliced lengthwise

8 ounces (250 g) mushrooms, thinly sliced

2 cups (100 g) bean sprouts, rinsed

3 scallions (spring onions), thinly sliced

Serves: 4–6
Preparation: 15 minutes
Cooking: 15–20 minutes
Level: 1

SPICY BEEF NOODLE STIR-FRY

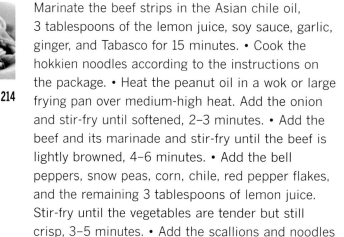

Marinate the beef strips in the Asian chile oil, 3 tablespoons of the lemon juice, soy sauce, garlic, ginger, and Tabasco for 15 minutes. • Cook the hokkien noodles according to the instructions on the package. • Heat the peanut oil in a wok or large frying pan over medium-high heat. Add the onion and stir-fry until softened, 2–3 minutes. • Add the beef and its marinade and stir-fry until the beef is lightly browned, 4–6 minutes. • Add the bell peppers, snow peas, corn, chile, red pepper flakes, and the remaining 3 tablespoons of lemon juice. Stir-fry until the vegetables are tender but still crisp, 3–5 minutes. • Add the scallions and noodles and stir-fry over high heat until well combined. • Serve hot.

1	pound (500 g) lean beef fillet, cut into thin strips
2	tablespoons Asian chile oil
6	tablespoons (90 ml) freshly squeezed lemon juice
1	tablespoon soy sauce
2	cloves garlic, finely chopped
1	teaspoon finely chopped fresh ginger
1	teaspoon Tabasco
12	ounces (350 g) hokkien noodles
2	tablespoons peanut oil
1	red onion, finely sliced
1	medium red bell pepper (capsicum), seeded and sliced
1	medium green bell pepper (capsicum), seeded and sliced
6	ounces (180 g) snow peas (mangetout), trimmed and chopped
1	cup (150 g) fresh or frozen corn
1	red chile, seeded and finely chopped
2	teaspoons crushed red pepper flakes
2	scallions (green onions), white and tender green parts only, sliced

Serves: 4
Preparation: 10 minutes
    + 15 minutes to marinate
Cooking: 10–15 minutes
Level: 1

EGGPLANT NOODLE STIR-FRY

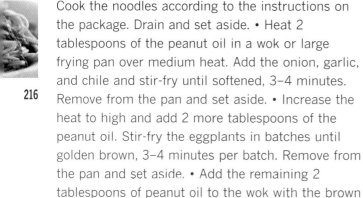

216

Cook the noodles according to the instructions on the package. Drain and set aside. • Heat 2 tablespoons of the peanut oil in a wok or large frying pan over medium heat. Add the onion, garlic, and chile and stir-fry until softened, 3–4 minutes. Remove from the pan and set aside. • Increase the heat to high and add 2 more tablespoons of the peanut oil. Stir-fry the eggplants in batches until golden brown, 3–4 minutes per batch. Remove from the pan and set aside. • Add the remaining 2 tablespoons of peanut oil to the wok with the brown sugar and stir-fry until caramelized, about 3 minutes. • Add the soy sauce, oyster sauce, sesame oil, and fish sauce and stir until heated through. • Add the noodles, onion mixture, and eggplants to the wok and toss well. • Top with the scallions and serve hot.

12	ounces (350 g) flat fresh or dried egg noodles (or tagliatelle)
6	tablespoons (90 ml) peanut or other vegetable oil
1	onion, finely chopped
1	clove garlic, sliced
1	fresh red chile, seeded and thinly sliced
8	baby eggplants, unpeeled, finely sliced on the diagonal
2	tablespoons dark brown sugar
2	tablespoons light soy sauce
2	tablespoons oyster sauce
1	teaspoon Asian sesame oil
1	tablespoon Vietnamese or Thai fish sauce
2	scallions (spring onions), white and tender green parts only, chopped

Serves: 4
Preparation: 15 minutes
Cooking: 20 minutes
Level: 1

217

BEEF AND SPINACH STIR-FRY

Combine the beef with the soy sauce, apple juice, red pepper flakes, garlic, papaya, and tomatoes in a large glass or stainless steel bowl. Use your hands to mix the ingredients for 5–10 minutes to ensure all the spices are well absorbed. The heat from your hands will help the tenderizing process. • Let marinate for 2 hours. • Cook the rice noodles according to the instructions on the package. Drain and set aside. • Heat a wok or large frying pan over high heat and add the oil. Stir-fry the celery and ginger until aromatic, 1 minute. • Add the beef and its marinade. Stir occasionally until all the liquid has evaporated and the meat is tender, about 5 minutes. • Add the spinach and noodles. Stir-fry until the spinach is wilted, about 2 more minutes. • Serve hot.

2 **pounds (1 kg) beef tenderloin, cut into thin strips**

5 **tablespoons dark soy sauce**

5 **tablespoons apple juice**

1 **teaspoon red pepper flakes**

2 **cloves garlic, finely chopped**

1 **medium papaya (pawpaw), peeled and cut into small cubes**

12 **cherry tomatoes, halved**

12 **ounces (350 g) thin rice noodles**

3 **tablespoons peanut oil**

2 **stalks celery, thinly sliced**

2 **tablespoons finely chopped fresh ginger**

6 **cups (300 g) leaf spinach, tough stems removed, finely shredded**

Serves: 6
Preparation: 15 minutes
    + 2 hours to marinate
Cooking: 10 minutes
Level: 1

STIR-FRIED CHILE BEEF NOODLES

220

Mix the kecap manis and chile peppers in a medium bowl. • Add the beef and let marinate for 1 hour. • Place the noodles in a medium bowl and let soak in boiling water for 5–10 minutes, or according to the time on the package. • Drain and set aside. • Place a wok over high heat. Add the beef and stir-fry for 2 minutes. • Add the bok choy and stir-fry for 2 more minutes. • Pour in any remaining marinade and add the noodles. Stir-fry for 2 minutes. • Toss well and serve hot.

½ cup (125 ml) kecap manis

3 small red chiles, thinly sliced

14 ounces (400 g) beef fillet, cut into thin strips

14 ounces (400 g) dried rice stick noodles

1 bunch bok choy, cut lengthwise into quarters

Serves: 4–6
Preparation: 10 minutes
  + 1 hour to marinate
Cooking: 10 minutes
Level: 1

■ ■ ■ *Kecap manis is a thick, syrupy Indonesian soy sauce. It is sweeter than ordinary soy sauce. If you can't find it, replace with the same quantity of dark soy sauce and 1 teaspoon of sugar.*

BREADS

SCONES

Preheat the oven to 425°F (210°C/gas 7). • Set out a baking sheet. Do not grease. • Sift the flour, baking powder, and salt into a large bowl. Stir in the sugar. • Rub the butter in with your fingertips until the mixture resembles coarse meal. • Using a rubber spatula or fork, stir in the cream until a sticky dough forms. • Turn the dough out onto a floured work surface and knead quickly until it comes together in a rough ball shape. Spread out on the work surface into a disk about 1/2 inch (1 cm) thick. • Transfer to the baking sheet. Use a heavy knife to score the mixture into 8–12 scones (just mark the top; don't cut through). • Bake until pale golden brown, 12–15 minutes. • Cut into scones along the score marks and use a steel spatula to transfer to a wire rack. Let rest for at least 10 minutes before serving. • Slice each scone in half and spread with butter and preserves.

2	cups (300 g) all-purpose (plain) flour
2	teaspoons baking powder
1/2	teaspoon salt
4	tablespoons sugar
5	tablespoons (75 g) unsalted butter, chopped + extra to serve
1	cup (250 ml) heavy (double) cream
1/2	cup (150 g) raspberry preserves (jam) to serve

Serves: 6–8
Preparation: 10 minutes
Cooking: 12–15 minutes
Level: 1

■ ■ ■ *These scones are quick and easy to make. Whip them up for breakfast on the weekend or as a snack for unexpected guests. If you don't have heavy (double) cream on hand, replace with the same quantity of milk. To make whole-wheat (wholemeal) scones, replace half the all-purpose (plain) flour with whole-wheat flour. Serve hot or at room temperature with butter and raspberry or other fruit preserves (jam).*

DAMPER (AUSTRALIAN BUSH BREAD)

Preheat the oven to 375°F (190°C/gas 5). • Sift the flour, baking powder, and salt into a large bowl.• Rub the butter in with your fingertips until the mixture resembles coarse meal. • Make a well in the center and pour in the water. Stir until a dough begins to form. Knead briefly, to bring the dough together. • Lightly oil a large baking sheet or line with parchment paper. • Shape the dough into an 8 inch (20 cm) disk and place on the baking sheet. • **Step 1:** Use a heavy knife to score the dough into 8 wedges. Don't cut through; just mark the top. • Bake for 20–25 minutes, until golden brown. • **Step 2:** When cooked, the base of the bread will sound hollow when tapped. • Serve warm with butter and jam or honey.

■ ■ ■ *This bread was invented by Australian drovers who cooked it in the coals of campfires. Far from home in remote areas ("the bush") for weeks at time, they used flour and water to make basic bread every day.*

3 **cups (450 g) all-purpose (plain) flour**

2 **teaspoons baking powder**

½ **teaspoon salt**

⅓ **cup (90 g) butter, cubed + extra to serve**

¾ **cup (180 ml) water**

Fruit preserves (jam) or honey, to serve

Serves: 4–6
Preparation: 10 minutes
Cooking: 20–25 minutes
Level: 1

■ SCORING DOUGH AND TESTING BREAD TO SEE IF COOKED

1. USE a heavy knife to score the dough into wedges. Don't cut all the way through; just mark the top.
2. WHEN COOKED tap the bottom of the bread with your knuckles. If ready, it will sound hollow.

CHILE CORN BREAD

Preheat the oven to 400°F (200°C/gas 6). • Lightly grease a square 8-inch (20-cm) cake pan with butter and set aside. • Sift the flour, baking soda, baking powder, and salt into a medium bowl. • Whisk the egg in a separate small bowl until frothy. • Whisk in the yogurt and half-and-half. • Gradually stir the egg mixture into the flour mixture with a wooden spoon. • Stir in the cornmeal in batches until well blended. • Mix in the chiles and scallions. • Spoon the batter into the prepared pan. • Bake for 25–30 minutes, until a skewer inserted into the center comes out clean. • Cool in the pan for 5 minutes. Cut into squares and serve warm.

½ cup (75 g) all-purpose (plain) flour

1 teaspoon baking soda (bicarbonate of soda)

1 teaspoon baking powder

1 teaspoon salt

1 large egg

1 cup (250 ml) plain yogurt

²/₃ cup (150 ml) half-and-half (single cream) or milk

1³/₄ cups (275 g) yellow cornmeal

3 tablespoons finely chopped roasted chiles

2 scallions (spring onions), finely chopped

Serves: 6–8
Preparation: 15 minutes
Cooking: 25–30 minutes
Level: 1

NAAN BREAD

Combine the water and yeast in a small bowl. Set aside in a warm place until frothy, about 10 minutes. • Combine the flour, sugar, salt, and baking soda in a large bowl. Add the nigella seeds and stir to combine. • Stir in the yogurt, oil, and yeast mixture to form a dough. • Turn the dough out onto a lightly floured work surface and knead until smooth and elastic, about 5 minutes. • Lightly oil a large bowl and put the dough in it. Cover with a clean kitchen towel and set aside in a warm place until doubled in bulk, 3–4 hours. • Put an oven shelf on the second-to-top rung if your oven has a broiler (grill), or on the top rung if it does not. • Preheat the oven to 475°F (250°C/gas 9). Place a pizza stone on the prepared shelf for at least 45 minutes. • Turn the dough out onto the work surface and knock back, punching all the air out. • **Step 1:** With oiled hands, shape the dough into ten even-size balls. • Roll each ball into an oval shape, about 5 inches (13 cm) long. **Step 2:** The naan can be rolled using a rolling pin or stretched into shape by hand. • Preheat the grill to high, if using. • **Step 3:** Lightly brush a piece of dough with water on both sides and place it on the preheated pizza stone. Work quickly as you want the oven to stay very hot. Cook for 2–3 minutes if you have a preheated oven broiler (grill) or for 2–3 minutes on each side if without. It should be golden brown. • **Step 4:** Remove from the oven and lightly brush with melted butter. • Wrap in a clean kitchen towel to keep warm.

1¼ cups (300 ml) lukewarm water + extra to brush

2 teaspoons (7 g) active dry yeast

3⅓ cups (500 g) all purpose (plain) flour

1 teaspoon sugar

1 teaspoon salt

¼ teaspoon baking soda (bicarbonate of soda)

1 teaspoon nigella seeds

¾ cup (180 ml) plain yogurt

3 tablespoons vegetable oil + extra to roll

2 tablespoons butter, melted to brush

Serves: 10
Preparation: 30 minutes + 3–4 hours to rise
Cooking: 50–60 minutes
Level: 2

Naan is a popular flatbread from South Asia and is served in Indian restaurants all over the world. In our recipe, we have flavored the dough with nigella seeds which are available in Asian food stores. If preferred, substitute with cumin seeds. Like all Indian breads, it is best served hot straight from the oven.

1. LIGHTLY OIL your hands and shape the dough into ten even-size balls. Roll each ball into an oval shape, about 5 inches (13 cm) long.

2. THE NAAN can be rolled using a rolling pin or stretched into shape by hand.

3. LIGHTLY BRUSH each piece of dough with water on both sides and place on the preheated pizza stone to cook.

4. REMOVE from the oven and lightly brush with melted butter. Wrap in a clean kitchen towel to keep warm.

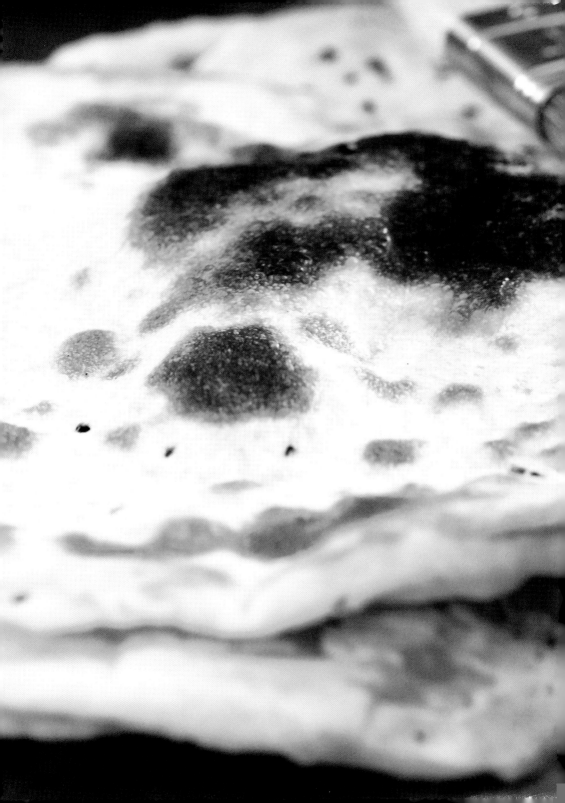

WHOLE-WHEAT SODA BREAD

Preheat the oven to 400°F (200°C/gas 6). • Oil a 9 x 5-inch (23 x 12-cm) loaf pan. • Combine the flour, brown sugar, salt, paprika, and baking soda in a large bowl and mix well. • Gradually add the yogurt and malt extract, if using. • Stir in as much milk as needed to make a moist dough. For best results, mix everything together with your hands, although the dough is very sticky. • Dust your hands with a little flour and transfer the dough to the pan. Dust the top with flour, and make a $2/3$-inch (1.5-cm) deep cut lengthwise down the center of the loaf with a knife. • Sprinkle with the pumpkin and sunflower seeds. • Bake for 15 minutes. • Decrease the oven temperature to 350°F (180°C/gas 4) and bake for 40–45 minutes more, until brown and crisp on top. • Cool on a wire rack. • Serve hot or toasted.

3   cups (450 g) whole-wheat (wholemeal) flour + extra to dust

1   tablespoon dark brown sugar

1   teaspoon salt

$1/2$ teaspoon sweet paprika

1   teaspoon baking soda (bicarbonate of soda)

2   cups (500 g) plain yogurt

1   teaspoon malt extract (optional)

$1/3$ cup (90 ml) lukewarm milk

$1/4$ cup (45 g) pumpkin seeds

1   tablespoon sunflower seeds

Serves: 6–8
Preparation: 15 minutes
Cooking: 55–60 minutes
Level: 1

■ ■ ■ *Malt extract for bread baking is readily available in supermarkets and health food stores in the UK and some other countries. Elsewhere it can be hard to find. Do make an effort to find it as it will not only help your bread to rise well but will also add extra flavor.*

BASIC FOCACCIA

Step 1: Put $1/2$ cup (125 ml) of warm water in a bowl and add the yeast and sugar. Stir with a fork until dissolved. • **Step 2:** Set aside until frothy, about 10 minutes. • **Step 3:** Sift the flour and salt into a large bowl. Pour in the yeast mixture, 2 tablespoons of oil, and most of the remaining water. Stir until the flour is absorbed, adding more water to make a firm dough as required. • Sprinkle a work surface with a little flour. Transfer the dough to the work surface. • **Step 4:** Shape into a compact ball and begin kneading. Press down on the dough with your knuckles to spread it. Take the far end of the dough, fold it a short distance toward you, then push it away again with the heel of your palm. Fold it toward you again, give it a quarter turn, then push it away. Repeat for 8–10 minutes. When ready, the dough should be smooth and elastic, show definite air bubbles beneath the surface, and spring back if you flatten it with your palm. • **Step 5:** Place in a large oiled bowl and cover with a cloth. Set aside until doubled in bulk, about 2 hours. • Preheat the oven to 425°F (230°C/gas 8). • Transfer the risen dough to a lightly floured work surface and knead for 2–3 minutes. • **Step 6:** Place on an oiled baking sheet and, using your hands, spread into a disk or oblong about $1/2$ inch (1 cm) thick. • Dimple the surface with your fingertips. • Drizzle with the remaining 2 tablespoons of oil and sprinkle with the sea salt, if using (salt is good for plain focaccia; it may clash with other toppings). • Bake until pale golden brown, 20–25 minutes. • Serve warm or at room temperature.

1   ounce (30 g) fresh compressed yeast or 2 ($1/4$-ounce/7-g) packages active dry yeast

1   teaspoon sugar

About $1^1/4$ cups (300 ml) warm water

$3^1/3$ cups (500 g) bread flour or all-purpose (plain) flour

1   teaspoon fine salt

4   tablespoons (60 ml) extra-virgin olive oil

1   tablespoon coarse sea salt (optional)

Serves: 6–8
Preparation: 30 minutes + 2 hours to rise
Cooking: 20–25 minutes
Level: 2

Focaccia is an Italian flatbread. The dough is often flavored with olives, rosemary, sage, oregano, or other herbs. Toppings can either be baked on top (onions, leeks, olives, cheese, tomatoes, herbs) or spread on the hot focaccia just after it comes out of the oven. However, be sure not to smother the bread with toppings; the bread itself should be enjoyed.

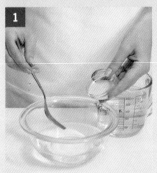

1. PUT $^1/_2$ cup (125 ml) of warm water in a bowl and add the yeast and sugar. Stir with a fork until dissolved.

2. SET ASIDE Set aside until frothy, about 10 minutes.

3. SIFT the flour and salt into a bowl. Add the yeast mixture, 2 tablespoons of oil, and most of the water. Stir until a dough forms. Transfer to a work surface.

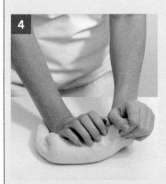

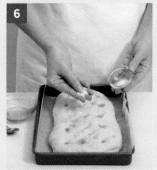

4. KNEAD the dough for 8–10 minutes. When ready it should be smooth and elastic and spring back if flattened with your palm.

5. PLACE in an oiled bowl to rise until doubled in bulk. Test by poking with a finger. If the indent remains, it's ready to cook.

6. PLACE in the baking sheet. Spread to $^1/_2$ inch (1 cm) thick. Dimple with your fingers, drizzle with oil, and sprinkle with salt.

FOCACCIA WITH CHERRY TOMATOES AND BASIL

Prepare the focaccia dough following the instructions on pages 236–237. Let rise in a warm place until doubled in bulk, about 2 hours.
• Preheat the oven to 425°F (230°C/gas 8). • Oil a 12-inch (30-cm) pizza pan. • Turn the dough out onto a lightly floured work surface and knead for 5 minutes. • Press the dough into the prepared pan using your fingers. • Cover with the tomatoes. Season with salt and pepper. Drizzle with the oil.
• Bake until the focaccia is golden brown, 20–25 minutes. • Garnish with the basil. Serve hot or at room temperature.

1 recipe Basic Focaccia Dough (see pages 236–237)

6 cherry tomatoes, sliced

Salt and freshly ground black pepper

2 tablespoons extra-virgin olive oil

Fresh basil leaves to garnish

Serves: 4–6
Preparation: 30 minutes
+ 2 hours to rise
Cooking: 20–25 minutes
Level: 2

■ ■ ■ *If preferred, drizzle the oil over the focaccia just after it comes out of the oven.*

HERB FOCACCIA

Prepare the focaccia dough following the instructions on pages 236–237. Let rise in a warm place until doubled in bulk, about 2 hours. • Preheat the oven to 425°F (230°C/gas 8). • Turn the dough out onto a lightly floured work surface and knead for 1–2 minutes. • Oil a large baking sheet. Spread the dough on it into a large round or oval shape using your fingers. It should be about $1/2$ inch (1 cm) thick. • Mix the onion, garlic, parsley, basil, rosemary, and oregano in a small bowl. Add the oil and season with salt and pepper. Spread the tomatoes over the focaccia and top with the herb mixture. • Bake until the focaccia is golden brown, 20–25 minutes. • Serve hot or at room temperature.

1 **recipe Basic Focaccia Dough (see pages 236–237)**

1 **medium onion, very finely chopped**

2 **cloves garlic, very finely chopped**

3 **tablespoons finely chopped fresh parsley**

2 **tablespoons finely chopped fresh basil**

1 **tablespoon finely chopped fresh rosemary**

1 **tablespoon finely chopped fresh oregano**

2 **tablespoons extra-virgin olive oil**

Salt and freshly ground black pepper

1 **cup (250 g) canned tomatoes, with juice**

Serves: 4–6
Preparation: 30 minutes
+ 2 hours to rise
Cooking: 20–25 minutes
Level: 2

■ ■ ■ *This topping is also good with whole-wheat (wholemeal) focaccia. You can make whole-wheat focaccia by replacing half the flour in the basic focaccia dough with whole-wheat flour.*

FOCACCIA WITH LEEKS AND BACON

Prepare the focaccia dough following the instructions on pages 236–237. Let rise in a warm place until doubled in bulk, about 2 hours. • Preheat the oven to 425°F (230°C/gas 8). • Turn the dough out onto a lightly floured work surface and knead for 1–2 minutes. • Oil a large baking sheet. Spread the dough on it into a large round or oval shape using your fingers. It should be about $1/2$ inch (1 cm) thick. • Heat 2 tablespoons of oil in a large frying pan over medium heat. Add the leeks and sauté until softened, 3–4 minutes. • Add the stock and simmer until tender, about 5 minutes. • Sauté the bacon in a separate frying pan over medium heat until crisp and lightly browned, about 5 minutes. • Stir the bacon and cheeses into the leeks. • Beat the egg yolk, milk, and thyme in a small bowl. • Drizzle the focaccia with the remaining 1 tablespoon of oil. Spread with the leek mixture. Drizzle with the egg mixture. • Bake until golden brown, about 30 minutes. • Serve hot or at room temperature.

1   **recipe Basic Focaccia Dough (see pages 236–237)**

3   **tablespoons extra-virgin olive oil**

4   **medium leeks, finely sliced**

¼   **cup (60 ml) vegetable stock**

3½ **ounces (100 g) bacon, chopped**

1   **cup (125 g) freshly grated Gruyère cheese**

2   **tablespoons freshly grated Parmesan cheese**

1   **large egg yolk**

¼   **cup (60 ml) milk**

1   **tablespoon finely chopped thyme**

Serves: 4–6
Preparation: 30 minutes
  + 2 hours to rise
Cooking: 40–45 minutes
Level: 2

FOCACCIA WITH PROSCIUTTO AND CHERRY TOMATOES

Prepare the focaccia dough following the instructions on pages 236–237. Let rise in a warm place until doubled in bulk, about 2 hours. • Preheat the oven to 425°F (230°C/gas 8). • Oil a 12-inch (30-cm) pizza pan. • Press the dough into the pan using your fingers. • Bake until golden brown, 20–25 minutes. • Remove from the oven and top with the prosciutto, arugula, Parmesan, and tomatoes. • Cut into wedges and serve hot.

1   recipe Basic Focaccia Dough (see pages 236–237)

4   large, thin slices prosciutto (Parma ham)

½   cup (25 g) arugula (rocket) leaves

3   ounces (90 g) coarsely grated Parmesan cheese

8   cherry tomatoes, halved

Serves: 4–6
Preparation: 30 minutes
    + 2 hours to rise
Cooking: 20–25 minutes
Level: 2

■ ■ ■ *This makes a great after-school snack or weekend lunch. Change the topping according to what you like and what you have on hand.*

FOUGASSE PROVENÇALE

Starter: Combine the yeast and water in a small bowl and let stand until frothy, about 10 minutes. • Put the flour in a large bowl and stir in the yeast mixture. Cover the bowl with plastic wrap (cling film) and let stand at room temperature for 12–16 hours. It should first triple in bulk and then deflate. It will have a ripe, yeasty smell.

Dough: Add the flour, salt, garlic,if using, oil, and enough of the water to the starter to make a soft dough. • Knead on a floured work surface until smooth and elastic, 5–10 minutes. • Place in an oiled bowl and let rise until doubled in bulk, about 1 hour. • Knead again for 2–3 minutes. Return to the bowl and let rise until doubled in bulk, about 1 hour. • Divide the dough into 8–10 pieces and shape into ovals about $1/2$ inch (1 cm) thick. Use a sharp knife to make diagonal cuts in the dough. Stretch to open up the holes. Brush with oil and sprinkle with sea salt. • Let rise for 30 minutes. • Preheat the oven to 400°F (200°C/gas 6). • Bake for 20–25 minutes, until golden brown. • Serve warm or at room temperature.

Starter

1   (¼-ounce/7-g) package active dry yeast or ½ ounce (15 g) fresh compressed yeast

$3/4$ up (180 ml) warm water

$1^{1/2}$ cups (250 g) bread flour or all-purpose (plain) flour

Dough

$1^{1/2}$ cups (250 g) bread flour or all-purpose (plan) flour

1   teaspoon salt

2   cloves garlic, minced (optional)

$1/3$ cup (90 ml) lukewarm water

2   tablespoons extra-virgin olive oil + extra to brush

Coarse sea salt or kosher salt, to sprinkle

Serves: 8–10
Preparation: 1 hour
    + $14^{1/2}$–$18^{1/2}$ hours
    to rise
Cooking: 20–25 minutes
Level: 3

TURKISH BREAD

Sift the flour and salt into a large bowl and make a well in the center. • Combine the yeast, sugar, and 1/2 cup (125 ml) of the water in a small bowl. Set aside until frothy, about 10 minutes. • Pour the yeast mixture into the flour. Add the oil and gradually pour in the remaining water, stirring until a dough begins to form. • Transfer to a lightly floured work surface and knead until smooth and elastic, 10–15 minutes. • Lightly oil a large bowl and place the dough inside. Cover with a clean kitchen towel and set aside in a warm place until doubled in bulk, about 2 hours. • Preheat the oven to 425°F (230°C/gas 8). • Turn the dough out onto a lightly floured work surface and knock back, punching all the air out. • **Step 1:** Shape the dough into three even-size balls. • Roll each ball into an oval about 8 inches (20 cm) long. • **Step 2:** Press your thumbs into the dough to make two rows of indentations. • Cover with a clean kitchen towel and let rise for 20 minutes. • Place two large baking sheets on the top and middle shelves of the oven to preheat. **Step 3:** Lightly brush the loaves with water and sprinkle with sesame seeds. • Transfer to the prepared baking sheets, stretching them out another 2–4 inches (4–8 cm) in length. • Bake for 8–10 minutes, until golden brown. • When cooked, the base of the bread will sound hollow when tapped. • Serve hot or warm.

4	cups (600 g) all-purpose (plain) flour
1	teaspoon salt
1/2	ounce (15 g) fresh compressed yeast or 1 (1/4-ounce/7-g) package active dry yeast
1/2	teaspoon sugar
1 1/2	cups (375 ml) lukewarm water
1/4	cup (60 ml) extra-virgin olive oil
	Sesame seeds to sprinkle

Serves: 10–12
Preparation: 30 minutes + 2 hours 20 minutes to rise
Cooking: 8–10 minutes
Level: 2

This is another Mediterranean/Middle-Eastern style flatbread. It is easy to prepare. You should note that rising times will vary according to the temperature and humidity of your kitchen and also depending on the type of yeast and flour you use.

251

1. SHAPE the dough into three even-size balls. Roll each ball into an oval about 8 inches (20 cm) long.

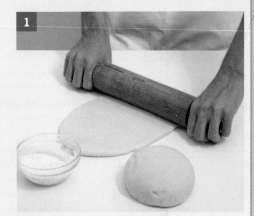

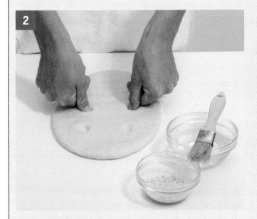

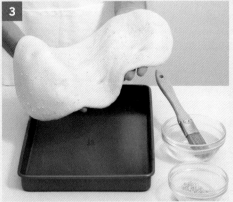

2. PRESS your thumbs into the dough to make two rows of indentations. Cover with a clean kitchen towel and let rise for 20 minutes.

3. LIGHTLY BRUSH with water and sprinkle with sesame seeds. Transfer to the baking sheets, stretching 2–4 inches (4–8 cm) more in length.

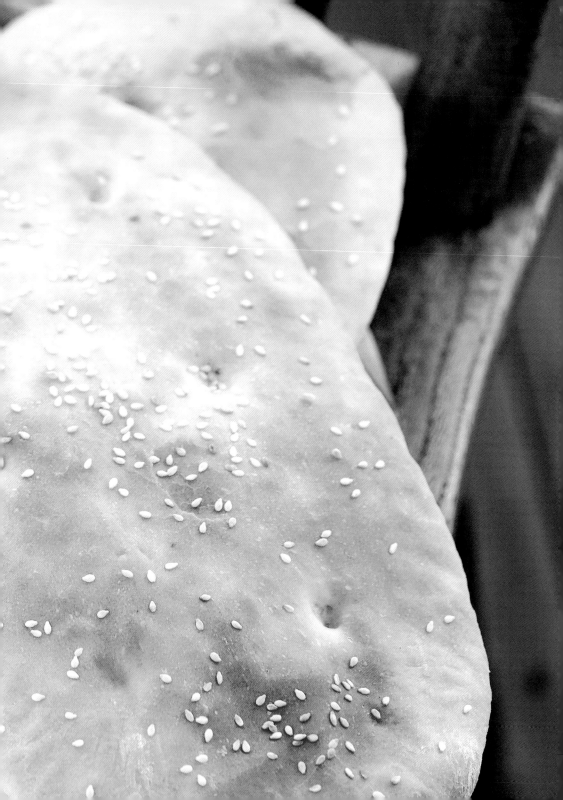

MOROCCAN BREAD

Sift both flours and the salt into a large bowl and make a well in the center. • Combine the yeast, sugar, and $1/2$ cup (125 ml) of the water in a small bowl. Set aside until frothy, about 10 minutes. • Pour the yeast mixture into the flour. Gradually add the remaining water, stirring until a dough begins to form. • Transfer the dough to a clean work surface and knead until smooth and elastic, 10–15 minutes. • Lightly oil two large baking sheets. Sprinkle with a fine layer of semolina. • Shape the dough into three even-size balls and place them on a large oiled baking sheet. Cover with a clean kitchen towel and let rise until doubled in bulk, about 2 hours. • Preheat the oven to 425°F (230°C/gas 8). • Flatten the balls of dough with the palm of your hand to make disks about 6 inches (15 cm) in diameter. • Sprinkle the tops with semolina and transfer to the prepared baking sheets. • Bake for 15–20 minutes, or until golden brown. Tap the bottom of the bread with your knuckles to see if it is cooked; it will sound hollow when ready. • Wrap in a clean kitchen towel until ready to serve.

2   cups (300 g) all-purpose (plain) flour

1½ cups (225 g) whole-wheat flour

2   teaspoons salt

1   ounce (30 g) fresh compressed yeast or 2 (¼-ounce/7-g) packages active dry yeast

2   teaspoons sugar

1¼ cups (300 ml) lukewarm water

Fine semolina to sprinkle

Serves: 8–10
Preparation: 35 minutes + 2 hours to rise
Cooking: 15–20 minutes
Level: 2

GRISSINI (BREAD STICKS)

Prepare the focaccia dough following the instructions on pages 236–237. Let rise in a warm place until doubled in bulk, about 2 hours. • Place the risen dough on a lightly floured work surface and knead for 2–3 minutes. • Divide the dough into three equal portions. • Lightly oil 3 large baking sheets. • **Step 1:** Heat the oil in a large frying pan over medium heat. Add the onion and sauté until softened, 3–4 minutes. Set aside to cool. • Knead the onion mixture into one portion of dough. Divide into pieces about the size of an egg, and shape into sticks about the thickness of your little finger and about 10 inches (25 cm) long. Sprinkle with flour and roll to coat evenly. • Transfer to an oiled baking sheet, keeping them a finger's width apart. • Cover with a cloth and set aside to rise for 1 hour. • **Step 2:** Divide the second portion of dough into pieces about the size of an egg. Shape into sticks. Sprinkle with the sesame seeds and roll to coat evenly. • Transfer to an oiled baking sheet, keeping them a finger's width apart. • Cover with a cloth and set aside to rise for 1 hour. • **Step 3:** Knead the Parmesan and paprika into the third portion of dough. Divide the third portion of dough into pieces about the size of an egg. Shape into sticks. Sprinkle with flour and roll to coat evenly. • Transfer to an oiled baking sheet, keeping them a finger's width apart. • Cover with a cloth and set aside to rise for 1 hour. • Preheat the oven to 475°F (250°C/gas 9). • Bake one sheet at a time until golden brown, about 5 minutes. • Let cool before removing from the sheets.

1   recipe Basic Focaccia Dough (see pages 236–237)

2   tablespoons extra-virgin olive oil

1   medium onion, finely chopped

½   cup (75 g) sesame seeds

½   cup (75 g) freshly grated Parmesan cheese

½   teaspoon hot paprika

Serves: 10–12
Preparation: 30 minutes + 2 hours to rise
Cooking: 15 minutes
Level: 2

PREPARING GRISSINI

Bread sticks, or grissini, are from Piedmont, in northern Italy. According to legend, they were invented in 1679 by the Turin baker Antonio Brunero when the doctor at the royal court asked for a long, crisp type of bread for his young patient and future king, Vittorio Amedeo di Savoia. They can be plain or flavored; here we have suggested three possible flavorings: onion, sesame, and cheese and paprika.

1. ONION GRISSINI Prepare the dough and the onion mixture as directed. Knead the onion mixture into one-third of the dough. Divide the dough into pieces about the size of an egg and shape into sticks about the thickness of your little finger and about 10 inches (25 cm) long. Sprinkle with flour and roll to coat evenly. Transfer to an oiled baking sheet, keeping them a finger's width apart. Cover with a cloth and let rise for 1 hour.

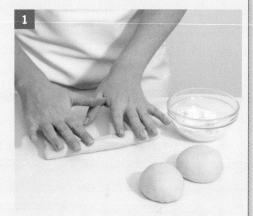

2. SESAME GRISSINI Prepare the grissini as above then roll in sesame seeds until well-coated. Let rise for 1 hour before baking.

3. PAPRIKA AND CHEESE GRISSINI Prepare the grissini as above. Knead the paprika and cheese into the dough. Let rise for 1 hour before baking.

WALNUT BREAD

Place the yeast in a small bowl. Add the sugar and half the water and stir until dissolved. Set aside until frothy, about 10 minutes. • Sift the flour and salt into a large bowl and stir in the yeast mixture, oil, cheese, and enough of the remaining water to obtain a fairly firm dough. • Knead on a floured work surface until smooth and elastic, about 10 minutes. • Add the walnuts and pepper and knead for 5 minutes more. • Place the dough in two $4^1/2$ x $8^1/2$-inch (11 x 21-cm) oiled loaf pans and let rise for 2 hours. • Preheat the oven to 425°F (230°C/gas 8). • Bake the loaves until well risen and golden brown, 30–35 minutes. • Serve warm or at room temperature.

1 ounce (30 g) fresh compressed yeast or 2 ($^1/4$-ounce/7-g) packages active dry yeast

1 teaspoon sugar

$1^1/2$ cups (375 ml) lukewarm water

$3^1/3$ cups (500 g) all-purpose (plain) flour

1 teaspoon salt

3 tablespoons extra-virgin olive oil

1 cup (120 g) freshly grated pecorino or Parmesan cheese

1 cup (150 g) coarsely chopped walnuts

$^1/2$ teaspoon freshly ground black pepper

Serves: 10–12
Preparation: 35 minutes
  + 2 hours to rise
Cooking: 30–35 minutes
Level: 2

GREEK EASTER BREAD

Red Eggs: Boil the eggs in a small saucepan until hard-boiled, 8–10 minutes. Drain and set aside.
• Combine the vinegar, water, and food coloring in a small bowl. • Dip and roll the eggs in the dye until red. Place on a wire rack to dry. • Dip a piece of paper towel in the oil and rub over the eggs to gloss.
Bread: Combine $1/2$ cup (125 ml) of milk, 1 tablespoon of sugar, and the yeast in a small bowl. Set aside in a warm place until frothy, about 10 minutes. • Sift the flour, mahlepi, and salt into a large bowl. Make a well in the center and pour in the yeast mixture. • Combine the remaining sugar, butter, and one of the beaten eggs in a small bowl.
• Stir into the flour mixture until a dough forms.
• Knead briefly. • Lightly oil a large bowl and put the dough in it. Cover with a clean cloth and set aside in a warm place until doubled in bulk, about 2 hours. • Preheat the oven to 350°F (180°C/gas 4).
• Line a large baking sheet with parchment paper.
• Turn the dough out onto a floured work surface and knock back, punching the air out. • **Step 1:** Divide in half and divide each half into three portions. Roll each portion into a long rope. • **Step 2:** Braid (plait) three ropes together to create a loaf. **Step 3:** Put an egg in the center and transfer to the baking sheet. Repeat with the remaining dough and egg. Cover with a clean cloth and set aside in a warm place until doubled in bulk, about 30 minutes. **Step 4:** Brush the loaves with the remaining beaten egg and sprinkle with almonds. • Bake for 30–40 minutes, until golden brown.

Red Eggs

2	large eggs
1	tablespoon white wine vinegar
1	teaspoon water
	Few drops red food coloring
1	teaspoon extra-virgin olive oil

Bread

1	cup (250 ml) lukewarm milk
$1/3$	cup (70 g) superfine (caster) sugar
1	tablespoon active dry yeast
3	cups (450 g) all-purpose (plain) flour
2	teaspoons mahlepi
$1/2$	teaspoon salt
2	tablespoons butter, melted
2	large eggs, lightly beaten, separately
$1/2$	cup toasted almond flakes

Serves: 10–12
Preparation: 1 hour
+ $2^1/2$ hours to rise
Cooking: 30–40 minutes
Level: 2

■ PREPARING GREEK EASTER BREAD

Tsoureki, or Greek Easter Bread, is traditionally served on Easter Sunday to celebrate the resurrection of Christ. Mahlepi is an aromatic spice made from the seeds of the St. Lucie cherry. It is used to flavor breads and other baked goods in many Eastern Mediterranean countries. You can find it in Mediterranean and Greek food stores or from online suppliers.

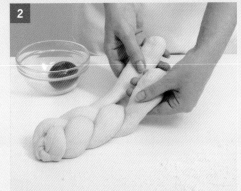

1. DIVIDE the dough in half and divide each half into three portions. Roll each portion into a long rope.

2. BRAID (plait) the three ropes together to create a loaf. Repeat with the remaining dough.

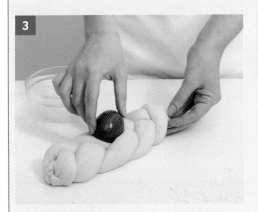

3. PLACE the red eggs at the center of each loaf. Transfer to the prepared baking sheet and let rise for 30 minutes.

4. BRUSH the loaves with the remaining beaten egg and sprinkle with the almonds. Bake for 30–40 minutes, until golden brown.

QUICHES
& SAVORY
PIES

■ PREPARING SHORTCRUST PASTRY

Shortcrust pastry (pâte brisée) is made from flour, fat (usually butter, sometimes lard or vegetable shortening), water, and salt. The butter and water must be very cold as this slows the development of the gluten in the flour, resulting in a flaky crust. Some acid, such as lemon juice or vinegar, can also be added; this also helps to retard the gluten.

$1^{1}/_{2}$ **cups (225 g) pastry flour or unbleached all-purpose (plain) flour**

$^{1}/_{2}$ **teaspoon salt**

$^{1}/_{2}$ **cup (125 g) chilled unsalted butter, cut in cubes**

1 teaspoon freshly squeezed lemon juice or cider vinegar (optional)

4 tablespoons (60 ml) ice-cold water

Serves: 6–8
Preparation: 15 minutes
   + $1^{1}/2$ hours to chill
Cooking: 10–15 minutes
Level: 2

1. BY HAND: Sift the flour and salt into a medium bowl. Add the butter and rub in by hand until the mixture resembles coarse meal.

2. ADD 3 tablespoons of iced water and the lemon juice, if using. Stir quickly until it comes together. Add the remaining water gradually, only if required.

3. BY MACHINE: Put the flour and salt in a food processor. Pulse to mix. Add the butter and pulse until coarse crumbs form, about 10 seconds.

4. ADD 3 tablespoons of iced water and the lemon juice, if using. Pulse quickly about 6 times until the mixture just comes together as a dough. Add the remaining water very gradually and only if necessary.

Work quickly and easily when making shortcrust pastry. The less you handle the dough the flakier the pastry will be. Once the dough is made, it is chilled for at least an hour. This relaxes the gluten in the dough. The chilled dough is rolled and fitted to the pan. It can then be either filled and baked, or "baked blind," which means partially or fully baked without the filling.

1. PRESS the dough into a disk and wrap in plastic wrap (cling film). Chill in the refrigerator for 1 hour (or up to 2 days) before rolling.

2. ROLL the dough out on a cool, floured work surface into a 12 inch (30 cm) circle. Roll from the center, using quick, firm strokes.

3. ROLL the dough loosely around the rolling pin and transfer to a 9-inch (23-cm) pie plate. Unroll the dough over the pan and press into the base and sides using your fingertips. Chill in the refrigerator for 30 minutes. Preheat the oven to 400°F (200°/gas 6).

4. PRESS a double sheet of aluminum foil over the dough. Fill with about 2 cups of ceramic or metal pie weights, or dried beans.

5. BAKE for 5–7 minutes, until pale and chalky-white (partially baked). Remove the pie weights and foil. Lower the oven temperature to 350°F

(180°C/gas 4) and bake for 5–7 minutes more, until golden brown. Some pies are filled when partially baked, others when completely baked.

QUICHE LORRAINE

Crust: Prepare the shortcrust pastry following the instructions on pages 268–269, up until the crust is partially baked, 5–7 minutes. Let cool a little while you prepare the filling.

Filling: Preheat the oven to 375°F (190°C/gas 5).
• Heat a large frying pan over medium heat. Add the bacon and fry until crisp and golden brown, about 5 minutes. Remove the bacon with a slotted spoon and let drain on paper towels. • Combine the eggs, egg yolks, cream, milk, salt, white pepper, and nutmeg in a medium bowl and whisk until smooth.
• Sprinkle the bacon and cheese evenly over the still-warm partially baked pie crust. Pour the whisked cream mixture carefully over the top. It should come to about $1/2$ inch (1 cm) beneath the top of the pan. • Bake for 25–30 minutes, until pale golden brown and a toothpick inserted into the center comes out clean. • Transfer to a rack to cool. Serve warm or at room temperature.

Crust

| 1 | recipe Shortcrust Pastry (see pages 268–269) |

Filling

8   ounces (250 g) bacon, rinds and fat removed, coarsely chopped

2   large eggs + 2 large egg yolks

1   cup (250 ml) heavy (double) cream

1   cup (250 ml) milk

$1/2$ teaspoon salt

$1/2$ teaspoon freshly ground white pepper

$1/8$ teaspoon freshly grated nutmeg

1   cup (120 g) freshly grated Emmental cheese

Serves: 6
Preparation: 15 minutes
   + time for the pastry
Cooking: 25–30 minutes
Level: 2

■■■*Quiche is a French term derived from the German word* kuchen *(cake or biscuit) and refers to a baked savory tart filled with beaten egg and cream. Quiche Lorraine, which comes from Lorraine on the French-German border, has an egg, bacon, and cream filling and is the original quiche. All others derive from it.*

SWISS CHARD AND WALNUT TART

272

Crust: Prepare the shortcrust pastry following the instructions on pages 268–269, up until the crust is fully baked, 10–15 minutes. Let cool a little while you prepare the filling.

Filling: Preheat the oven to 350°F (180°/gas 4). • Melt the butter in a large frying pan over medium heat. Add the onions and sauté until softened, 3–4 minutes. • Add the chard stems and walnuts. Sauté until the stems begin to soften, 2–3 minutes. Mix in the chard leaves and cook until wilted, 1–2 minutes. Season with salt and pepper. • With a slotted spoon, transfer the chard mixture to the pastry shell, discarding any juice. • Whisk the eggs, egg yolk, and crème fraîche in a bowl. Stir in the cheese and pour over the chard filling, making sure it oozes down through the filling. • Bake for 25–30 minutes, until golden and set. • Serve hot or at room temperature.

Crust

1   recipe Shortcrust Pastry (see pages 268–269)

Filling

¼   cup (60 g) unsalted butter

2   medium onions, finely sliced

8   ounces (250 g) Swiss chard (silverbeet), leaves and stems separated and thinly sliced

1½   cups (150 g) walnuts, coarsely chopped

    Salt and freshly ground black pepper

2   large eggs + 1 large egg yolk

1   cup (250 ml) crème fraîche or sour cream

½   cup (60 g) freshly grated Gruyère cheese

Serves: 6
Preparation: 35 minutes
 + time for the pastry
Cooking: 35 minutes
Level: 2

ONION AND SPINACH TARTLETS

Crust: Prepare the shortcrust pastry following the instructions on pages 268–269, up until ready to roll the dough (page 269, step 2). • Roll the dough out on a lightly floured work surface to $1/8$ inch (3 mm) thick. Cut out four rounds large enough to line the base and sides of four 4-inch (10-cm) tartlet pans. Line the pans and chill in the refrigerator for 30 minutes.

Filling: Preheat the oven to 350°F (180°C/gas 4). • Combine the onions and oil in a heavy saucepan over low heat and simmer, stirring often, until caramelized, about 30 minutes. • Remove the tartlet pans from the refrigerator. Cover each one with a square of aluminum foil and fill with pie weights or dried beans. • Bake for 5–7 minutes, until the pastry has just begun to color. • Combine the caramelized onions, spinach, and salt in a medium bowl. • Fill the tart shells with spinach and onion filling. • Bake for 10 minutes, or until the pastry is pale golden brown. • Serve hot or at room temperature.

Crust

1   **recipe Shortcrust Pastry (see pages 268–269)**

Filling

4   **large yellow onions, sliced**

2   **tablespoons extra-virgin olive oil**

4   **large handfuls baby spinach leaves**

$1/2$ **teaspoon salt**

Serves: 4
Preparation: 30 minutes
  + time for the pastry
Cooking: 45–50 minutes
Level: 2

QUICHE WITH ZUCCHINI FLOWERS

276

Crust: Prepare the shortcrust pastry following the instructions on pages 268–269, up until the crust is partially baked, 5–7 minutes. Let cool a little while you prepare the filling.

Filling: Preheat the oven to 375°F (190°C/gas 5). • Heat the oil in a small frying pan over medium heat. Add the zucchini flowers and sauté for 2 minutes. Drain well on paper towels. • Beat the eggs and cream in a large bowl. Season with salt and pepper. • Sprinkle the partially baked crust with the Parmesan and Emmental. • Add the zucchini flowers and pour the egg mixture over the top. • Bake for 25–30 minutes, or until the pastry is golden brown and the filling has set. • Serve warm.

Crust

1   recipe Shortcrust Pastry (see pages 268–269)

Filling

2   tablespoons extra-virgin olive oil

10   zucchini flowers (courgette blooms), stamen and green part removed, halved

5   large eggs

1   cup (250 ml) heavy (double) cream

    Salt and freshly ground black pepper

$1^{1}/_{4}$ cups (150 g) freshly grated Parmesan cheese

$1^{1}/_{4}$ cups (150 g) freshly grated Emmental cheese

Serves: 6
Preparation: 30 minutes + time for the pastry
Cooking: 30–35 minutes
Level: 2

■■■ *Zucchini flowers, also known as courgette blooms, are delicate in flavor and pretty to see. If liked, reserve 1-2 zucchini flowers, leave them raw, and lay them on the cooked quiche as a garnish. Zucchini flowers are usually only available fresh in spring and summer. Use 4-6 sliced tender baby zucchini when the flowers are not available.*

QUICHE WITH PEAS AND CHEESE

Crust: Prepare the shortcrust pastry following the instructions on pages 268–269, up until the crust is partially baked, 5–7 minutes. Let cool a little while you prepare the filling.

Filling: Preheat the oven to 375°F (190°C/gas 5). • Heat the oil in a large frying pan over medium heat. Add the scallions and sauté until softened, 3–4 minutes. • Add the peas and sauté for 5 minutes. • Beat the eggs and milk in a bowl. Season with salt and pepper. • Spoon the pea mixture into the partially baked pastry case. Add the Gorgonzola. Pour in with the egg mixture. • Bake until set and golden brown, 25–30 minutes. • Serve hot or at room temperature.

Crust

1   recipe Shortcrust Pastry (see pages 268–269)

Filling

2   tablespoons extra-virgin olive oil

3   scallions (green onions), chopped

2   cups (300 g) frozen peas

2   large eggs

$1/3$ cup (90 ml) milk

     Salt and freshly ground black pepper

8   ounces (250 g) Gorgonzola cheese, cut into small cubes

Serves: 6
Preparation: 20 minutes
    + time for the pastry
Cooking: 25–30 minutes
Level: 2

GOAT CHEESE
AND MINT TARTLETS

Crust: Prepare the shortcrust pastry following the instructions on pages 268–269, up until ready to roll the dough (page 269, step 2). • Roll the dough out on a lightly floured work surface to $1/8$ inch (3 mm) thick. Cut out four rounds large enough to line the base and sides of four 4-inch (10-cm) tartlet pans. Line the pans and chill in the refrigerator for 30 minutes.

Filling: Preheat the oven to 350°F (180°C/gas 4). • Remove the tartlet pans from the refrigerator. Cover each one with a square of aluminum foil and fill with pie weights or dried beans. • Bake for 5–7 minutes, until the pastry has just begun to color. • Whisk the eggs in a medium bowl. • Add the goat cheese and mint and stir well to combine. • Fill the tart shells with this mixture. Season with cracked pepper. • Bake for about 10 minutes, until the filling turns golden. • Serve warm or at room temperature, garnished with the mint leaves.

Crust

1   recipe Shortcrust Pastry (see pages 268–269)

Filling

3   large eggs

8   ounces (250 g) soft goat cheese, crumbled

3   tablespoons coarsely chopped fresh mint leaves + whole leaves to garnish

     Cracked pepper

Serves: 4
Preparation: 30 minutes + time for the pastry
Cooking: 15–20 minutes
Level: 2

ONION TARTE TATIN

282

Crust: Prepare the shortcrust pastry following the instructions on pages 268–269, up until ready to roll the dough (page 269, step 2).

Filling: Melt 4 tablespoons (60 g) of butter in a large frying pan over low heat. Add the onions, cover, and sweat until very soft, about 30 minutes. Stir often during the cooking time. • Uncover, add the honey, and increase the heat, stirring constantly, until caramelized and the juice reduces to a sticky glaze. • Stir in the peppercorns, pine nuts, and 3 tablespoons of Parmesan. Season with salt and pepper. • Preheat the oven to 375°F (190°C/gas 5). • Melt the remaining 2 tablespoons of butter and use them to brush a 9-inch (23-cm) pie pan. Sprinkle with the remaining 2 tablespoons Parmesan. • Spoon the onions into the pan. • Roll out the pastry into an 10-inch (25-cm) disk. Place over the onions, press down gently, and tuck in the edges between the onions and the pan. • Bake for 25–30 minutes, until golden brown. • Let cool for 10 minutes, then run a knife around the edges. Place a plate on top and turn over. Serve warm.

Crust

1   recipe Shortcrust Pastry (see pages 268–269)

Filling

6   tablespoons (90 g) butter

3   large white onions, sliced into wedges about $2/3$ inch (1.5 cm) thick

3   large red onions, sliced into wedges about $2/3$ inch (1.5 cm) thick

1   tablespoon honey

1   tablespoon brine-cured green peppercorns, drained

1   tablespoon pine nuts

5   tablespoons freshly grated Parmesan cheese

  Salt and freshly ground black pepper

Serves: 6
Preparation: 30 minutes
  + time for the pastry
Cooking: 60–65 minutes
Level: 2

BASTELA (MOROCCAN PIE)

Put the chicken, onion, oil, butter, garlic, ginger, salt, turmeric, pepper, and saffron in a large saucepan. Cover and simmer over low heat, stirring often, for 30 minutes. • Add the water, cover, simmer until the meat is falling off the bones, about 45 minutes.

284

Almond Filling: Heat the oil in a large frying pan over medium heat. Add the almonds and toss until golden brown. Remove with a slotted spoon and drain on paper towels. • Chop the almonds and sugar in a food processor to make fine crumbs. • Remove the chicken from the saucepan, reserving the liquid. • Remove the meat from the bones, discarding the skin and any fat. Shred the meat. • Preheat the oven to 400°F (200°C/gas 6). • Return the pan to the heat and bring the reserved liquid to a simmer. Add the parsley, cilantro, lemon juice, sugar, and cinnamon. • Gradually add the eggs, stirring until thickened. Set aside. • **Step 1:** Grease deep a 12-inch (30-cm) pizza pan with melted butter. • Brush nine filo sheets with butter and fold in half. • **Step 2:** Place a sheet in the pan. Arrange the remaining sheets, overlapping, around the pan, so that it is covered and there is overhang to encase the filling. • **Step 3:** Drain any excess liquid off the egg mixture. Spread in the pastry case. Cover with a layer of chicken and a final layer of almond mixture. • **Step 4:** Wrap the overhanging wrappers over the filling to encase, brushing between each with melted butter to seal. • **Step 5:** Brush the edge of the bastela with egg yolk and lay the final sheet of filo on top. Tuck the edges under. Brush with melted butter and egg yolk. • Pierce a few holes in the top with a knife to let steam escape. • Bake for 15–20 minutes, until golden brown. • Dust with confectioners' sugar and create a spoke pattern of cinnamon lines on top.

1	chicken, about 3 pounds (1.5 kg), quartered
2	large onions, chopped
1/2	cup (125 ml) vegetable oil
1/4	cup (60 g) butter, cubed
2	cloves garlic, bruised
2	teaspoons ground ginger
2	teaspoons salt
2	teaspoons turmeric
1	teaspoon freshly ground pepper
	Pinch saffron threads
1 1/4	cups (300 ml) water
3	cups (150 g) coarsely chopped fresh parsley
1/2	cup (25 g) coarsely chopped cilantro (coriander)
2	tablespoons (30 ml) lemon juice
1 1/2	tablespoons sugar
1	teaspoon cinnamon + extra to dust
10	large eggs, lightly beaten + 1 large egg yolk to brush
1/2	cup (125 g) butter, melted
10	sheets filo pastry
	Confectioners' (icing) sugar, to decorate

Almond Filling

3	tablespoons vegetable oil
2 1/2	cups (375 g) blanched almonds
2	tablespoons sugar

■ PREPARING BASTELA

Bastela is a classic Moroccan pie. Traditionally it was made with pigeon, but chicken is normally used outside Morocco. In Morocco a special, time-consuming pastry is made; we have replaced this with filo pastry so that the recipe is a little easier. The pie is usually served at parties as an appetizer, but you can also serve it as a main course.

1. GREASE a 12-inch (30-cm) deep pizza pan with melted butter. Brush nine of the filo sheets with butter and fold in half.

2. PLACE a sheet in the pan. Arrange the remaining sheets, overlapping, around the pan, so that it is covered and there is overhang to encase the filling.

3. DRAIN any excess liquid out of the egg mixture. Spread the egg mixture in the pastry case. Create a second layer with the chicken and a final layer with the almond mixture.

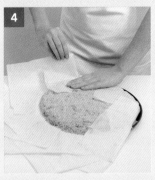

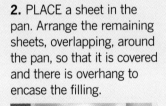
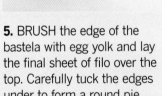
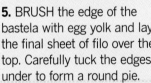

4. WRAP the overhanging wrappers over the filling to encase, brushing in between each with melted butter to seal.

5. BRUSH the edge of the bastela with egg yolk and lay the final sheet of filo over the top. Carefully tuck the edges under to form a round pie.

Serves: 8–10

Preparation: 45 minutes

Cooking: 1 1/2–2 hours

Level: 3

GOAT CHEESE TURNOVERS

288

Sift the flour into a large bowl. Add 3 tablespoons of oil and the water. Mix to make a smooth dough. • Shape into a ball and wrap in plastic wrap (cling film). Chill in the refrigerator for 1 hour. • Put the goat cheese in a small bowl and stir until smooth. • Add the thyme and season with salt and pepper. • Preheat the oven to 400°F (200°C/gas 6). • Oil a large baking sheet. • Divide the dough into 8 equal pieces. Roll out on a lightly floured work surface into ovals about $1/8$-inch (3-mm) thick. • Spread the cheese mixture on half of each oval, leaving a $3/4$ inch (2 cm) border around the edges. • Beat the egg white and water in a small bowl. Brush the edges of the pastry with this mixture. • Fold the dough over the filling. Pinch the edges together to seal. • Place on the prepared sheet. Brush with some of the remaining 3 tablespoons of oil. • Bake for 5 minutes. Brush with the remaining oil. • Bake until puffed and golden brown, 5–10 minutes. • Serve hot.

$1^2/3$	cups (250 g) all-purpose (plain) flour
6	tablespoons (90 ml) extra-virgin olive oil
$1/3$	cup (90 ml) water
5	ounces (150 g) soft fresh goat cheese
2	tablespoons finely chopped fresh thyme
	Salt and freshly ground black pepper
1	large egg white
2	tablespoons water

Serves: 4
Preparation: 30 minutes
 + 1 hour to chill
Cooking: 10 minutes
Level: 1

MACEDONIAN SPINACH PIE

Preheat the oven to 400°F (200°C/gas 6). • Steam the spinach until wilted, 1–2 minutes. Drain and chop finely. Squeeze out excess moisture. • Heat the oil in a frying pan over medium heat. Add the onion and sauté until softened, 3–4 minutes. Remove from the heat and add the spinach, garlic, thyme, oregano, and sage. Season with salt, pepper, and nutmeg. Stir in the cheese. • Oil a 9-inch (23-cm) springform pan. • Cut an 11-inch (28-cm) circle out of one pastry sheet. Line the bottom and sides of the prepared pan with the pastry. • Sprinkle with bread crumbs and spoon in the filling. • Make four hollows in the filling and break an egg into each. • Cut a 9-inch (23-cm) circle from the remaining pastry. Place on the pie. Cut two small holes in the center to let steam escape. • Beat the remaining egg and brush the pie with it. Sprinkle with sesame seeds. • Bake for 30–35 minutes, until puffed and golden brown. • Serve hot.

2	pounds (1 kg) fresh spinach
2	tablespoons extra-virgin olive oil
1	white onion, finely chopped
2	cloves garlic, thinly sliced
3	tablespoons finely chopped fresh thyme
1	tablespoon finely chopped fresh oregano
2	sage leaves, chopped
	Salt and freshly ground black pepper
	Grating of nutmeg
5	ounces (150 g) soft goat cheese or feta cheese, diced
2	(9$\frac{1}{4}$ x 9$\frac{1}{2}$-inch/ 24 x 24-cm) sheets ready-rolled puff pastry
1	tablespoon fresh bread crumbs
5	small eggs
2	tablespoons white sesame seeds

Serves: 6
Preparation: 45 minutes
Cooking: 35–40 minutes
Level: 2

DOWNUNDER MEAT PIES

Crust: Prepare the shortcrust pastry following the instructions on pages 268–269, up until ready to roll the dough (page 269, step 2).

Filling: Preheat the oven to 425°F (220°C/gas 7).

• Lightly grease four deep 5-inch (12-cm) pie pans.
• Heat the oil in a medium saucepan over medium heat. Add the onion and sauté until softened, 3–4 minutes. • Add the beef and sauté, stirring to break up any lumps, until browned, 8–10 minutes. • Pour in half the stock and bring to a boil. • Combine the cornstarch, Worcestershire sauce, and remaining stock in a small bowl to make a paste. • Add the paste to the beef and cook, stirring, until thickened. Season with salt and pepper. Remove from the heat and set aside to cool. • Roll the dough out on a lightly floured work surface to $1/8$ inch (3 mm) thick. • **Step 1:** Cut out four pastry rounds, using the pie pans or a 7 inch (18 cm) plate as a guide. • **Step 2:** Line the bases and sides of the prepared pie pans. • Cut out another four slightly larger rounds with the remaining pastry and set aside to use as the pie lids. • **Step 3:** Fill the pies with the beef filling. Lightly brush the edges of the pastry with water and cover with the lids. Press around the edges with a fork to seal. • **Step 4:** Make small holes in the center of the lid with a skewer or knife to allow the steam to escape during baking. Brush the tops with egg. • Bake for 20–25 minutes, until pastry is puffed and golden brown. • Serve hot with ketchup.

Crust

2 recipes Shortcrust Pastry (see pages 268–269)

Filling

2 tablespoons extra-virgin olive oil

1 medium onion, finely chopped

1 pound (500 g) ground (minced) beef

$3/4$ cup (180 ml) beef stock (see pages 62–63)

1 tablespoon cornstarch (cornflour)

1 tablespoon Worcestershire sauce

Salt and freshly ground pepper

1 small egg, lightly beaten

Ketchup (tomato sauce) to serve

Serves: 4
Preparation: 30 minutes
  + time for the pastry
Cooking: 35–40 minutes
Level: 2

■ PREPARING DOWNUNDER MEAT PIES

Meat pies are a favorite takeaway food in Australia and New Zealand (Downunder). Made fresh at home, with handmade shortcrust pastry and a simple ground beef filling, they are a gourmet delight. Be sure to serve them hot with plenty of ketchup; it's traditional!

1. CUT OUT four pastry rounds, using the pie pan or a 7 inch (18 cm) plate as a guide.

2. LINE the bases and sides of the prepared pie pans. Cut out another four slightly larger rounds with the remaining pastry to use as pie lids.

3. FILL with the beef filling. Lightly brush the edges of the pastry with water and cover with the lids. Press around the edges with a fork to seal.

4. MAKE small holes in the center of the lid with a skewer or knife to allow the steam to escape during baking.

SEAFOOD

SPANISH MUSSELS

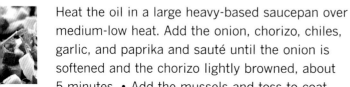

Heat the oil in a large heavy-based saucepan over medium-low heat. Add the onion, chorizo, chiles, garlic, and paprika and sauté until the onion is softened and the chorizo lightly browned, about 5 minutes. • Add the mussels and toss to coat. • Increase the heat to medium-high and pour in the wine and tomatoes. Bring to a boil, cover, and simmer until the mussels have opened, 5–10 minutes. Discard any mussels that have not opened. • Stir in the parsley and season with salt and pepper. • Serve hot garnished with lemon wedges.

■ ■ ■ *When you buy mussels in their shells remember that the mollusk inside should still be alive. Healthy, fresh mussels will be tightly closed and have very little odor. Discard any that are cracked or broken. If the mussels are muddy or sandy, soak them in cold, salted water for 1–2 hours, changing the water several times. Cultivated mussels do not generally require soaking. To clean, use a wire brush or small sharp knife to scrub or scrape off any seaweed or grit.*

2	tablespoons extra-virgin olive oil
1	small onion, coarsely chopped
1	spicy chorizo sausage, thinly sliced into rounds
3	long red chiles, seeded and finely chopped
2	cloves garlic, finely chopped
2	teaspoons smoked paprika
3	pounds (1.5 kg) mussels, in shell
3/4	cup (180 ml) dry white wine
2	cups (400 g) canned tomatoes, with juice
1/2	cup (25 g) coarsely chopped fresh parsley
	Salt and freshly ground pepper
	Lemon wedges to serve

Serves: 4–6
Preparation: 15 minutes
Cooking: 10–15 minutes
Level: 1

CURRIED SCALLOPS

Chile Pickle: Heat the oil in a small saucepan over low heat. Add the onion, garlic, red and green chiles, and ginger and sauté softened but not browned, 8–10 minutes. • Stir in the fish sauce, lime zest and juice, and the curry leaves. Simmer until the mixture is very soft, about 15 minutes. • Stir in the cilantro and cook for 2 minutes. Season the with salt and pepper, remove from the heat, and let cool a little. • Spoon about 1 1/2 tablespoons of the chile pickle into each scallop shell. Transfer to a serving dish and set aside while you prepare the scallops.

Scallops: Brush each scallop with oil and season with salt and pepper. Dust with curry powder and cayenne pepper. • Heat a grill pan or griddle over medium-high heat. Cook the scallops for 1 minute, then rotate to form crisscross marks, and cook for 1 more minute on that side. Turn the scallops over and cook for another 1 1/2 minutes on the other side. • Put the scallops crisscross side up in the prepared shells. Garnish with lime wedges and serve hot or at room temperature.

■ ■ ■ *If possible, ask your fishmonger to shuck (open) the scallops for you. If shucking yourself, place each shell flat side down on a board and slide a thin-bladed knife between the two halves. Prise open and slide the knife under the scallop, keeping the blade flat. With a gentle sawing motion sever the ligament attaching the scallop to the shell. Scoop it out with a tablespoon. Pull off and discard the ligament. Wash the scallop and pat dry. Wash the shell halves and reserve.*

Chile Pickle

2 tablespoons extra-virgin olive oil
1 red onion, finely chopped
2 cloves garlic, finely chopped
2 green chiles, seeded and finely chopped
1 small red chile, seeded and finely chopped
1 heaped teaspoon finely chopped fresh ginger
2 tablespoons Thai fish sauce
Zest and juice of 4 fresh limes
5 fresh curry leaves or 1 tablespoon dry curry leaves
3 tablespoons finely chopped fresh cilantro (coriander)
Salt and freshly ground black pepper

Scallops

12 medium king scallops, with coral, on half-shell
1–2 tablespoons extra-virgin olive oil
1/2 teaspoon sea salt
1/4 teaspoon freshly ground black pepper
1 tablespoon curry powder
1/4 teaspoon cayenne pepper
Lime wedges, to serve

Serves: 4–6
Preparation: 15 minutes
Cooking: 25–30 minutes
Level: 1

SINGAPORE CHILE CRAB

Step 1: Turn the crabs over and remove and discard the apron. • **Step 2:** Remove and discard the intestines and grey gills. • **Step 3:** Cut each crab in half lengthwise and then again crosswise, leaving the legs and claws intact. • **Step 4:** Crack the large front claws with the back of a heavy-handled knife or a meat pounder and rinse to remove any shell particles. Pat dry with paper towels and set aside. • Heat the oil in a large wok over medium-high heat. Add the shallots, garlic, and ginger and stir-fry until softened, 2–3 minutes. • Add the chiles, jaggery, coriander, cumin, pepper, turmeric, and salt and stir-fry until fragrant, about 30 seconds. • Add the crabs and stir-fry until they begin to change color, 3–4 minutes. • Add the water and oyster and soy sauces, toss to coat, and bring to a boil. Cover and steam until crabs have completely changed color and the flesh is opaque, 3–5 minutes. • Add the cilantro and toss to coat. • Serve hot.

3   pounds (1.5 kg) blue or brown (hard shell) crabs, scrubbed clean

¼   cup (60 ml) peanut oil

2   shallots, finely chopped

3   cloves garlic, finely chopped

1½ tablespoons finely grated fresh ginger

2   small red chiles, seeded and finely chopped

2   teaspoons coarsely grated jaggery (palm sugar) or raw sugar

½   teaspoon ground coriander

½   teaspoon ground cumin

½   teaspoon freshly ground black pepper

¼   teaspoon ground turmeric

¼   teaspoon salt

¼   cup (60 ml) water

2   tablespoons oyster sauce

2   tablespoons soy sauce

2   tablespoons finely chopped fresh cilantro (coriander)

Serves: 4
Preparation: 30 minutes
Cooking: 8–12 minutes
Level: 3

■ ■ ■ *The only possible way to eat these crabs is using your hands so be sure to serve the dish with a little bowl of water and lemon juice for each guest to rinse their fingers.*

PREPARING SINGAPORE CHILE CRAB

Crabs are either sold live, cooked, or frozen. You will need live crabs for this recipe. When buying, make sure they are lively and active; if they are not moving, don't buy them. If you are not used to them, whole crabs can look a little "icky," but they are not hard to prepare.

1. TURN the crabs over and remove and discard the apron.

2. REMOVE and discard the intestines and grey gills.

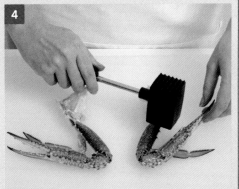

3. CUT each crap in half lengthwise and then again crosswise, leaving the legs and claws intact.

4. CRACK the large front claws with the back of a heavy-handled knife or a meat pounder. Rinse to remove any shell particles.

VIETNAMESE SHRIMP ROLLS

Sweet Chile Dipping Sauce: Combine all the sauce ingredients in a small saucepan and simmer over low heat until the sugar has dissolved and the liquid is slightly syrupy, 5–7 minutes. • Set aside to cool.
Shrimp Rolls: Place the noodles in a medium bowl, cover with hot water and soak until soft, 2–3 minutes. Drain and chop coarsely into short lengths.
Step 1: Soak the rice papers one at a time in a large bowl of warm water until softened, about 30 seconds. • Lay on a damp kitchen towel. • Place half a lettuce leaf and 1–2 tablespoons of noodles just below the center of the rice paper, allowing enough space at the sides to fold over. Lay a few mint and cilantro leaves, a little bell pepper and bean sprouts, and 2 shrimp halves on top. • **Step 2:** Fold the base and the sides of the rice paper over the filling and roll until firmly enclosed. Repeat with the remaining wrappers and filling. • Serve with the dipping sauce.

Sweet Chile Dipping Sauce

1	cup (250 ml) rice vinegar
1/4	cup (60 ml) water
4	tablespoons sugar
1	red chile, finely chopped
2	teaspoons salt
1	clove garlic, minced

Shrimp Rolls

3	ounces (90 g) vermicelli rice noodles
12	rice paper sheets (wrappers)
6	butter lettuce or other soft lettuce leaves
1/2	cup (25 g) fresh mint
1/2	cup (25 g) fresh cilantro (coriander)
1	red bell pepper (capsicum) seeded and thinly sliced lengthwise
1	cup (50 g) bean sprouts
8	cooked shrimp (prawns), peeled and halved lengthwise

Serves: 4–6
Preparation: 30 minutes
Cooking: 10 minutes
Level: 2

▮ PREPARING VIETNAMESE SHRIMP ROLLS

1. SOAK the rice papers one at a time in a large bowl of warm water until softened, about 30 seconds.
2. FOLD the base and the sides of the rice paper over the filling and roll until firmly enclosed.

SPICY BATTERED SHRIMP

Shrimp: Prepare the shrimp as shown on the opposite page. For this recipe you will need to remove the tails too. • Bring 3 cups (750 ml) of water to a boil in a medium saucepan over high heat. Add the shrimp and simmer until they turn pink, 2–5 minutes, depending on their size. • Drain well and place on a clean kitchen towel to dry.

Batter: Mix the milk, egg, chile paste, Tabasco, and garlic salt in a small bowl and whisk until combined. • Put the flour in a separate bowl and mix with the salt, pepper, and paprika. • Dip each shrimp in the spiced milk mixture and dredge in the spiced flour. • Pour the oil into a deep-fryer or deep saucepan over medium heat and heat to 365°F (190°C). If you don't have a frying thermometer, test the oil temperature by dropping a small piece of bread into the hot oil. If the bread immediately bubbles to the surface and begins to turn golden, the oil is ready. • Deep-fry the shrimp in batches until golden and crisp, 2–3 minutes per batch. • Remove with a slotted spoon and drain on paper towels.

To Serve: Place the hot shrimp on a serving platter with the lemon wedges. • Whisk the ketchup with the Tabasco and serve with the shrimp for dipping.

Shrimp

12	ounces (350 g) small or medium shrimp (prawns), peeled and deveined

Batter

2	tablespoons milk
1	large egg, lightly beaten
1/2	teaspoon chile paste or Harissa Paste (see page 312)
1/4	teaspoon Tabasco
1/8	teaspoon garlic salt
3/4	cup (125 g) all-purpose (plain) flour
1/4	teaspoon salt
1/4	teaspoon freshly ground black pepper
1/4	teaspoon hot paprika
4	cups (1 liter) vegetable oil to deep-fry

To Serve

	Lemon wedges
1	cup (250 ml) tomato ketchup
1/2	teaspoon Tabasco

Serves: 4–6
Preparation: 30 minutes
Cooking: 10–15 minutes
Level: 2

Shrimp (prawns) come in an amazing array of sizes and varieties but the basics for preparing them are the same. The best quality shrimp is sold whole, either fresh or frozen. In most cases you will want to remove the heads, peel, and devein them before cooking.

1. GRASP the shrimp firmly with the thumb and index finger of one hand and use the other thumb and index finger to twist and pull off the head.

2. TURN OVER and peel off the shell, taking care to keep the shrimp intact. You can remove the tail or leave it on, depending on the recipe.

3. MAKE a shallow cut along the front with a sharp knife to expose the dark intestinal vein.

4. USE a toothpick to lift the vein up. Pull it out and discard.

HARISSA SHRIMP

Harissa Paste: Dry-fry the chiles, peppercorns, fennel, cumin, and coriander seeds in a small frying pan over medium-high heat until fragrant, 2–3 minutes. • Transfer to a mortar and pestle or spice grinder and grind to a fine paste. • Place the spice mix and garlic in a food processor and blend, gradually adding 3 tablespoons of the oil to form a moist paste.
Shrimp: Place the vegetable stock in a small saucepan over medium-high heat and bring to a boil. Add the couscous, remove from the heat, and cover with plastic wrap (cling film). Let stand until the liquid is completely absorbed, about 5 minutes. • Stir gently with a fork to separate the grains. • Meanwhile, preheat a wok or large frying pan over medium-high heat. Add the oil and stir-fry the onion until transparent, about 2 minutes. • Add the harissa paste, shrimp, and tomatoes and stir-fry until the shrimp has changed color and is cooked through, 3–4 minutes. • Spoon the couscous onto serving plates. Top with the shrimp mixture and a dollop of yogurt. • Garnish with the cilantro and serve hot.

Harissa Paste

5 large red dried chiles, chopped

2 teaspoons whole white peppercorns

2 teaspoons fennel seeds

1 teaspoon cumin seeds

1 teaspoon coriander seeds

2 cloves garlic, chopped

3 tablespoons extra-virgin olive oil

Shrimp

1½ cups (325 ml) Vegetable Stock (see page 94)

1½ cups (225 g) couscous

1 tablespoon extra-virgin olive oil

1 onion, thinly sliced

2 pounds (1 kg) shrimp (prawns), peeled and deveined

2 medium tomatoes, finely chopped

½ cup (125 g) plain yogurt

3 tablespoons finely chopped fresh cilantro (coriander) + extra to garnish

Serves: 4–6
Preparation: 15 minutes
Cooking: 10 minutes
Level: 1

GRILLED BABY OCTOPUS

Place the baby octopus in a shallow glass or ceramic bowl. • Whisk the sweet chili sauce, lime juice, fish sauce, and sesame oil in a small bowl. • Pour the marinade over the octopus, cover with plastic wrap (cling film), and marinate in the refrigerator for 4 hours or overnight. Drain and reserve the marinade. • Divide the salad greens evenly among four serving plates. Top with the bean sprouts, cucumber, and tomatoes. • Preheat a barbecue plate or grill pan to very hot. Add the baby octopus all at once and toss until cooked through, 2–3 minutes. Remove and set aside. Do not overcook. • Place the reserved marinade in a small saucepan and bring to a boil. • Arrange the baby octopus on top of the salad. Drizzle with the hot marinade and garnish with the cilantro and lime wedges. • Serve at once.

12	ounces (350 g) fresh baby octopus, cleaned
$1/3$	cup (90 ml) Thai sweet chili sauce
2	tablespoons freshly squeezed lime juice
1	tablespoon Thai fish sauce
1	tablespoon sesame oil
2	cups (100 g) mixed salad greens
1	cup (50 g) bean sprouts
1	cucumber, with peel, thinly sliced
8	ounces (250 g) cherry tomatoes, halved
$1/2$	cup (25 g) fresh cilantro (coriander) leaves
	Lime wedges, to serve

Serves: 4
Preparation: 20 minutes
  + 4–12 hours to
  marinate
Cooking: 2–3 minutes
Level: 1

■ ■ ■ *Be sure to cook the baby octopus on a very hot barbecue or grill pan for no more than 2–3 minutes. If you cook them for longer they will become rubbery.*

TUNA AND EGG BRIK

Combine the tuna, preserved lemon peel, onion, cilantro, capers, and cayenne pepper in a medium bowl. Season with salt and pepper. • Because you need to cook the briks as soon as they are formed (otherwise the wrapper will go soggy), heat the oil in a large frying pan over medium high-heat just before you begin the make the first brik. • Lightly dust a clean work surface with cornstarch. • Lay out a spring roll wrapper, keeping the remaining wrappers covered with plastic wrap (cling film) to prevent them from drying out. • **Step 1:** Place one quarter of the filling in the center of the spring roll wrapper. Make a well in the middle and crack an egg inside. • **Step 2:** Brush the beaten egg around all four edges of the spring roll wrapper and prepare to fold. • **Step 3:** Fold two of the wrappers over to enclose the filling, pressing the edges moistened with beaten egg together to seal. • **Step 4:** Fold the remaining edges in, pressing down gently to seal without causing the egg to run, to make a square parcel. • Fry the brik immediately in the hot oil until golden brown and crisp, 20–30 seconds on each side. The egg yolk will still be runny in the center. • Remove using a slotted spoon and drain on paper towels. Repeat with the remaining filling and wrappers. • Serve hot.

6	ounces (180 g) canned tuna in spring water, drained
½	Moroccan Preserved Lemon (see page 373), pulp and membrane discarded and peel finely chopped
½	small red onion, finely chopped
2	tablespoons finely chopped fresh cilantro (coriander)
2	teaspoons finely chopped capers
½	teaspoon cayenne pepper
	Salt and freshly ground black pepper
1	cup (250 ml) vegetable oil to fry
	Cornstarch (cornflour) to dust
4	(8½ inch/21 cm) spring roll wrappers
4	small eggs + 1 small egg, lightly beaten

Serves: 4
Preparation: 30 minutes
Cooking: 5 minutes
Level: 3

Briks are a classic Tunisian dish made by wrapping a thin layer of pastry around a filling of tuna, egg, and seasonings. This is the traditional recipe, but other fillings include ground meat, chicken, or cheese. In Tunisia, a special pastry called *warka* is used. We have simplified things by using spring roll wrappers which are readily available in Asian food stores.

1. PLACE a quarter of the filling in the center of the spring roll wrapper. Make a well in the middle and crack an egg inside.

2. BRUSH the beaten egg around all four edges of the spring roll wrapper and prepare to fold.

3. FOLD two of the wrappers over to enclose the filling, pressing the edges with beaten egg together to seal.

4. FOLD the remaining edges in, pressing down gently to seal without causing the egg to run, to make a square parcel.

5. FRY the brik immediately in the hot oil until golden brown and crisp, 20–30 seconds on each side.

CEVICHE

Combine the fish and lime and lemon juice in a medium glass or stainless steel bowl. Cover and refrigerate, stirring occasionally, until the fish turns from opaque to white, about 4 hours. • Drain the fish, reserving 3 tablespoons of the marinade. • Combine the fish, tomatoes, onion, avocado, cilantro, and chile on a serving platter. • Whisk the reserved marinade and oil in a small bowl. Season with salt and pepper. • Drizzle over the fish and toss gently to coat. • Garnish with the cilantro and serve.

1½ pounds (750 g) firm skinless fish fillets (such as mackerel, halibut, tuna, sea bass), boned and thinly sliced

Freshly squeezed juice of 6 limes

Freshly squeezed juice of 2 lemons

2 medium tomatoes, diced

1 small red onion, halved and thinly sliced

1 avocado, pitted and diced

½ cup (25 g) coarsely chopped fresh cilantro (coriander) + extra to garnish

2 small green chiles, seeded and thinly sliced

2 tablespoons extra-virgin olive oil

Salt and freshly ground black pepper

■ ■ ■ *Ceviche is a specialty of the Spanish-speaking peoples of Central and South America, especially Mexico, Ecuador, and Peru. The raw fish fillets are marinated in a citrus juice mixture until they turn white. The chemical process is similar to cooking, although the fish is not exposed to heat.*

Serves: 6–8
Preparation: 15 minutes
 + 4 hours to marinate
Level: 1

THAI FISH CAKES

Dipping Sauce: Place the water, vinegar, and sugar in a small saucepan over low heat. Simmer for 5 minutes, stirring occasionally, until the sugar has dissolved. • Increase the heat and simmer until slightly syrupy, about 5 minutes. • Transfer into a small bowl. Add the fish sauce, cucumber, chile, and peanuts. Stir to combine then set aside to cool.
Fish Cakes: Place the fish, curry paste, fish sauce, and egg white in a food processor and blend until smooth. Transfer to a medium bowl. • Add the shallots, beans, kaffir lime leaves, and cilantro and stir to combine. Season with salt and pepper. • Shape the fish mixture into 16 fish cakes. • Heat the oil in a wok over medium-high heat until hot enough to brown a piece of bread when tested. • Fry the fish cakes in batches until cooked through and golden brown, 5–7 minutes per batch. Drain on paper towels. • Serve hot with the dipping sauce and lime wedges.

Dipping Sauce

½   cup (125 ml) water

¼   cup (60 ml) white wine vinegar

⅓   cup (70 g) sugar

2   tablespoons Thai fish sauce

½   cucumber, peeled, seeded, and finely diced

1   large red chile, seeded and finely diced

2   tablespoons roasted peanuts, finely chopped

Fish Cakes

1   pound (500 g) firm fish fillets (ling, monkfish, mahi-mahi, grouper, mackerel, etc), skin and bones removed and coarsely chopped

1½   tablespoons Thai red curry paste

1½   tablespoons Thai fish sauce

1   large egg white

2   shallots, finely chopped

2   snake or green beans, finely sliced

2   kaffir lime leaves, finely chopped

2   tablespoons finely chopped fresh cilantro (coriander)

     Salt and freshly ground black pepper

1   cup (250 ml) vegetable oil, to fry

2   limes, cut into wedges

Serves: 4–6
Preparation: 30 minutes
Cooking: 15–20 minutes
Level: 1

BREADED FISH WITH TARTAR SAUCE

Tartar Sauce: Place the egg yolks, mustard, lemon juice, salt, and pepper in a food processor or blender. Turn the machine on and add the oil in a thin, steady stream. After you have added about half the oil, the mixture will begin to thicken. Keep adding the oil until it has all been absorbed. • Stir in the cornichons and shallot. • Chill in the refrigerator until ready to serve.

Breaded Fish: Put the bread crumbs in a large plate or shallow bowl. • Press the fish fillets into the bread crumbs so that they are thoroughly coated on both sides; set aside. • Heat the oil in a large frying pan over medium heat. • Cook the fish until the flesh flakes easily and the crumbs are golden, about 3 minutes on each side. • Place the fish and salad greens on serving plates. • Serve hot with the tartar sauce.

■ ■ ■ *Tartar (or Tartare) sauce is a classic sauce for fish. It is really just fresh mayonnaise with cornichons added. If using olive oil, use only top quality, cold-pressed, extra-virgin. If you can't get that, or if you find the flavor of olive oil too strong, use canola or sunflower oil instead.*

Tartar Sauce

2 large egg yolks

1 teaspoon Dijon mustard

1 tablespoon freshly squeezed lemon juice

   Salt and freshly ground black pepper

1 cup (250 ml) extra-virgin olive oil

1 tablespoon finely chopped cornichons (pickled gherkins)

1 shallot, finely chopped

Breaded Fish

1½ cups (90 g) fresh bread crumbs

4 (8-ounce/250-g) fillets firm white fish (snapper, John Dory, whiting, blue-eye, cod, flounder, grouper, halibut, etc)

½ cup (125 ml) canola oil

3 cups (150 g) mixed salad greens

Serves: 4
Preparation: 15 minutes
Cooking: 6 minutes
Level: 2

Most of the fish we buy today is cleaned industrially and arrives at fish counters ready to cook. Even when it is fresh and whole, many fish stores and supermarkets have qualified people on hand to scale, gut, and fillet your fish before your eyes. However, there are times when you may have to do it yourself.

1. FINS: Pull the fins away from the body and use a pair of sharp kitchen scissors to snip them off.

2. SCALING: Use a fish scaler, spoon, or the back of a knife. Wet the fish, grip it firmly by the tail, and scrape upward from the tail with short strokes.

3. GUTTING: Beginning at its vent, cut up to the gill openings. Pull out the guts, then scrape out the kidneys attached to the backbone. Rinse.

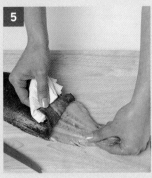

4. GILLING: Lift the gill covers and cut the gills out with sharp kitchen scissors or a knife.

5. SKINNING: Make a small cut just above the tail. Lift the skin away from the flesh and pull upward from the tail.

6. FILLETING: Using the point of a sharp knife, feel for the central bone, and run the knife along it. Peel back the meat.

CORFU FISH SOUP

328

Heat 3 tablespoons of oil in a large saucepan over medium heat. • Add the onions, 3 cloves of garlic, and the parsley and sauté until the garlic is pale gold, 3–4 minutes. • Add the potatoes and sauté for 5 minutes. • Add the tomatoes and bring to a boil. Simmer for 10–15 minutes. • Add the fish and enough water to cover. Cover the pan and simmer until the fish is very tender, 5–10 minutes. • Season with salt and pepper. Stir in the remaining 1 tablespoon oil and 1 clove of garlic and let stand for 5 minutes before serving.

4 **tablespoons (60 ml) extra-virgin olive oil**

2 **medium onions, coarsely chopped**

4 **cloves garlic, finely chopped**

2 **tablespoons finely chopped fresh parsley**

2 **pounds (1 kg) potatoes, scrubbed and cubed**

2 **cups (400 g) canned tomatoes, with juice**

2 **pounds (1 kg) firm fish fillets (scorpion fish, dogfish, catfish, cod, red snapper, turbot, grouper, etc.)**

Water

Salt and freshly ground white pepper

Serves: 4
Preparation: 10 minutes
Cooking: 25–35 minutes
Level: 2

GOAN FISH CURRY

330

Curry Paste: Step 1: Put the chiles, garlic, ginger, turmeric, coriander, peppercorns, and cumin in a large mortar and pestle or food processor and grind or chop to make a coarse paste.

Curry: Heat the ghee in a medium saucepan or wok over medium-low heat. Add the onion and stir-fry until softened, 3–4 minutes. • Add the curry paste, green chiles, and mustard seeds and stir-fry until the seeds begin to pop and the spices are fragrant, about 30 seconds. • Pour in the water, stir to combine, and bring to a boil. • Pour in the coconut milk and return to a boil. Decrease the heat, add the curry leaves, and simmer until the sauce thickens, about 10 minutes. • Add the fish and simmer until the fish is cooked, 5–10 minutes. • Season with salt and serve hot with the rice.

Curry Paste

6	dried red chiles, coarsely chopped
4	cloves garlic, coarsely chopped
2	teaspoons finely grated ginger
2	tablespoons ground turmeric
1	tablespoon coriander seeds
½	teaspoon whole black peppercorns
¼	teaspoon cumin seeds

Curry

3	tablespoons ghee or vegetable oil
1	large onion, finely chopped
2	small green chiles, seeded and finely sliced
½	teaspoon black mustard seeds
½	cup (125 ml) water
2	cups (500 ml) coconut milk
8	curry leaves
1½	pounds (750 g) firm white fish fillets (halibut, monkfish, ocean perch, porgy, cod, dogfish, etc.) boned and cut into bite-size chunks
	Salt
	Steamed basmati rice to serve

Serves: 4–6
Preparation: 15 minutes
Cooking: 20–25 minutes
Level: 1

■ PREPARING CURRY PASTE

1. PUT the chiles, garlic, ginger, turmeric, coriander, peppercorns, and cumin in a large mortar and pestle or food processor and grind or chop to make a coarse paste.

THAI RED FISH CURRY

Curry Paste: Place all of the curry paste ingredients in a large mortar and pestle or food processor and grind or chop to make a coarse paste.

Curry: Heat the oil in a medium saucepan or wok over medium-low heat. Add the curry paste and stir-fry until fragrant, about 30 seconds. • Pour in the coconut milk, stir to combine and bring to a boil. Decrease the heat and simmer until the cream splits, 4–5 minutes. • Pour in the water and return to a boil. Decrease the heat, add the fish sauce, jaggery, and lime juice and leaves and simmer for 5 minutes. • Add the green beans and bell pepper and simmer for 5 minutes. • Add the fish and gently simmer until the fish and vegetables are cooked, about 10 minutes. Season with salt. • Serve hot topped with bean shoots and with jasmine rice.

Curry Paste

3	shallots, chopped
4	long red chiles, seeded and chopped
2	cloves garlic, chopped
1	stalk lemongrass, white part only, chopped
1	(1-inch/2.5-cm) piece ginger, finely chopped
2	coriander roots, chopped
1	teaspoon hot paprika
½	teaspoon shrimp paste
¼	teaspoon black peppercorns
¼	teaspoon ground coriander
¼	teaspoon ground turmeric
¼	teaspoon salt

Curry

2	tablespoons vegetable oil
4	cups (1 liter) coconut milk
½	cup (125 ml) water
2	tablespoons Thai fish sauce
1	tablespoon coarsely grated jaggery (palm sugar) or brown sugar
1	tablespoon lime juice
5	kaffir lime leaves
5	ounces (150 g) green beans, halved
1	red bell pepper (capsicum), diced
1¼	pounds (600 g) firm white fish fillets, cut into bite-size chunks
	Salt
	Steamed jasmine rice
1	cup (50 g) bean shoots

Serves: 4
Preparation: 30 minutes
Cooking: 20 minutes
Level: 1

ZARZUELA (SPANISH FISH STEW)

Place a medium saucepan of water on high heat and bring to a boil. Score a cross in the base of the tomatoes and remove the cores. Blanch the tomatoes in the boiling water for 20 seconds. Remove using a slotted spoon and plunge into iced water. Peel, cut into quarters, remove and discard the seeds. • Heat 4 tablespoons of oil in a large saucepan over medium heat. Add the almonds and sauté until golden, 3–5 minutes. • Add the garlic and sauté until softened, 3–4 minutes. Remove from the heat. • Chop the almond mixture and 1 cup (50 g) of parsley in a food processor to make a paste. Set aside. • Heat the remaining 4 tablespoons of oil in the same pan. Add the onion and sauté until softened, 3–4 minutes. • Add the tomatoes, chile, saffron mixture, and bay leaves and simmer for 10 minutes. • Stir in the tomato paste, paprika, and brandy. Carefully light, tilting the pan towards the flame. The flame will burn out when all the alcohol has burnt off. • Add the wine and bring to a boil. Add the fish stock and almond and parsley paste and bring back to a boil. Decrease the heat and simmer to infuse the flavors, about 5 minutes. • Add the fish, squid, and mussels, cover, and cook until the fish begins changes from opaque to white, about 5 minutes. Add the shrimp, cover, and simmer until shrimp have changed color, the mussels are open, and the fish is tender and cooked. Discard any unopened mussels. • Stir in the remaining parsley and season with salt and pepper. • Garnish with lemon and serve hot with the bread.

3 large tomatoes

8 tablespoons (125 ml) extra-virgin olive oil

1/3 cup (50 g) blanched almonds

4 cloves garlic, coarsely chopped

2 cups (100 g) fresh parsley leaves

1 onion, finely sliced

1 large chile, seeded and finely chopped

1 teaspoon saffron threads, soaked in 2 tablespoons water

2 bay leaves

1 tablespoon tomato paste

1 teaspoon smoked paprika

3 tablespoons brandy

1/2 cup (125 ml) dry white wine

1 1/4 cups (300 ml) fish stock

1 1/2 pounds (750 g) two varieties firm white fish fillets, such as blue eye, snapper or monk-fish, cut into bite-size pieces

12 ounces (350 g) squid, cut into rings

12 mussels, cleaned

12 shrimp (prawns), peeled

Salt and freshly ground pepper

Lemon wedges to serve

Crusty bread to serve

Serves: 6
Preparation: 30 minutes
Cooking: 30–35 minutes
Level: 2

SALMON STEAKS WITH PAK CHOY

336

Season the salmon steaks with salt and pepper and set aside. • Cut the leaves from the pak choy stalks. Coarsely shred the leaves with a large knife and cut the stalks into small pieces. • Heat the oil in a wok or deep frying pan over medium heat. Add the onion, ginger, and pak choy stalks and cook, stirring frequently, until the onion is golden, 5–6 minutes. • Add the tomatoes, chile, and sugar and simmer for 5 minutes, mixing well. • Pour in the coconut milk and water. Season with salt and a good grinding of pepper. Bring to a boil, stirring often, then simmer over low heat for 15 minutes. • Stir in the pak choy leaves, soy sauce, and lime juice. • Place the salmon steaks in a single layer on top of the sauce, spooning some of it over the fish. Cover with a tight-fitting lid or aluminum foil. Increase the heat to medium and bring back to simmering. Simmer until the fish is cooked through, 8–10 minutes. • Transfer the steaks with the sauce onto a serving dish. Spoon the remaining sauce over the top and sprinkle with the cilantro. Serve hot.

4	salmon steaks
	Salt and freshly ground black pepper
1	pak choy, 5–6 stalks Swiss chard (silver-beet), or 2½ cups (250 g) spinach
3	tablespoons peanut oil
1	large onion, thinly sliced
1	tablespoon finely chopped fresh ginger
3	large tomatoes, peeled and chopped
1	long red chile, seeded and thinly sliced
1	teaspoon sugar
³/₄	cup (200 ml) coconut milk
³/₄	cup (200 ml) water
1	teaspoon soy sauce
	Freshly squeezed juice of 1 lime
½	cup (25 g) chopped fresh cilantro (coriander) leaves

Serves: 4–6
Preparation: 15 minutes
Cooking: 10–15 minutes
Level: 1

SOLE MEUNIÈRE

Place the flour on a plate and dredge the sole in it until well coated. Shake off any excess. • Melt half the butter in a large frying pan over medium heat. Add the sole in a single layer (or cook in two batches) and sauté until golden on one side, about 3 minutes. Season with salt. Use a spatula to turn the fish over and cook until golden brown on the other side, about 2 minutes. • Remove the fish from the pan carefully with the spatula, making sure it doesn't break. Place on serving dishes and keep warm. • Melt the remaining 4 tablespoons of butter in the same frying pan over medium heat. Simmer until it begins to turn golden. Add the lemon juice, and parsley and simmer for 30 seconds. • Spoon the sauce over the sole and serve at once.

$^1/_2$ **cup (75 g) all-purpose (plain) flour**

4 **sole (6–8 ounces/ 200–250 g) each, gutted**

8 **tablespoons (125 g) butter**

Freshly squeezed juice of 1 lemon

Salt

2 tablespoons finely chopped fresh parsley

Serves: 4
Preparation: 15 minutes
Cooking: 15 minutes
Level: 1

▨ ▨ ▨ *This simple dish is a classic of French cuisine. Normally a true Dover Sole should be used. This is the dish that is said to have been Julia Child's epiphany, inspiring her life-long love of French cooking.*

BAKED FISH
WITH VEGETABLES

340

Preheat the oven to 350°F (180°C/gas 4).
• Combine the oil, 4 cloves of garlic, cumin,
$1/4$ cup (60 ml) of lemon juice, salt, and pepper
in an ovenproof baking dish. • Place a layer of
potatoes, carrots, and tomatoes on top and cover
with the fish fillets. Arrange the remaining
vegetables over the fish. • Bake for 40–45 minutes,
or until the fish and vegetables are tender. • Just
before the fish comes out of the oven, process the
pine nuts, parsley, remaining $1/2$ cup (125 ml) of
lemon juice, and remaining 1 clove of garlic in a
food processor until smooth. • Spoon the sauce
over the fish and vegetables. • Serve hot.

$1/4$ cup (60 ml) extra-virgin olive oil

5 cloves garlic, finely chopped

1 teaspoon ground cumin

$3/4$ cup (180 ml) freshly squeezed lemon juice

Salt and freshly ground black pepper

4 medium potatoes, with skins, thinly sliced

4 medium carrots, thinly sliced

2 large tomatoes, finely chopped

2 pounds (1 kg) firm, white fish fillets (sea bass, grouper, cod, porgy, red snapper, mullet, etc.)

$1/2$ cup (90 g) pine nuts

1 bunch fresh parsley

Serves: 6
Preparation: 20 minutes
Cooking: 40–45 minutes
Level: 1

ROAST FISH STEAKS
WITH TOMATOES

342

Preheat the oven to 400°F (200°C/gas 6).
• Combine the tomatoes and olives in a medium baking dish and drizzle with the oil. Bake for 5 minutes. • Add the fish and bake for 10–15 minutes, or until the flesh flakes easily. • Remove the fish and keep warm. • Stir the arugula with the roasted tomatoes and olives. Divide evenly among four serving dishes and place the fish on top.
• Serve hot.

6 plum (roma) tomatoes, halved

1/2 cup (50 g) black olives

1/4 cup (60 ml) extra-virgin olive oil

4 (8-ounce/250-g) firm white fish steaks(cod, snapper, ling, or warehou, etc.) cut about 3/4 inch (2 cm) thick

2 cups (100 g) arugula (rocket) leaves

Serves: 4
Preparation: 5 minutes
Cooking: 15–20 minutes
Level: 1

■ ■ ■ *Another very simple dish that can be prepared in no time.*

SNAPPER STUFFED WITH DATES

Preheat the oven to 350°F (180°C/gas 4). • Bring a small saucepan of water to a boil. Add the rice and cook for 3 minutes. Drain and set aside to cool. • Melt the butter in a small frying pan over medium-low heat. Add the onion, cinnamon, and ginger and sauté until softened and fragrant, 5–7 minutes. • Combine the cooled rice, spiced onion, dates, flaked almonds, and ground almonds in a medium bowl, mixing well. • **Step 1:** Stuff the filling inside the fish cavity. Secure using toothpicks. • Lay the fish on a sheet of aluminum foil large enough to encase the whole fish. Drizzle with oil and season with salt and pepper. Wrap the fish so that it is completely enclosed in the foil. • Bake 20–25 minutes, until cooked through and the flesh flakes easily. • Remove the toothpicks and serve hot.

4	pounds (2 kg) whole snapper, scaled and cleaned
1/4	cup (50 g) long-grain rice, rinsed
2	tablespoons butter
1	small onion, finely chopped
1/2	teaspoon ground cinnamon
1/2	teaspoon ground ginger
4	ounces (125 g) fresh dates, pitted and coarsely chopped
1/4	cup (40 g) flaked almonds
2	tablespoons ground almonds
	Olive oil
	Salt and freshly ground black pepper

Serves: 4
Preparation: 15 minutes
Cooking: 30–35 minutes
Level: 1

SECURING FISH WITH TOOTHPICKS

1. STUFF the filling inside the fish cavity. Secure using toothpicks.

FISH STEAMED BANANA LEAF

Spice Paste: Place the chiles, candlenuts, shallots, garlic, ginger, lemongrass, turmeric, coriander, shrimp, and salt in a large mortar and pestle or food processor and grind or blend to make a coarse paste. **Fish:** Heat the oil in a medium frying pan over medium heat. Add the spice paste and stir-fry until fragrant, about 30 seconds. • Strain the tamarind and discard the pulp. Add the tamarind liquid, water, and jaggery to the pan and bring to a boil. Decrease the heat to low and simmer until the liquid has evaporated, 3–5 minutes. Transfer to a small bowl and set aside to cool. • Dice the fish and place in a medium bowl. Add $1/2$ cup (125 ml) of the spice paste mixture and the tomato wedges. Toss to coat. • **Step 1:** Divide the fish mixture evenly among the banana leaves, spooning it onto the center of each. • **Step 2:** Fold the banana leaves to encase the filling. **Step 3:** Secure each parcel with toothpicks. • Chill in the refrigerator for 1 hour to marinate. • Preheat a barbecue hot plate on medium-low heat. • Cook the banana leaf parcels until firm and cooked through, 4–5 minutes on each side. • Serve hot or at room temperature with steamed jasmine rice.

■ ■ ■ *Store surplus spice paste in an airtight container in the refrigerator for up to 1 week.*
If you can't find banana leaves, use corn husks or wrap in parchment paper or aluminum foil.

Spice Paste

10 large red chiles, seeded and coarsely chopped

$1/2$ cup (60 g) candlenuts, coarsely chopped

2 shallots, coarsely chopped

2 cloves garlic, coarsely chopped

1 tablespoon finely grated fresh ginger

1 stalk lemongrass, white part only, coarsely chopped

2 teaspoons ground turmeric

1 teaspoon coriander seeds

1 teaspoon dried shrimp

1 teaspoon salt

Fish

$1/4$ cup (60 ml) vegetable oil

1 tablespoon tamarind pulp, soaked in 2 tablespoons water

1 teaspoon finely grated jaggery (palm sugar)

$1^1/2$ pounds (750 g) blue eye, snapper, or other firm white fish

4 young banana leaves, cut into eight 6 x 5-inch (15 x 13-cm) pieces

2 large tomatoes, each cut into 6 wedges

Steamed jasmine rice

$1/2$ cup (125 ml) water

Serves: 4
Preparation: 45 minutes
+ 1 hour to marinate
Cooking: 10 minutes
Level: 2

◼ PREPARING BANANA LEAF PARCELS

This dish comes from Indonesia. Banana leaves are used in many Southeast Asian dishes to wrap food which is then barbecued, baked, or steamed. They lend the food a little of their delicate, natural flavor and are also pretty to serve. Banana leaves can be found in Asian food stores and markets. Sometimes you will find them fresh, but they are also available frozen.

1. DIVIDE the fish mixture evenly among the banana leaves, spooning it onto the center of each.

2. FOLD the banana leaves over to encase the filling.

3. SECURE each parcel with toothpicks and chill in the refrigerator for 1 hour to marinate.

COD WITH POTATOES AND ROSEMARY

350

Heat the oil and butter in a large frying pan over medium heat. Add the onion and sauté until softened, 3–4 minutes. • Add the potatoes and sauté for 5 minutes. • Add the fish, rosemary, and lemon zest. Pour in the milk and enough water to cover the ingredients. Season with salt and pepper. • Simmer until the fish and potatoes are tender and the sauce has reduced to half its original volume, 5–10 minutes. • Sprinkle with the parsley and garnish with sprigs of rosemary. • Serve hot.

2 tablespoons extra-virgin olive oil

1 tablespoon butter

1 large onion, cut into rings

2 pounds (1 kg) potatoes, peeled and cut into thin wedges

1¼ pounds (600 g) cod, hake, or other firm white fish fillets

1 tablespoon finely chopped fresh rosemary + extra sprigs to garnish

Zest of ½ lemon, very finely sliced

¼ cup (60 ml) milk

½ cup (125 ml) water

Salt and freshly ground black pepper

1 tablespoon finely chopped fresh parsley

Serves: 4
Preparation: 10 minutes
Cooking: 12–18 minutes
Level: 1

DEEP FRIED FISH WITH THREE-FLAVORED SAUCE

Three-Flavored Sauce: Place the shallots, chiles, garlic and coriander root in a large mortar and pestle or food processor and grind or chop to make a coarse paste. • Heat the oil in a medium frying pan over medium-low heat. Add the spice paste and stir-fry until fragrant, about 30 seconds. • Strain the tamarind, discarding the solids. Add the tamarind water, jaggery, and fish sauce to the spice paste. Stir to combine and bring to a boil. Decrease the heat to low and gently simmer until thickened and syrupy, 4–5 minutes. Set aside.

Fish: • Pour the oil into a deep-fryer or deep saucepan over medium heat and heat to 365°F (190°C). If you don't have a frying thermometer, test the oil temperature by dropping a small piece of bread into the hot oil. If the bread immediately bubbles to the surface and begins to turn golden, the oil is ready. • Fry the basil leaves until crisp, 10 seconds. Remove using a slotted spoon and drain on paper towels. • Score the fish, making three or four diagonal cuts on both sides. • Dredge the fish in the flour and deep-fry, one at a time, until crisp and golden, 15–20 minutes. Remove carefully and drain on paper towels. Keep warm. • Meanwhile, reheat the sauce over low heat. • Drizzle over the fish, scatter with basil leaves, and serve hot.

Three-Flavored Sauce

5 shallots, coarsely chopped
5 long red chiles, seeded and coarsely chopped
6 cloves garlic, coarsely chopped
5 coriander roots, chopped
3 tablespoons vegetable oil
3 tablespoons tamarind paste soaked in ½ cup (125 ml) water
4 tablespoons coarsely grated jaggery (palm sugar) or brown sugar
¼ cup (60 ml) Thai fish sauce

Fish

4 cups (1 liter) vegetable oil
2 (1½-pound/750-g) whole snapper (or other firm white fish), cleaned and scaled
1 cup (50 g) Thai or ordinary basil leaves
All-purpose (plain) flour to coat

Serves: 4
Preparation: 15 minutes
Cooking: 30–40 minutes
Level: 2

MOROCCAN CHERMOULA FISH

Chermoula: Combine the fresh cilantro, parsley, garlic, lemon juice, oil, paprika, cumin, and ground coriander in a medium bowl. Season with salt and pepper. • **Step 1:** Score the fish twice in the thickest part, near the head, to ensure even cooking. • Place the fish in a large dish and coat in chermoula, filling the cavity and cuts where it has been scored. • Cover and refrigerate for at least 6 hours or overnight to marinate. • Preheat the oven to 375°F (190°C/gas 5). • Lay half of the onion slices in the base of a large baking pan. Place the fish on top and scatter with the remaining onion. • Bake for 25–30 minutes, until cooked through and the flesh flakes easily. • Serve hot with lemon wedges.

Chermoula

1	cup (50 g) finely chopped fresh cilantro (coriander) leaves
1	cup (50 g) finely chopped fresh parsley
3	cloves garlic, minced
3	tablespoons freshly squeezed lemon juice
2	tablespoons extra-virgin olive oil
2	teaspoons hot paprika
1	teaspoon ground cumin
1	teaspoon ground coriander
	Salt and freshly ground black pepper
4	pounds (2 kg) whole snapper (or other firm white fish), scaled and cleaned
1	large red onion, sliced into rounds
	Lemon wedges to garnish

Serves: 4
Preparation: 25 minutes
    + 6–12 hours to marinate
Cooking: 25–30 minutes
Level: 2

■ SCORING FISH

When cooking whole fish, you can score the fish by making several deep cuts along it sides. This allows the heat to penetrate evenly so that the whole fish is cooked at the same time.

1. SCORE the fish 2–3 times in the thickest part, working downward from the head, to ensure even cooking.

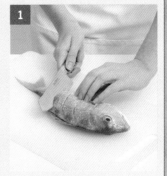

POULTRY

BANG BANG CHICKEN

Chicken: Place the chicken, onion, and ginger in a medium saucepan, cover with water, and bring to a boil. Decrease the heat and simmer until the chicken is cooked, 10–12 minutes. • Remove the chicken, reserving 3 tablespoons of the stock (cooking liquid), and set aside until cool enough to handle. • Shred into thin strips with your fingers and set aside.
Sesame Sauce: Dry-fry the peppercorns in a small frying pan over medium-low heat until very fragrant, 2–3 minutes. • Transfer to a mortar and pestle or spice grinder and grind to a powder. • Combine the Szechuan pepper powder and remaining sauce ingredients in a small bowl. • Add the reserved chicken stock and stir to combine. • Cut the cucumber into thirds crosswise and into quarters lengthwise. Remove and discard the seeds. Slice the quarters into thin lengthwise strips and place in a medium bowl. • Cut the celery in the same way and add to the cucumber. • Add the scallions and cilantro and toss to combine. • To serve, arrange the cucumber mixture on a serving plate. Top with the chicken and drizzle with sauce. Garnish with the cilantro and serve.

■ ■ ■ *This dish comes from the Szechuan region of China. Apparently its name is derived from the sound made by the rolling pin used to tenderize the chicken before shredding.*
Szechuan pepper is not related to black pepper or chiles, although it has a similar flavor but with lemony overtones. Buy it in Asian food stores or online.

Chicken

1½ pounds (750 g) boneless skinless chicken breasts

1 small onion, quartered

1 (2-inch/5-cm) piece ginger, thinly sliced

1 cucumber

2 stalks celery

2 scallions, (spring onions), thinly sliced

1 cup (50 g) fresh cilantro (coriander) + extra to garnish

Sesame Sauce

½ teaspoon Szechuan peppercorns

2 cloves garlic, minced

2 teaspoons finely grated fresh ginger

3 tablespoons tahini (sesame paste)

2 tablespoons light soy sauce

1 tablespoon sesame oil

1 tablespoon rice wine vinegar

2 teaspoons sugar

¼ teaspoon chile paste

Serves: 4–6
Preparation: 30 minutes
Cooking: 15–20 minutes
Level: 1

GRILLED CHICKEN WITH SPINACH AND MANGO

Marinade: Whisk all the marinade ingredients in a small bowl. Set aside.

Chicken: Place the chicken in a large glass or ceramic bowl. Add 1/2 cup (125 ml) of the marinade and marinate for 2 hours. • Preheat the oven to 450°F (220°C/gas 8). • Season the tomatoes with the basil, mint, salt, pepper, and sugar. • Add the sesame oil to a baking dish large enough to hold the tomatoes cut-side up in a single layer. Add the tomatoes and roast for 15 minutes. Reduce the oven temperature to 300°F (150°C/gas 2) and roast until the tomatoes have shrivelled to about half their original size, about 1 1/2 hours. Let cool. • Heat a grill pan on high heat. Drain the chicken, reserving the marinade, and grill until tender and cooked through, 4–5 minutes each side. Baste with the marinade during cooking. Set aside and keep warm.

To assemble: Steam the asparagus until just tender then refresh under cold water. Drain well. • Put the spinach in a large bowl and add the asparagus, scallions, mushrooms, and roasted tomatoes. • Add the remaining marinade and toss gently. • Divide evenly among six serving plates. • Top with the mango and avocado cubes. Cover with the chicken and nuts and serve.

360

Marinade
- 3 tablespoons raspberry vinegar
- 2 tablespoons balsamic vinegar
- 2 tablespoons soy sauce
- 2 teaspoons Dijon mustard
- 2 teaspoons honey
- 1 inch (2.5-cm) piece ginger, finely chopped
- 2 cloves garlic, chopped
- 1 teaspoon chile paste
- 2 tablespoons freshly squeezed lemon juice
- 2 tablespoons extra-virgin olive oil

Chicken
- 4 boneless skinless chicken breast halves
- 6 tomatoes, halved
- 10 fresh basil leaves, torn
- 10 fresh mint leaves, torn
- Salt and pepper
- 1/2 teaspoon sugar
- 2 tablespoons sesame oil

To Assemble
- 1 bunch asparagus
- 2 cups (100 g) baby spinach leaves
- 4 scallions (spring onions), sliced
- 8 button mushrooms, sliced
- 1 mango, pitted and diced
- 1 avocado, pitted and diced
- 1 cup (120 g) toasted hazelnuts

Serves: 6
Preparation: 1 hour + 2 hours to marinate
Cooking: 1 3/4 hours
Level: 2

CHICKEN BALLS

362

Soak the bread in the milk in a small bowl for
5 minutes. Drain well, squeezing out excess milk.
• Mix the chicken, soaked bread, and egg in a large
bowl. Season with salt and pepper. • Use your
hands to bind the mixture and shape into balls the
size of large marbles. • Roll the balls in the flour.
• Heat the oil to very hot in a large deep frying pan.
• Fry the chicken balls in batches until golden
brown, about 5 minutes each batch. • Drizzle with
the lemon juice just before serving and serve hot.

2	slices white sandwich bread, crusts removed
¼	cup (60 ml) milk
1	pound (500 g) ground (minced) chicken
1	large egg, lightly beaten
	Salt and freshly ground black pepper
½	cup (75 g) all-purpose (plain) flour
1	cup (250 ml) vegetable oil for frying
	Freshly squeezed juice of ½ lemon

Serves: 2–4
Preparation: 15 minutes
    + 5 minutes to soak
Cooking: 10–15 minutes
Level: 1

■ ■ ■ *These delicious little balls can be served as an*
appetizer (for four people) or with a salad and rice or
potatoes as a light lunch or supper (for two people).

THAI CHICKEN AND SHRIMP MONEY BAGS

364

Dipping Sauce: Combine the rice wine vinegar, sugar, and fish sauce in a small saucepan and bring to a simmer over medium heat, stirring to dissolve the sugar. • Remove from the heat, add the chile and set aside to cool.

Money Bags: Place the shrimp in a food processor and chop until well ground. Transfer to a medium bowl. • Add the chicken, chestnuts, garlic, ginger, scallions, cilantro, and salt and stir to combine. • Lightly dust a clean kitchen towel with cornstarch and lay half of the wonton wrappers on top. Step 1: Divide half of the chicken filling evenly among the wrappers, placing small spoonfuls in the center of each. Lightly brush around the filling with egg yolk. Step 2: Bring the corners of the wrappers together. Step 3: Tie a chive around the top to create a "money bag." • Lightly dust a tray with cornstarch and place the money bags on top. • Repeat with the remaining filling and wonton wrappers. • Pour the oil into a deep-fryer of deep saucepan over medium heat and heat to 365°F (190°C). If you don't have a frying thermometer, test the oil temperature by dropping a small piece of bread into the hot oil. If the bread immediately bubbles to the surface and begins to turn golden, the oil is ready. • Step 4: Deep-fry the money bags in batches until crisp, golden, and cooked through, 3–4 minutes each batch. • Remove with a slotted spoon and drain on paper towels. • Serve hot with the dipping sauce.

Dipping Sauce

- ½ cup (125 ml) rice wine vinegar
- 5 tablespoons sugar
- 1 tablespoon Thai fish sauce
- 1 red chile, seeded and finely chopped

Money Bags

- 5 ounces (150 g) shrimp (prawns), peeled, deveined, and chopped
- 8 ounces (250 g) ground (minced) chicken
- 8 ounces (250 g) canned water chestnuts, drained and finely chopped
- 1 clove garlic, minced
- 1 teaspoon finely grated fresh ginger
- 2 scallions (spring onions), thinly sliced
- 1 tablespoon finely chopped fresh cilantro (coriander)
- 1 teaspoon salt
- 30 wonton wrappers
- 30 chives
- 2 large egg yolks, lightly beaten
- Cornstarch (cornflour) to dust
- 4 cups (1 liter) vegetable oil for frying

Serves: 6–8
Preparation: 30 minutes
Cooking: 20 minutes
Level: 3

PREPARING MONEY BAGS FOR THAI CHICKEN AND SHRIMP

Prepare a platter of these nifty little money bags for a party buffet or as an entrée. They can be prepared ahead of time and chilled in the refrigerator. Deep-fry just a few minutes before serving.

1. DIVIDE half the filling evenly among the wrappers, placing small spoonfuls in the center of each. Lightly brush around the filling with egg yolk.

2. BRING the corners of the wrappers together.

3. TIE a chive around the top of each one to create a "money bag."

4. DEEP-FRY in batches until crisp, golden, and cooked through, 3–4 minutes each. Remove with a slotted spoon and drain on paper towels.

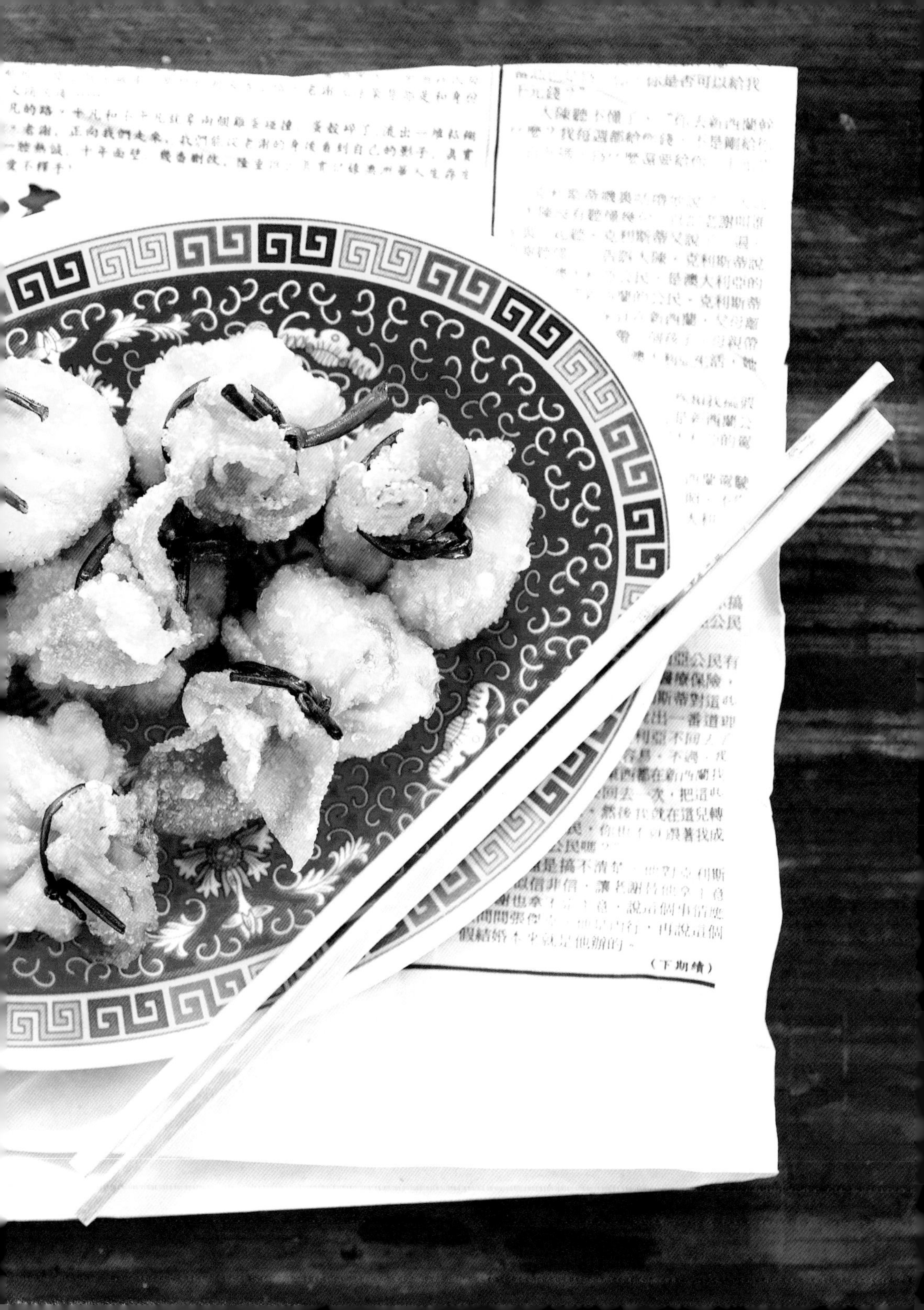
(下期續)

THAI GREEN CHICKEN CURRY

Curry Paste: Dry-fry the coriander and cumin seeds in a small frying pan over medium heat until fragrant, about 30 seconds. • Combine the coriander and cumin and remaining curry paste ingredients in a large mortar and pestle or food processor and grind or blend to make a coarse paste.

Curry: Heat the oil in a medium heavy-based saucepan or wok over medium heat. Add the curry paste and stir-fry until fragrant, about 30 seconds. • Pour in the cream of coconut, stir to combine, and bring to a boil. Decrease the heat to low and simmer until the cream splits, 4–5 minutes. • Pour in the coconut milk and water and return to a boil. Decrease the heat, add the fish sauce, jaggery, and lime juice and leaves and simmer for 5 minutes. • Add the chicken and simmer for 5 minutes. • Add the eggplant and simmer until the chicken and eggplant are completely tender, 5–10 minutes. Season with salt. • Garnish with cilantro and serve hot with the rice.

Curry Paste

1	teaspoon coriander seeds
1/2	teaspoon cumin seeds
4	long green chiles, seeded and halved lengthwise
3	shallots, chopped
4	cloves garlic, chopped
3	coriander roots, chopped
2	stalks lemongrass, white part only, chopped
1	(2-inch/5-cm) piece fresh ginger, coarsely chopped
2	teaspoons finely grated kaffir lime zest
1½	teaspoons shrimp paste

Curry

2	tablespoons vegetable oil
2	cups (400 ml) canned cream of coconut
2	cups (400 ml) canned coconut milk
1/2	cup (125 ml) water
2	tablespoons Thai fish sauce
1	tablespoon coarsely grated jaggery (palm sugar) or brown sugar
1	tablespoon freshly squeezed lime juice
5	kaffir lime leaves
1½	pounds (750 g) chicken breast or thigh fillets, sliced
1	eggplant (aubergine), with skin, diced
	Salt
	Fresh cilantro (coriander) leaves to garnish
	Steamed jasmine rice

Serves: 4
Preparation: 25 minutes
Cooking: 20–25 minutes
Level: 2

CHICKEN AND SAUSAGE GUMBO

Season the chicken thighs generously with salt and white pepper. • Heat 2 tablespoons of the oil in a large Dutch oven or saucepan over medium-high heat. Add the chicken in 2 batches and sauté until well browned and crisp, about 10 minutes each batch. Set aside. • Wipe the pot clean and add the remaining 6 tablespoons (90 ml) of oil. Place over medium heat for 2 minutes. Gradually stir in the flour, mixing with a wooden spoon until the mixture is a deep, red-brown color, about 10 minutes. • Add the onions, celery, garlic, marjoram, salt, and pepper. Simmer, stirring often, until the vegetables begin to soften, about 10 minutes. • Add the chicken stock a little at a time, stirring constantly with the wooden spoon so that no lumps form. • Add the bay leaves and chicken and simmer for 30 minutes. • Add the sausage and simmer for 30 minutes more. • Remove from the heat. Remove the bay leaves. Stir in the parsley and scallions and serve hot.

■ ■ ■ *Gumbo is a spicy dish somewhere between a soup and a stew. It is a famous Cajun recipe from the state of Louisiana. There are many different versions; this one is based on chicken and sausage. Cajun andouille sausage is spicy (the French version is milder); if you can't find it, substitute with another type of smoked, spicy sausage.*

3	pounds (1.5 kg) chicken thighs
	Salt and freshly ground white pepper
8	tablespoons (125 ml) vegetable oil
½	cup (75 g) all-purpose (plain) flour)
2	onions, finely chopped
1	stalk celery, finely chopped
6	cloves garlic, finely chopped
1	teaspoon dried marjoram
8	cups (2 liters) Chicken Stock (see pages 34–35)
2	bay leaves
1	pound (500 g) andouille sausage, cut in short chunks
2	tablespoons finely chopped fresh parsley
2	scallions (spring onions), tender white and green parts only, sliced

Serves: 6
Preparation: 30 minutes
Cooking: About 2 hours
Level: 2

CHICKEN TAGINE WITH PRESERVED LEMON

Chicken Tagine: Heat the oil in a medium-large tagine or heavy-based saucepan over medium heat. Add the chicken, onion, garlic, ginger, cumin, turmeric, saffron, salt, and pepper and sauté until the chicken is browned and the spices fragrant, 5–10 minutes. • Pour in the water or stock and bring to a boil. Reduce the heat to low, cover, and simmer for 20 minutes. • Slice the preserved lemon thinly lengthwise. • Scatter the lemon and olives around the chicken. Sprinkle with cilantro. • Cover and simmer until the chicken is cooked, 20–25 minutes. • Serve hot.

Preserved Lemons: Step 1: Soak the lemons in cold water for 3–4 days, changing the water daily. • **Step 2:** Without slicing all the way through, cut each lemon vertically into four. Open them out carefully, salt generously, then press the quarters back together to make whole lemons. • **Step 3:** Insert the lemons into two sterilized 1 quart (1 liter) preserving jars, packing them tightly together. Seal the jars. • Store in a cool dark place for 1 month before using.

Chicken Tagine

3   tablespoons extra-virgin olive oil

1   chicken, about 3½ pounds (1.8 kg), cut into 8 pieces

1   large onion, sliced

2   cloves garlic, finely chopped

1   teaspoon ground ginger

1   teaspoon ground cumin

¼   teaspoon ground turmeric

    Pinch of saffron threads, crushed

½   teaspoon salt

¼   teaspoon freshly ground black pepper

1½   cups (375 ml) water, Chicken or Vegetable stock (see pages 34–35 or 94)

1   preserved lemon, rinsed, quartered, pulp discarded

½   cup (75 g) green olives

3   tablespoons finely chopped fresh cilantro (coriander)

Serves: 4
Preparation: 20 minutes
Cooking: 45–50 minutes
Level: 1

Preserved Lemons

2   pounds (1 kg) organic lemons

1   cup (250 g) coarse sea salt or kosher salt

Makes: 2 pounds (1 kg)
Preparation: 30 minutes
    + 3–4 days to soak
    + 1 month to store
Level: 1

■ PREPARING MOROCCAN PRESERVED LEMONS

Preserved lemons are used in many Moroccan and North African dishes. You can buy them in Middle Eastern and Mediterranean food stores, but they are also easy to make at home. They must be stored for one month before use and during that time they will produce enough juice to marinate, enriching their full flavor. Serve them with meat or seafood tagines, but also with vegetables, rice, and couscous.

1. SOAK the lemons in cold water for 3–4 days, changing the water daily.

2. WITHOUT slicing all the way through, cut each lemon vertically into four. Open out, salt generously, then press the quarters back together to make whole lemons.

3. INSERT the lemons into two sterilized 1 quart (1 liter) preserving jars, packing them tightly together. Seal the jars and store for 1 month.

DUCK AND FIG TAGINE

Melt the butter in a tagine or heavy-based saucepan over medium heat. • Add the duck, onions, and garlic and sauté until nicely browned, 8–10 minutes. • Add the ginger, turmeric, and salt. Pour in the water. • Cover and simmer over very low heat until the duck is tender, 40–45 minutes. • Add the honey and cinnamon and simmer for 10 minutes. • Stir in the figs and cook for 5 more minutes. • Garnish with the mint or basil and serve hot.

⅓	cup (90 g) butter
1	duck, weighing about 4 pounds (2 kg), cut into 8–10 pieces
2	onions, finely chopped
2	cloves garlic, finely chopped
1	teaspoon finely chopped fresh ginger
1	teaspoon ground turmeric
	Salt
1½	cups (375 ml) water
2	tablespoons honey
1	teaspoon ground cinnamon
1¾	pounds (800 g) fresh figs, quartered
	Fresh mint or basil leaves to garnish

Serves: 6
Preparation: 15 minutes
Cooking: 65–70 minutes
Level: 2

■ ■ ■ *This recipe calls for fresh figs, but when figs are out of season, dried may be used. You will need about 14 ounces (400 g) of dried figs. Cut into quarters and soak in lukewarm water for about 15 minutes and add an extra 5 minutes or so to the cooking time.*

CHICKEN MOLE

Preheat the oven to 350°F (180°C/gas 4). • Dry-fry the chiles in a small frying pan over low heat, turning frequently, until toasted, 2–3 minutes. • Combine the chiles and 1 cup (250 ml) of the chicken stock in a small saucepan and bring to a boil. Decrease the heat and simmer for 10 minutes. Remove from the heat and set aside to cool. • Remove the chiles, reserving the stock. Skin and remove the seeds. • Combine the chiles and reserved stock in a food processor and blend until smooth. Transfer to a small bowl and set aside. • Place the onion, garlic, chile powder, cinnamon, oregano, cumin, and cloves in a food processor and blend to a smooth paste. Transfer to a small bowl and set aside. • Place the tomatoes in a food processor and blend until smooth. • Heat the oil in a large saucepan over medium-low heat. Add the spiced onion mixture and cook until fragrant, 1–2 minutes. • Pour in the chile water and tomatoes and bring to a boil. Decrease the heat and simmer for 5 minutes. • Add the remaining stock and bring back to a boil. Decrease the heat, add the chocolate, and stir to combine. • Place the chicken in a medium ovenproof dish. Pour the sauce over the chicken, cover, and bake until tender, abut 1 hour. • Season with salt and pepper. • Serve hot with rice or floured tortillas.

4	large dried chipotle chiles
4	cups (1 liter) Chicken Stock (see pages 34–35)
1	large onion, coarsely chopped
3	cloves garlic, coarsely chopped
1	tablespoon mild chile powder
1	teaspoon ground cinnamon
1	teaspoon dried oregano
1/2	teaspoon ground cumin
1/4	teaspoon ground cloves
2	cups (400 ml) canned tomatoes, with juice
2	tablespoons extra-virgin olive oil
1	chicken, about 3 pounds (1.5 kg), cut into 8 pieces
1	ounce (30 g) Mexican or semisweet dark chocolate
	Salt and freshly ground black pepper
	Steamed rice or flour tortillas to serve

Serves: 4
Preparation: 45 minutes
Cooking: About 1^1/2 hours
Level: 2

TANDOORI CHICKEN

Marinade: Combine all the marinade ingredients in a medium bowl and stir to combine.

Chicken: Step 1: Score the chicken thighs, legs, and breasts, making diagonal cuts into the flesh using a sharp knife. • **Step 2:** Coat the chicken in the marinade, working it into the cuts and cavity. • Cover and refrigerate, turning occasionally, for at least six hours, or overnight, to marinate. • Preheat the oven to 350°F (180°C/gas 4). • Place the chicken in a large baking pan and cook, basting occasionally with the marinade, for 1 hour. • Decrease the heat to 275°F (140°C/gas 1). • Brush the chicken with ghee and cook until juices run clear from the thickest part when tested with a skewer, 30–45 minutes. • Serve hot with lemon wedges.

Marinade

1 cup (250 g) plain yogurt

3 tablespoons freshly squeezed lemon juice

2 cloves garlic, minced

2 teaspoons finely grated fresh ginger

2 teaspoons ground coriander

1 teaspoon ground cumin

1 teaspoon garam masala

1 teaspoon ground turmeric

1 teaspoon chile powder

½ teaspoon salt

¼ teaspoon freshly ground black pepper

Chicken

3 pounds (1.5 kg) chicken pieces

3 tablespoons melted ghee or extra-virgin olive oil

Lemon wedges to serve

Serves: 4–6
Preparation: 20 minutes
+ 6–12 hours to marinate
Cooking: $1^1/2$–$1^3/4$ hours
Level: 2

◼ PREPARING THE CHICKEN FOR TANDOORI CHICKEN

1. SCORE the chicken thighs, legs, and breasts, making diagonal cuts into the flesh using a sharp knife.

2. COAT the chicken in the marinade, working it into the cuts and cavity. Cover and marinate for 6–12 hours.

MOROCCAN CHICKEN STUFFED WITH COUSCOUS

Stuffing: Place the couscous in a large shallow bowl. • Combine the water and salt in a medium bowl. Gradually sprinkle ½ cup (125 ml) of the water over the couscous, rubbing it through and separating the grains with your hands. Set aside until the grains have swelled and dried out slightly, about 10 minutes. • Fill the base of a steamer pot with water and bring to a boil. • Rub your fingers through the couscous again, separating the grains. Place the couscous in the top of the steamer pot and set over the boiling water, ensuring that the top steamer section is not touching the water. Watch to see when the steam begins to rise through the couscous. Now steam for 10 minutes. • Turn the couscous out into a shallow bowl. Sprinkle with the remaining water and the olive oil and rub with your hands, separating the grains. Set aside for 10 minutes to swell and dry out a little. • Meanwhile, heat the vegetable oil in a medium frying pan over medium-low heat. Add the almonds and sauté until golden brown, 3–4 minutes. Remove with a slotted spoon, drain on paper towels, and chop coarsely. • Separate the couscous grains again using your fingers and return to the top of the steamer. When the steam begins to rise through the couscous, steam for 10 more minutes. • Tip the couscous back

Stuffing

1	cup (180 g) couscous
1¼	cups (300 ml) water
1	teaspoon salt
2	tablespoons extra-virgin olive oil
2	tablespoons vegetable oil
1	cup (150 g) blanched almonds
2	tablespoons butter
½	cup (90 g) raisins, soaked in water for 10 minutes and drained
2	teaspoons caster sugar
1	teaspoon ground cinnamon
Salt and freshly ground black pepper	

Chicken

1	chicken, about 4 pounds (2 kg)
1	large onion, grated
3	tablespoons honey
2	tablespoons butter
1	teaspoon ground cinnamon

½ teaspoon ground ginger

Pinch of saffron threads, crushed and soaked in 1 tablespoon water for 10 minutes

1 cup (250 ml) water

Serves: 4
Preparation: 45 minutes
Cooking: 2 hours
Level: 2

into the shallow bowl. • Add the butter, almonds, raisins, sugar, and cinnamon and rub in using your fingers to separate the grains. Season with salt and pepper.

Chicken: Preheat the oven to 400°F (200°C/gas 6). • Wash the chicken, including the cavity thoroughly with cold running water and pat dry with paper towels. • Stuff the cavity with the stuffing, fold over the two flaps of skin and secure together using toothpicks. Truss the legs together using kitchen string. • Combine the onion, honey, butter, cinnamon, ginger, saffron and its water together in a medium bowl. • Spread the onion mixture in the base of a large baking pan. Place the chicken on top and pour in the water. Cover with aluminum foil and bake for 45 minutes. • Uncover the chicken and return to the oven to cook, basting occasionally, for a 45 minutes, or until the juices run clear from the thickest part of the thigh when tested. • Serve hot.

STUFFED TURKEY MIDDLE EASTERN STYLE

Preheat the oven to 325°F (170°C/gas 3). • Set out a large roasting pan. • Rinse the turkey and dry well. Rub inside and out with a generous seasoning of salt and pepper. Rub with the allspice. • Heat the oil in a large frying pan over medium heat. Sauté the garlic, parsley, and pine nuts until golden, about 5 minutes. • Add the beef and sauté until browned, 8–10 minutes. • Stir in the rice, nutmeg, cinnamon, cumin, and 1 cup (250 ml) water. Season with salt and pepper. • Bring to a boil and simmer until the rice is tender, 15–20 minutes. • Spoon the mixture into the turkey cavity and sew up the cavity with kitchen string. • Rub the turkey with the butter and place in the roasting pan. • Pour the remaining 1 cup (250 ml) water into the pan and cover with aluminum foil. • Roast for 1 1/2 hours. Remove the foil and roast until very tender, 30–60 minutes more. • Serve hot or at room temperature.

1	turkey, about 10 pounds (4–5 kg)
	Salt and freshly ground black pepper
1	teaspoon ground allspice or pumpkin pie spice
1/4	cup (60 ml) extra-virgin olive oil
2	cloves garlic, finely chopped
2	tablespoons finely chopped fresh parsley
1/2	cup (90 g) pine nuts
1	pound (500 g) ground (minced) beef
2	cups (400 g) long-grain rice
1	teaspoon freshly grated nutmeg
1	teaspoon ground cinnamon
1/2	teaspoon cumin seeds
2	cups (500 ml) water
1/4	cup (60 g) butter, cut up

Serves: 8–10
Preparation: 30 minutes
Cooking: 2 1/2–3 hours
Level 1

SPICY CHICKEN AND PORK TAMALES

Filling: Place the chicken, pork, water, onion, garlic, bay leaves, and peppercorns in a large saucepan over high heat and bring to a boil. Decrease the heat to low and simmer for 2 hours. • Skim the surface frequently to remove impurities and excess fat. • Remove from the heat, transfer the chicken and pork to a large bowl and set aside to cool slightly. • Strain the stock through a fine-mesh sieve. Discard the bay leaves and peppercorns. • Return the onion and garlic to the stock and blend, using a hand held blender, until smooth. Set aside. • Remove the fat, skin, and bones from the chicken and pork and shred the meat. • Finely chop the meat in a food processor. Transfer to a medium bowl. • Add about $1/2$ cup (125 ml) of the stock to the meat to moisten. • Melt the butter in a small frying pan over low heat. Add the onion, garlic, and chile powders, paprika, salt, and pepper and stir to combine. • Pour the spiced butter into the meat. Mix well and set aside.

Corn Paste: Place the cornmeal in a medium bowl. Gradually add the stock, stirring to incorporate. • Melt the butter in a small frying pan. Add the chile, cumin, salt, and pepper and stir to combine. • Pour the spiced butter into the corn paste and stir to combine. The paste should be sticky, with the consistency of peanut butter. Add a little more stock if necessary.

To Assemble and Cook: Step 1: Spread a large spoonful of corn paste down two-thirds of one of the corn husks. The sides and top third should be free of

Filling

1¼	pounds (600 g) chicken thighs
1¼	pounds (600 g) pork rump
8	cups (2 liters) water
1	large onion, halved
4	whole garlic cloves, peeled
3	bay leaves
½	teaspoon peppercorns
¼	cup (60 g) butter
1	teaspoon onion powder
½	teaspoon garlic powder
½	teaspoon chile powder
½	teaspoon hot paprika
½	teaspoon salt
¼	teaspoon freshly ground black pepper

Corn Paste

2	cups (500 g) yellow cornmeal
4	cups (1 liter) reserved stock (from filling)
1	cup (250 g) butter
2	tablespoons chile powder
1	tablespoon ground cumin
1	teaspoon salt

½ teaspoon freshly ground black pepper

To Serve

Corn fresh or dried husks from 8 corn ears (cobs) (If using dried husks, soak in cold water for 2 hours to soften)

Steamed long-grain rice

Mexican-style salsa

Serves: 4
Preparation: 1 hour
Cooking: About 2¹/2 hours
Level: 3

paste so it can be folded into a parcel. Spread a spoonful of filling down the center and fold over to enclose, making a long parcel. Seal both ends, or leave one end open. • Tie a thin strip of corn husk around the parcel to secure. Repeat with the remaining filling and corn husks. • **Step 2:** Put the corn parcels upright in a large steamer with the open end (if applicable) facing upward. • Place over a pot of boiling water, cover, and steam until firm, about 20 minutes. • Serve hot with the rice and salsa.

■ ■ ■ *The filling can also be wrapped in banana leaves or parchment paper. However corn husks are more authentic and add to the flavor.*
The tamales can be made in advance and frozen in a freezer-proof container for up to 2–3 weeks. If cooking from frozen, add an extra 10 minutes to the cooking time.

■ ASSEMBLING AND COOKING TAMALES

1. SPREAD a spoonful of corn paste down two-thirds of a corn husk. The sides and top third should be free of paste. Put meat filling down the center, fold, and tie with a strip of corn husk.
2. STEAM until firm, about 20 minutes.

COQ AU VIN

Heat the oil in a large saucepan over medium heat. Add the chicken and sauté until well browned, 8–10 minutes. • Sprinkle the chicken with the flour, letting it soak up the oil. Remove and set aside. • Add the bacon, mushrooms, onions, and shallots to the same pan and sauté over medium heat until lightly browned, about 10 minutes. • Add the garlic, tomato paste, and bouquet garni. Season with salt and pepper. • Pour in the wine and stock. Return the chicken to the pan. Cover and simmer over low heat until the chicken is very tender, 30–45 minutes. The sauce should be thick. • Remove the bouquet garni. Garnish with fresh herbs and serve hot with the rice or potatoes.

3	tablespoons extra-virgin olive oil
1	chicken, 4–5 pounds (2 kg), cut into 8 pieces
2	tablespoons all-purpose (plain) flour
2	cups (250 g) diced bacon
8	ounces (250 g) button mushrooms
2	onions, finely chopped
2	shallots, finely chopped
3	cloves garlic, finely chopped
1	teaspoon tomato paste (concentrate)
1	bouquet garni (see note) + fresh herbs to garnish
	Salt and freshly ground black pepper
2	cups (500 ml) full-bodied dry red wine
1½	cups (375 ml) Beef Stock (see page 62–63)
	Freshly cooked short-grain rice or boiled potatoes, to serve

Serves: 4–6
Preparation: 20 minutes
Cooking: 50–65 minutes
Level: 1

▓ ▓ ▓ *A bouquet garni is a bunch of fresh herbs, such as bay leaves, thyme, and parsley, tied together with kitchen string. It is added to a dish to give flavor during cooking and then removed before serving.*

CHICKEN PROVENÇAL

Heat the oil in a large frying pan over medium-high heat. Add the chicken and sauté until lightly browned, 8–10 minutes. • Season with salt and pepper. Remove the chicken from the pan and set aside. • In the same pan, sauté the onion, garlic, and tomatoes until the tomatoes begin to break down, about 10 minutes. Season with salt. • Lower the heat and pour in the wine. Stir in the rosemary, thyme, and olives. Simmer for 10 minutes. • Return the chicken to the pan and season with salt and pepper. • Cover and simmer over low heat until the chicken is very tender, 30–40 minutes. • Serve hot garnished with fresh thyme.

¼ cup (60 ml) extra-virgin olive oil

1 chicken, 3–4 pounds (1.5–2 kg), cut into bite-size chunks

Salt and freshly ground black pepper

1 onion, finely chopped

3 cloves garlic, finely chopped

6 firm-ripe tomatoes, peeled and coarsely chopped

2 cups (500 ml) dry white wine

1 tablespoon finely chopped fresh rosemary

1 tablespoon finely chopped fresh thyme + extra to garnish

1 cup (100 g) black olives

Serves: 6
Preparation: 30 minutes
Cooking: 50–60 minutes
Level: 2

SPANISH DUCK WITH PEAR SAUCE

Season the duck with salt and pepper. • Heat the butter in a Dutch oven (casserole) over medium heat. Add the pears and onion and sauté until softened and lightly browned, 5–7 minutes.
• Increase the heat to high and add the seasoned duck, turning until browned all over, 8–10 minutes.
• Pour in the wine and simmer for 2–3 minutes.
• Pour in the stock and season with salt and pepper. Partially cover the pan and simmer over low heat until the stock has reduced by half and the duck is tender, 40–50 minutes. • Remove the duck from the pan and set aside. • Process the cooking juices with a hand-held blender until smooth. • Carve the duck and serve hot with the cooking juices.

1	duck, 3–4 pounds (1.5–2 kg)
	Salt and freshly ground white pepper
8	firm ripe pears, quartered
1	red onion, finely chopped
1/4	cup (60 g) butter, cut up
1/2	cup (125 ml) dry white wine
4	cups (1 liter) Chicken Stock (see page 34–35)

Serves: 4
Preparation: 35 minutes
Cooking: 1 hour
Level: 2

CURRIED CHICKEN AND PEANUT STEW

Heat the oil over medium heat in a saucepan. Add the chicken and sauté until well browned, 8–10 minutes. Remove the chicken and set aside. • Add the onion, garlic, and ginger and sauté until the onion is softened, 3–4 minutes. • Stir in the salt, paprika, chile powder, turmeric, bell peppers, and tomato paste and sauté until the bell peppers are beginning to wilt, 5–10 minutes. • Return the chicken to the pan and add chicken stock. Cover and simmer over low heat until the chicken is tender, about 45 minutes. • Just before the chicken is ready, place the peanut butter in a small bowl and stir in about 1/2 cup (125 ml) of the cooking juices, stirring until smooth. • Stir the peanut mixture and black-eyed peas into the sauce and simmer until heated through. • Garnish the dish with cilantro and jalapeños and serve hot with the rice or naan.

1/4 cup (60 ml) peanut oil

1 chicken, 3–4 pounds (1.5–2 kg), cut into 8 pieces

1 large onion, chopped

2 cloves garlic, finely chopped

1 teaspoon minced fresh ginger

1 teaspoon salt

1 teaspoon sweet paprika

1 teaspoon chile powder

1/2 teaspoon ground turmeric

2 red bell peppers (capsicums), seeded and sliced

3 tablespoons tomato paste (concentrate)

6 cups (1.5 liters) Chicken Stock, boiling (see pages 34–35)

1/2 cup (125 g) peanut butter

2 cups (400 g) canned black-eyed peas or lima beans, drained

Handful of finely chopped fresh cilantro (coriander)

2 fresh green jalapeño chiles, seeded and chopped

Steamed long-grain rice or naan bread to serve

Serves: 4–6
Preparation: 15 minutes
Cooking: 1 hour
Level: 1

DUCK WITH ORANGE

Preheat the oven to 425°F (220°C/gas 7). • Season the duck with salt. • Truss the duck and place it, breast-side up, in a roasting pan. Roast in the oven for 30 minutes. • Decrease the heat to 350°F (180°C/gas 4). • Roast for 45–60 minutes more. Test the thickest part of the thigh with a skewer, the juices will run pink when ready. • Meanwhile, combine the sugar and vinegar in a medium saucepan. Simmer over medium-low heat until the liquid caramelizes to a golden brown color. • Gradually pour in the chicken stock, stirring to combine. Add the Grand Mariner and bring to a boil. Decrease the heat to low and simmer until thickened slightly, about 10 minutes. • Place a small saucepan of water on high heat and bring to a boil. • Cut the zest off one of the oranges and blanch in the boiling water for 10 seconds. Drain and discard the water. Bring a fresh saucepan of water to a boil and blanch the zest for a second time. Drain and thinly slice lengthwise. • Juice two of the oranges and strain the juice through a fine-mesh sieve. • Add the orange zest and juice to the sauce and simmer until thickened slightly, about 10 minutes. • Peel and segment the remaining oranges using a small knife and set aside. • Gradually add the butter, one cube at a time, to the sauce, whisking continuously until incorporated. • Serve the duck hot with the orange segments and glazed with the sauce.

1	duck, about 4–5 pounds (2 kg)
1/2	teaspoon salt
1/4	cup (50 g) superfine (caster) sugar
1/4	cup (60 ml) cider vinegar
2	cups (500 ml) Chicken Stock (see pages 34–35)
1/3	cup (90 ml) Grand Mariner
4	oranges
3	tablespoons cold unsalted butter, cubed

Serves: 6–8
Preparation: 20 minutes
Cooking: $1^1/4$–$1^1/2$ hours
Level: 2

BUTTERFLIED QUAIL WITH LEMON AND SAGE

402

Preheat the oven to 350°F (180°C/gas 4). • Mix 3 tablespoons of the oil, the lemon juice and zest, and garlic in a small bowl. Season with salt and pepper. Set aside. • Heat the remaining 2 tablespoons of oil in a large frying pan over medium-high heat. Add the quail and sage and sauté until well browned, about 10 minutes. • Transfer to a baking dish. • Add the lemon marinade and chicken stock to the pan. Return to the heat, bring to a boil, and simmer for 1 minute, stirring with a wooden spoon. • Pour the pan juices over the quail. • Bake until tender and cooked through, about 25 minutes. • Serve hot garnished with arugula.

5	tablespoons (75 ml) extra-virgin olive oil
2	tablespoons freshly squeezed lemon juice
½	teaspoon finely grated lemon zest
1	clove garlic, finely chopped
	Salt and freshly ground black pepper
4	quails, butterflied
2	tablespoons coarsely chopped fresh sage leaves
¼	cup (60 ml) Chicken Stock (see page 34–35)
	Arugula (rocket), to serve

Serves: 4
Preparation: 25 minutes
Cooking: 35 minutes
Level: 2

▦ ▦ ▦ *To butterfly the quail, place on a cutting board breast-side up and insert a knife into the cavity. Cut down through the backbone from neck to tail, then open the bird up and flatten with your hands. Cut off and discard the wing tips. If you can't find fresh quail, substitute with cornish hens.*

ROAST GUINEA FOWL WITH ROSEMARY AND LEMON

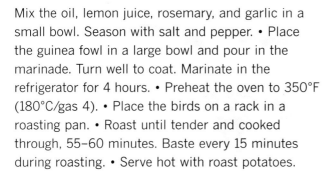

404

Mix the oil, lemon juice, rosemary, and garlic in a small bowl. Season with salt and pepper. • Place the guinea fowl in a large bowl and pour in the marinade. Turn well to coat. Marinate in the refrigerator for 4 hours. • Preheat the oven to 350°F (180°C/gas 4). • Place the birds on a rack in a roasting pan. • Roast until tender and cooked through, 55–60 minutes. Baste every 15 minutes during roasting. • Serve hot with roast potatoes.

¼ cup (60 ml) extra-virgin olive oil

2 tablespoons freshly squeezed lemon juice

1 tablespoon coarsely chopped fresh rosemary

1 clove garlic, finely chopped

Salt and freshly ground black pepper

2 guinea fowl, cut in half

Roasted potatoes, to serve

Serves: 4
Preparation: 10 minutes
  + 4 hours to marinate
Cooking: 55–60 minutes
Level: 1

▩ ▩ ▩ *If you can't find guinea fowl, substitute with lean young chicken.*
You can roast the potatoes under the rack in the same pan in which you roast the guinea fowl. They will take about 45 minutes to cook.

TEX-MEX CHICKEN

Marinade: Blend the chiles and chili paste in a food processor until smooth. • Combine both oils in a large saucepan and warm over low heat. Add the garlic and blended chile paste and simmer over very low heat until the garlic is soft but not browned, 35–40 minutes. Leave to cool. • Stir in the salt, lime juice, and cilantro.

Chicken: Marinate the chicken in the chile mixture in the refrigerator for 6–8 hours. • Heat a grill pan or barbecue until very hot. • Drain the chicken and place in the pan. Grill, basting often with the marinade, until the chicken is tender, about 15 minutes. • Slice and serve hot with tortillas.

Marinade

8 red Thai chiles, seeded and chopped

1–2 tablespoons chipotle chile paste

3/4 cup (200 ml) extra-virgin olive oil

3/4 cup (200 ml) corn oil

15 large cloves garlic, coarsely chopped

1 heaped teaspoon salt

Freshly squeezed juice of 2–3 limes

3 tablespoons finely chopped fresh cilantro (coriander)

Chicken

10 boneless skinless chicken breast halves or drumsticks

Tortillas, to serve

Serves: 10
Prep: 20 minutes + 6–8 hours to marinate
Cooking: 50–65 minutes
Level: 2

■ ■ ■ *Tex-Mex refers to Mexican food as it is prepared in Texas. The term became popular in the 1940s and is now widely used. The use of chiles is a key theme in Tex-Mex cooking.*
The marinade in this recipe can also be brushed over vegetables while grilling.

CHICKEN WITH CHERMOULA CRUST AND POLENTA

Chicken: Lightly spray or brush a flat non-reactive casserole or baking dish with the oil. Place the chicken in a single layer in the dish.

Chermoula: Place the parsley, cilantro, lemon zest, cumin, paprika, black pepper, saffron, lemon juice, and oil in a food processor. Using the pulse button, process until just combined—take care not to process until smooth. • Spoon the chermoula over the chicken. Cover and marinate in the refrigerator for at least 1 hour or overnight. • Preheat the oven to 350°F (180°C/gas 4). • Move the chicken and chermoula to a baking dish. Drizzle with the wine. • Bake for 20–30 minutes or until the chicken is cooked through.

Polenta: Place the stock, water, milk, bay leaves, and rosemary in a large saucepan over medium heat. Bring to a boil. Remove and discard the bay leaves and rosemary. • Gradually stir in the polenta. Reduce the heat and simmer, stirring occasionally, until mixture thickens and leaves the sides of the pan, 35–40 minutes. Add more liquid if the mixture becomes too thick; for this dish you want to keep it very soft. • Spoon the polenta onto serving plates. Place chicken on top. Drizzle with some of the cooking juices and serve hot.

Chicken

- ¼ cup (60 ml) extra-virgin olive oil
- 1½ pounds (750 g) skinless chicken breasts or thigh fillets, cut into large pieces

Chermoula

- 4 tablespoons finely chopped fresh parsley
- 4 tablespoons finely chopped fresh cilantro (coriander)
- 2 tablespoons minced lemon zest
- 1 teaspoon ground cumin
- 1 teaspoon paprika
- ½ teaspoon freshly ground black pepper
- Pinch saffron powder or threads
- 2 tablespoons freshly squeezed lemon juice
- 1 tablespoon extra-virgin olive oil
- ¼ cup (60 ml) dry white wine

Polenta

- 2 cups (500 ml) chicken stock (see pages 34–35)
- 1½ cups (375 ml) water
- 1 cup (250 ml) milk
- 2 bay leaves
- 1 sprig fresh rosemary
- 1½ cups (250 g) polenta

Serves: 6
Preparation: 25 minutes + 1–12 hours to marinate
Cooking: 1 hour
Level: 2

MEATS

MOROCCAN LAMB
KEFTA BRIOUATS

412

Heat the extra-virgin oil in a large frying pan over medium heat. Add the onion, garlic, cumin, paprika, cinnamon, cayenne, and tumeric and sauté until softened and fragrant, 3–4 minutes. • Add the lamb and sauté until browned and just cooked through, about 5 minutes. • Add the eggs and parsley and sauté until cooked, 1–2 minutes. • Season with salt and pepper. Transfer the meat mixture to a bowl and set aside for 10 minutes. • Cover and refrigerate until cold, about 30 minutes. • Lightly dust a clean work surface with flour. Lay a spring roll wrapper on the work surface (keep the remaining wrappers covered to stop them drying out.) • **Step 1:** Cut the wrapper in half lengthwise and place a spoonful of filling at the end of each half. Fold the bottom left corner over the filling to cover, creating a small triangular parcel. • **Step 2:** Continue folding the wrapper over, in a back and forth motion, until the filling is completely enclosed. • **Step 3:** Brush the end of the wrappers with the egg yolk and press to seal. Repeat the process with the remaining filling and wrappers. • Pour the oil into a deep-fryer or deep saucepan over medium heat and heat to 365°F (190°C). If you don't have a frying thermometer, test the oil temperature by dropping a small piece of bread into the hot oil. If the bread bubbles to the surface and begins to turn golden, the oil is ready. • **Step 4:** Fry the briouats in batches until golden brown and crisp, about 5 minutes each batch. • Remove with a slotted spoon and drain on paper towels. • Serve hot.

3 tablespoons extra-virgin olive oil
1 large onion, grated
2 cloves garlic, minced
2 teaspoons ground cumin
2 teaspoons hot paprika
1 teaspoon ground cinnamon
1/2 teaspoon cayenne pepper
1/4 teaspoon turmeric
1 pound (500 g) ground (minced) lamb
4 large eggs, lightly beaten + 1 large egg yolk, lightly beaten
1 tablespoon finely chopped fresh parsley
Salt and freshly ground black pepper
All-purpose (plain) flour to dust
10 spring roll wrappers
4 cups (1 liter) vegetable oil for frying

Serves: 6–8
Preparation: 45 minutes + 30 minutes to chill
Cooking: 20–30 minutes
Level: 3

Briouats are a triangular or cylinder-shaped pastry with savory or sweet fillings. In Morocco, they are wrapped in a paper-thin pastry called *warka*. We have simplified the recipe a little by using spring roll wrappers which are readily available in Asian markets and food stores.

413

1. CUT the wrapper in half lengthwise. Place a spoonful of filling at the end of each length. Fold the bottom left corner over the filling to create a triangular parcel.

2. CONTINUE folding the wrapper over, in a back and forth motion, until the filling is completely enclosed.

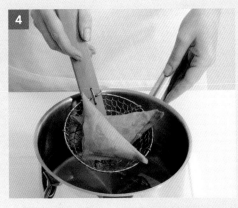

3. BRUSH the end of the wrappers with the egg yolk and press to seal.

4. FRY in batches until golden brown and crisp, about 5 minutes each batch. Remove with a slotted spoon and drain on paper towels.

SPANISH MEATBALLS WITH RISONE

Meatballs: Place the meat, onion, almonds, parsley, paprika, cumin, garlic, and egg in a bowl. Mix to combine. • Shape into balls about 2 inches (5 cm) in diameter. Place on a plate and cover with plastic wrap (cling film). Refrigerate until ready to cook.

Wine and Tomato Sauce: Heat the oil in a large frying pan over medium heat. Add the onion and sauté until softened, 3–4 minutes. • Add the fennel seeds. Sauté until fragrant, about 1 minute. • Stir in tomato paste. Simmer until it becomes deep red and develops a rich aroma, 3–4 minutes. • Add the tomatoes, wine, beef stock, and vinegar and bring to a boil. • Decrease the heat to low. Carefully add the meatballs. Cover and simmer for 15 minutes. Turn the meatballs. Cover and simmer until cooked through, about 15 minutes. Add a little more stock or water if sauce becomes too thick. • Meanwhile, cook the risone in a large pot of salted boiling water until al dente. • Drain the risone and divide among heated serving bowls. Spoon the meatballs and sauce over the top and serve hot.

416

Meatballs

1½ pounds (750 g) ground (minced) lean beef or lamb
1 onion, finely chopped
2 tablespoons finely chopped roasted unsalted almonds
2 tablespoons finely chopped fresh parsley
2 teaspoons sweet paprika
1 teaspoon ground cumin
1 clove garlic, crushed
1 egg, lightly beaten

Wine and Tomato Sauce

1 tablespoon extra-virgin olive oil
1 onion, finely chopped
2 teaspoons fennel seeds
1 tablespoon tomato paste (concentrate)
2 cups (400 g) canned tomatoes, with juice
1 cup (250 ml) red wine
½ cup (125 ml) Beef Stock + extra as required (see page 62–63)
1 tablespoon red wine vinegar
12 ounces (350 g) risone

Serves: 6
Preparation: 20 minutes
Cooking: 40 minutes
Level: 2

SOUVLAKI

Tzatziki: Combine the yogurt, garlic, and lemon juice together in a small bowl. Add the cucumber and mint and season with salt. • Cover with plastic wrap (cling film) and refrigerate until required.
Lamb: Combine the oil, lemon juice, vinegar, oregano, garlic, and cumin in a large bowl. Season with salt and pepper. • Add the lamb to the marinade and toss to coat. Cover with plastic wrap and refrigerate for at least 6 hours or overnight, to marinate. • Preheat a barbecue grill or hot plate to medium heat. • Drain the lamb, reserving the marinade. Thread the lamb onto 8 metal skewers. • Cook the skewers, basting frequently with the reserved marinade, until cooked to your liking, about 4–5 minutes each side.
To Serve: Serve the skewers hot with pita bread, salad, tomatoes, onions, lemon wedges, and the tzatziki spooned over the top.

■ ■ ■ *This is a classic Greek dish. If you don't have metal skewers, soak 8 bamboo skewers in cold water for 30 minutes before cooking.*

Tzatziki

1   cup (250 g) plain yogurt

1   clove garlic, minced

1   tablespoon freshly squeezed lemon juice

1   cucumber, peeled, seeded, and finely chopped

1   tablespoon finely chopped fresh mint

Lamb

1/3 cup (90 ml) extra-virgin olive oil

2   tablespoons freshly squeezed lemon juice

2   tablespoons red wine vinegar

2   tablespoons dried oregano

1   clove garlic, minced

1   teaspoon ground cumin

    Salt and freshly ground black pepper

1½ pounds (750 g) lamb leg, boned, cut into 1 inch (2.5 cm) cubes

To Serve

4   pita breads, to serve

    Mixed salad greens

    Sliced tomatoes

    Thinly red sliced onion

    Lemon wedges

Serves: 4
Preparation: 15 minutes + 6–12 hours to marinate
Cooking: 8–10 minutes
Level: 1

SANG CHOI BAU (VIETNAMESE SPICED PORK)

Separate the lettuce leaves to make lettuce cups. Set aside. • Heat both oils in a large wok over medium-low heat. Add the celery, garlic, ginger, and chile and stir-fry until softened, 3–4 minutes. • Increase the heat to medium-high, add the shiitake mushrooms and water chestnuts and stir-fry until golden, about 5 minutes. • Add the pork and stir-fry, breaking up the lumps, until browned, about 10 minutes. • Pour in the soy sauce and rice wine. Add the spice powder and simmer until the liquid is absorbed, about 5 minutes. • Stir in the bean sprouts, scallions, cilantro, and mint and transfer to a serving bowl. • To serve, scoop the spiced pork into the prepared lettuce cups, wrap to enclose, and eat with your hands.

■ ■ ■ *Sang choi bau can be a little messy to eat. Have plenty of napkins (serviettes) on hand! Five-spice powder is a mixture of 5 spices. There are many variations, but the most mix includes star anise, cloves, cinnamon, Szechuan pepper, and ground fennel seeds. Five-spice powder is widely available in Asian food stores.*

1	small iceberg lettuce
1	tablespoon peanut oil
1	tablespoon sesame oil
1	stalk celery, finely chopped
3	cloves garlic, finely chopped
2	teaspoons finely grated fresh ginger
1	large red chile, seeded and finely chopped
1½	ounces (45 g) dried shiitake mushrooms, soaked in boiling water for 20 minutes and thinly sliced
4	ounces (125 g) canned water chestnuts, drained and finely chopped
1	pound (500 g) ground (minced) pork
¼	cup (60 ml) soy sauce
2	tablespoons rice wine
1	teaspoon Chinese five-spice powder
2	cups (100 g) bean sprouts
3	scallions (spring onions), thinly sliced
3	tablespoons finely chopped fresh cilantro (coriander)
2	tablespoons finely chopped fresh mint

Serves: 4–6
Preparation: 20 minutes + 20 minutes to soak
Cooking: 15 minutes
Level: 1

CHILLI CON CARNE

422

Heat the oil in a large heavy-based saucepan over medium-low heat. Add the onion and garlic and sauté until softened, 3–4 minutes. • Add the beef, cumin, chile, paprika, and oregano and sauté, breaking up the lumps, until browned, about 5 minutes. • Add the tomatoes, tomato paste, beef stock, vinegar, and jalapeño pepper and bring to a boil. Decrease the heat and simmer, skimming the surface of excess fat occasionally, until thick and flavorsome, $1^1/2$–2 hours. • Season with salt and pepper and serve warm with tortillas.

2	tablespoons extra-virgin olive oil
1	large onion, finely chopped
3	cloves garlic, finely chopped
2	pounds (1 kg) coarsely ground (minced) beef
2	tablespoons cumin
2	tablespoons chile powder
1	tablespoon sweet paprika
2	teaspoons dried oregano
2	medium tomatoes, peeled and chopped
2	tablespoons tomato paste (concentrate)
2	cups (500 ml) Beef Stock (see pages 62–63)
1	tablespoon cider vinegar
1	tablespoon sliced jalapeño chile
	Salt and freshly ground black pepper
	Warm tortillas to serve

■ ■ ■ *Chilli con carne is best when prepared a day before serving as this gives the flavors the chance to develop fully.*

Serves: 4–6
Preparation: 15 minutes
Cooking: About 2 hours
Level: 1

BABY BACK RIBS WITH PARMESAN MASH

424

Baby Back Ribs: Preheat the oven to 350°F (180°C/gas 4). • Season the ribs generously with salt and pepper. • Cut holes in the meat with a sharp knife and push the garlic in. • Place the spare ribs in a large baking pan with the rosemary. • Roast, turning often, until cooked through and deep golden brown, 1–2 hours (depending on the size of the ribs).

Parmesan Mash: Boil the potatoes in a large pot of salted water until tender, about 25 minutes. • Drain and mash until smooth. • Return to the large pot used to cook the potatoes. Place over medium heat and add the polenta and buckwheat flour, mixing well. Stirring constantly, gradually add as much of the boiling water as the mixture will absorb. Simmer, stirring constantly, until the polenta is tender, 8–10 minutes. • Heat the butter and oil in a small saucepan over medium heat. Add the onion and sauté until softened, 3–4 minutes. • Add the onion mixture to the polenta. Season with salt and pepper and stir in the Parmesan. Stir for 5 more minutes. • When the ribs are cooked, turn the Parmesan mash out onto a heated serving dish and top with the ribs. • Serve hot.

Baby Back Ribs

2 pounds (1 kg) baby back ribs or spare ribs

Salt and freshly ground black pepper

4 cloves garlic, halved

Fresh rosemary

Parmesan Mash

2 pounds (1 kg) potatoes, peeled

½ cup (75 g) quick-cooking polenta (coarse-grain yellow cornmeal)

½ cup (75 g) buckwheat flour

1-2 cups (250-500 ml) boiling water

3 tablespoons butter

3 tablespoons extra-virgin olive oil

1 onion, finely chopped

Salt and freshly ground black pepper

1 cup (150 g) freshly grated Parmesan cheese

Serves: 6–8
Preparation: 45 minutes
Cooking: 1–2 hours
Level: 2

MASSAMAN BEEF

Curry Paste: Dry-fry the coriander, cumin, chiles, and peppercorns in a small frying pan over medium-low heat until fragrant, 1–2 minutes.
• Transfer to a large mortar and pestle or food processor and grind or blend to make a coarse powder. • Add the remaining curry paste ingredients and blend to make a smooth paste.
Curry: Dry-fry the cardamom and cinnamon in a medium heavy-based saucepan over medium heat until very fragrant, 1–2 minutes. Remove and set aside in a small bowl. • Heat the oil in the same saucepan over medium heat. Add the curry paste and stir until fragrant, 1–2 minutes. • Add the beef and sauté until browned, about 5 minutes. • Pour in 2 cups (500 ml) of the coconut cream and bring to a boil. Decrease the heat and simmer until the cream splits, 4–5 minutes. • Pour in the remaining 2 cups (500 ml) of coconut cream and the water and bring to a boil. Decrease the heat and simmer, uncovered, for 1 hour. • Add the potatoes, peanuts, tamarind water, jaggery, and fish sauce and stir to combine. Simmer until the meat and potatoes are tender, 30–40 minutes. Season with salt.
• Serve hot.

▥ ▥ ▥ *This is a delicious Thai curry with potatoes and peanuts. It is good with jasmine rice but can also be served on its own as a one-dish meal.*

Curry Paste

1½	tablespoons coriander seeds
1	teaspoon cumin seeds
2	red chiles, seeded and halved lengthwise
¼	teaspoon black peppercorns
3	shallots, chopped
3	cloves garlic, chopped
1	stalk lemongrass, white part only, finely chopped
2	teaspoons finely grated galangal or fresh ginger
½	teaspoon shrimp paste
¼	teaspoon ground cloves
	Pinch ground nutmeg

Curry

5	cardamom pods
1	cinnamon stick
3	tablespoons peanut oil
1¼	pounds (600 g) braising beef, diced
4	cups (1 liter) canned cream of coconut
1	cup (250 ml) water
3	potatoes, diced
½	cup (80 g) peanuts, roasted
2	teaspoons tamarind paste, soaked in 2 tablespoons water, strained, water reserved
2	tablespoons coarsely grated jaggery (palm sugar) or brown sugar
1	tablespoon Thai fish sauce
	Salt

Serves: 4
Preparation: 30 minutes
Cooking: About 2 hours
Level: 2

BEEF RENDANG

Spice Paste: Place all of the spice paste ingredients, except the vegetable oil, in a large mortar and pestle or food processor and grind or blend to make a coarse paste. • Gradually add the oil and continue blending until a smooth paste is formed.

Curry: Place a large heavy-based saucepan over medium heat. Add the spice mix and cook until fragrant, about 30 seconds. • Add the beef, lemongrass, and cinnamon and sauté until coated in the spice paste. • Pour in the coconut milk, add the jaggery, and bring to a boil. Decrease the heat and simmer, uncovered, stirring occasionally, until all the liquid has evaporated leaving the meat to fry in the oil that remains, 2–2^1/$_2$ hours. • Simmer until all the oil has been absorbed, about 15 minutes. Remove the lemongrass and cinnamon and season with salt. • Serve hot with steamed rice.

■ ■ ■ *This Indonesian beef curry is cooked very slowly until the beef is almost falling to pieces. Use a braising steak, such as chuck or blade, which will become very tender during the long cooking time.*

Spice Paste

- ½ cup (60 g) shredded coconut, lightly toasted
- 4 shallots, coarsely chopped
- 6 long red chiles, seeded and finely chopped
- 2 cloves garlic, chopped
- 2 teaspoons finely grated ginger
- 2 teaspoons ground coriander seeds
- 2 teaspoons ground cumin
- 1 teaspoon ground turmeric
- 3 tablespoons vegetable oil

Curry

- 3 pounds (1.5 kg) braising steak, cut into 2 inch (5 cm) chunks
- 2 stalks lemongrass
- 1 cinnamon stick
- 5 cups (1.2 liters) canned coconut milk
- 1 tablespoon coarsely grated jaggery (palm sugar) or brown sugar

  Salt

  Steamed long-grain rice

Serves: 6
Preparation: 30 minutes
Cooking: 2^1/$_4$–2^3/$_4$ hours
Level: 2

LAMB ROGAN JOSH

Spice Paste: Dry-fry the almonds, coriander seeds, cloves, cinnamon, and peppercorns in a medium frying pan over medium heat until fragrant, about 1 minute. • Add the cumin, chile, turmeric, and nutmeg and sauté until fragrant, about 30 seconds. • Transfer to a large mortar and pestle or food processor and grind or blend into a coarse powder. • Add the garlic and ginger and blend, gradually adding the water, to make a smooth paste.

Curry: Heat 2 tablespoons of the ghee in a medium heavy-based saucepan over medium-high heat. Add the meat a little at a time and sauté until browned, 8–10 minutes. • Transfer the meat to a medium bowl and set aside. • Heat the remaining 2 tablespoons of ghee in the same pan. Add the onion and sauté until softened, 3–4 minutes. • Add the spice paste and sauté for 1 minute. • Pour in the water and bring to a boil. Decrease the heat, return the meat to the pan, cover, and simmer for 30 minutes. • Stir in the yogurt and tomato paste, cover, and simmer until the meat is tender and the sauce is thick, about 30 minutes. • Season with salt and serve hot with naan bread.

■ ■ ■ *Rogan josh is an almond and meat curry from Kashmir. Its name comes from two Persian words; "rogan," which means oil and "josh," meaning heat or passion.*

430

Spice Paste

1/4   **cup (40 g) blanched almonds, coarsely chopped**

2   **tablespoons coriander seeds**

5   **whole cloves**

1/2   **cinnamon stick**

1/2   **teaspoon black peppercorns**

1   **tablespoon ground cumin**

1   **teaspoon chile powder**

1/2   **teaspoon ground turmeric**

1/4   **teaspoon ground nutmeg**

6   **cloves garlic, coarsely chopped**

1   **tablespoon coarsely grated fresh ginger**

1/4   **cup (60 ml) water**

Curry

4   **tablespoons (60 ml) ghee or vegetable oil**

2   **pounds (1 kg) stewing lamb, cut into 1 inch (2.5 cm) chunks**

1   **large onion, finely chopped**

1   **cup (250 ml) water**

3/4   **cup (180 g) plain yogurt**

1/4   **cup (60 g) tomato paste (concentrate)**

Naan bread, to serve

Serves: 6
Preparation: 30 minutes
Cooking: 1^1/4 hours
Level: 1

LAMB KORMA

Spice Mix: Dry-fry the cashews, cardamom, coriander, cumin, cinnamon, and cloves in a medium frying pan over medium-low heat until browned and very fragrant, 1–2 minutes. • Transfer to a large mortar and pestle or food processor. Add the garlic, ginger, and saffron and grind or blend to make a coarse paste. • Gradually add the water, blending to make a smooth paste.

Korma: Heat the ghee in a medium heavy-based saucepan over medium heat. Add the onion and sauté until softened and golden brown, 8–10 minutes. • Add the spice paste and sauté for 1 minute. • Add the meat and sauté until well coated in the spice mix and browned, 3–4 minutes. • Pour in the yogurt and water and bring to a gentle boil. • Cover and simmer for 1 hour over low heat. • Add the cream, cover, and simmer until the meat is tender and sauce is thick, about 30 minutes. • Season with salt and serve hot with basmati rice.

■ ■ ■ *A korma is an Indian or Pakistani dish in which meat is slowly braised with a spice mix and a yogurt and cream (or coconut milk) sauce.*

Spice Mix

¼ cup (40 g) cashews, coarsely chopped

1 teaspoon cardamom seeds

1 teaspoon coriander seeds

½ teaspoon cumin seeds

½ teaspoon ground cinnamon

3 whole cloves

1 clove garlic, coarsely chopped

2 teaspoons finely grated fresh ginger

Pinch saffron threads, crumbled

¼ cup (60 ml) water

Korma

3 tablespoons ghee or vegetable oil

1 large onion, finely chopped

2 pounds (1 kg) stewing lamb, cut into 1 inch (2.5 cm) chunks

1 cup (250 g) plain yogurt

½ cup (125 ml) water

⅓ cup (90 ml) light (single) cream

Salt

Steamed basmati rice to serve

Serves: 4–6
Preparation: 20 minutes
Cooking: 1³/4 hours
Level: 1

TAFAYA (MOROCCAN LAMB TAGINE)

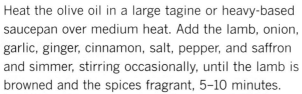

434

Heat the olive oil in a large tagine or heavy-based saucepan over medium heat. Add the lamb, onion, garlic, ginger, cinnamon, salt, pepper, and saffron and simmer, stirring occasionally, until the lamb is browned and the spices fragrant, 5–10 minutes. • Pour in the water and bring to a boil. Reduce the heat to low, cover, and simmer for $1^1/2$ hours. • Add the cilantro and a little more water if necessary, and stir to combine. Cook until the meat is tender and sauce is thick, about 30 minutes. • Meanwhile, heat the vegetable oil in a medium frying pan over medium-low heat. Add the almonds and sauté until golden brown. • Remove with a slotted spoon and drain on paper towels. • Cut the eggs in half lengthwise. • To serve, scatter the almonds over the meat and arrange the eggs around the edges of the dish. Serve hot.

3 tablespoons extra-virgin olive oil

3 pounds (1.5 kg) boneless lamb shoulder or leg, trimmed of fat and cut into 2 inch (5 cm) pieces

2 medium onions, grated

2 cloves garlic, finely chopped

1 teaspoon ground ginger

$^1/2$ teaspoon ground cinnamon

$^1/2$ teaspoon salt

$^1/4$ teaspoon freshly ground black pepper

Pinch saffron threads, crushed

$1^1/2$ cups (375 ml) water

$^1/2$ cup (25 g) finely chopped fresh cilantro (coriander)

2 tablespoons vegetable oil

$1^1/4$ cups (190 g) blanched almonds

6 hard-boiled eggs

▨ ▨ ▨ *Lamb is slowly braised in this Moroccan tagine. It is served with toasted almonds and sliced boiled eggs.*

Serves: 6–8
Preparation: 20 minutes
Cooking: About 2 hours
Level: 1

STOUT STEW WITH DUMPLINGS

Stew: Mix the flour and mustard. Season with $1/4$ teaspoon of the salt and pepper and coat the beef with this mixture. • Melt 1 teaspoon of the butter in a large saucepan over high heat. Add the meat in small batches and brown, adding more butter between batches and transferring the browned meat to a separate plate. • Add any remaining butter and the onions to the juices in the saucepan. Cook over low heat until the onions are soft and golden, about 10 minutes. • Return the meat to the pan. Stir in the carrots, the remaining $1/4$ teaspoon of salt, and bay leaves. • Mix the stout, brown sugar, tomato paste, and stock. Pour the mixture over the meat. If the liquid does not cover the meat, add more water or stock. Stir well to make sure you have scraped up any bits from the bottom of the pan and bring to a boil. Cover and simmer over low heat until the meat is tender, about $1 3/4$ hours. Stir the stew after 1 hour, adding more water if the stew begins to dry out. • Season with salt and pepper. Discard the bay leaf.

Dumplings: Mix the flour, butter, and enough water together to make a firm dough. Divide into 6–8 dumplings and place on top of the stew about 25 minutes before the stew is ready. • If more liquid is needed to cook the dumplings, add some boiling water. Cover and simmer for 20 minutes more.
• Serve hot sprinkled with the parsley.

Stew

1   tablespoon all-purpose (plain) flour

1   teaspoon English mustard

$1/2$ teaspoon salt + more as needed

    Freshly ground black pepper

2   pounds (1 kg) stew beef, cut into small chunks

3   tablespoons butter or cooking juices from a roasted meat

2   medium onions, finely chopped

4   medium carrots, cut into large chunks

2   bay leaves

2   cups (500 ml) stout or dark beer

1   tablespoon dark brown sugar

1   tablespoon tomato paste (concentrate)

$1 2/3$ cups (400 ml) Beef Stock (see pages 62–63)

1   tablespoon finely chopped fresh parsley

Dumplings

1 cup (150 g) all-purpose (plain) flour

$1/4$ cup (60 g) butter or beef suet

$1/4$ cup (60 ml) water + more as required

Serves: 4–6
Preparation: 15 minutes
Cooking: $2 1/4$ hours
Level: 2

SPICED GREEK STEW

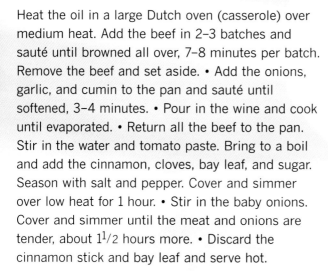

Heat the oil in a large Dutch oven (casserole) over medium heat. Add the beef in 2–3 batches and sauté until browned all over, 7–8 minutes per batch. Remove the beef and set aside. • Add the onions, garlic, and cumin to the pan and sauté until softened, 3–4 minutes. • Pour in the wine and cook until evaporated. • Return all the beef to the pan. Stir in the water and tomato paste. Bring to a boil and add the cinnamon, cloves, bay leaf, and sugar. Season with salt and pepper. Cover and simmer over low heat for 1 hour. • Stir in the baby onions. Cover and simmer until the meat and onions are tender, about 1 1/2 hours more. • Discard the cinnamon stick and bay leaf and serve hot.

1/4	cup (60 ml) extra-virgin olive oil
4	pounds (2 kg) stew beef, cut into small chunks
2	onions, finely chopped
2	cloves garlic, finely chopped
1	teaspoon ground cumin
1	cup (250 ml) dry red wine
2	cups (500 ml) water
2	tablespoons tomato paste (concentrate)
1	(2-inch/5-cm) cinnamon stick
8	cloves
1	bay leaf
2	teaspoons sugar
	Salt and freshly ground black pepper
2	pounds (1 kg) baby onions

Serves: 6–8
Preparation: 20 minutes
Cooking: 2 3/4 hours
Level: 2

BOEUF BOURGUIGNON

Place the flour in a plastic bag and season generously with salt and pepper. Add the beef. Shake the bag until the meat is well coated. • Heat $1/2$ tablespoon of oil in a large, heavy-based saucepan over medium heat. Sauté the bacon until it releases its fat and becomes crisp, about 5 minutes. • Remove the bacon from the pan and set aside. • Add the shallots to the pan and sauté over low heat until nicely colored, 7–8 minutes. Remove the shallots and set aside. • Pour in the remaining $31/2$ tablespoons of oil into the pan. Sauté the beef in small batches until browned all over, about 5 minutes each batch. Shake the pan so that the fat absorbs all the flour. • Pour in the wine and stock and bring to a boil. • Stir in the beef, garlic, thyme, parsley, bay leaves, and tomato paste. Cover and simmer over very low heat for $11/2$ hours. Add a little more stock if the mixture begins to dry out—the liquid should only just cover the meat. • Add the bacon, shallots, and mushrooms. Simmer until the meat is very tender, 40–60 minutes, stirring occasionally to prevent it from sticking. Season with salt and pepper. • Garnish with thyme and serve hot with the potatoes or rice.

■ ■ ■ *This is a classic French dish from Burgundy. Recipes vary according to the cook's interpretation and taste, but the secret lies in gently simmering the beef in red wine until tender. You can make this dish in advance—its flavors are only enhanced with reheating.*

2	tablespoons all-purpose (plain) flour
	Salt and freshly ground black pepper
3	pounds (1.5 kg) stew beef, trimmed and cut into small chunks
$1/4$	cup (60 ml) extra-virgin olive oil
5	ounces (150 g) bacon, finely chopped
8	shallots, peeled
1	bottle (750 ml) dry red wine
$1/2$	cup (125 ml) Beef Stock + more as needed (see pages 62–63)
1	clove garlic, chopped
$1/2$	tablespoon fresh thyme + extra sprigs to garnish
2	tablespoons finely chopped fresh parsley
2	bay leaves
1	tablespoon tomato paste (concentrate)
8	ounces (250 g) button mushrooms, stalks removed
	Boiled potatoes or rice, to serve

Serves: 6–8
Preparation: 25 minutes
Cooking: 2³/4 hours
Level: 2

TOULOUSE CASSOULET

Place the beans in a cassoulet, Dutch oven, or flameproof casserole dish. Fill with cold water and bring to a gentle boil. Simmer until tender, about 1 hour. • Drain and set aside. • In the same pan, heat 1 tablespoon of duck fat over medium-high heat. Brown the duck legs, if using, 8–10 minutes. Remove the legs, retaining the fat. • Sauté the bacon in the fat over high heat until crisp, about 3 minutes. • Add 1 tablespoon of duck fat (or 2 tablespoons if the bacon did not produce much fat) and heat until hot and sizzling. Add the onion, celery, and garlic and sauté over low heat until softened, about 10 minutes. • Scrape up the bits from the bottom of the pan as you stir the mixture. Remove with a slotted spoon and set aside. • Add the lamb and pork in batches and brown, 8–10 minutes, adding more fat if needed. Season the meat with salt and pepper and set aside. • Return the reserved ingredients to the cassoulet except for the duck legs. Stir in the tomatoes and tomato paste. Season with salt and pepper. Add three-quarters of the beans and the chicken stock. Bring to a boil and simmer over low heat for 3 minutes, stirring constantly. • Add the duck legs, if using, carrot, and the bouquet garni. Top with the sausage and cover with the remaining beans. Make sure the liquid comes about halfway up and add water if needed. Cover and simmer for 1 hour. Stir twice during that time and add a little more water if the

$1\frac{1}{2}$ cups (250 g) dried haricot beans, soaked overnight and drained

2–3 tablespoons duck fat or extra-virgin olive oil

4 duck legs (optional)

12 ounces (350 g) unsmoked bacon or pancetta, diced

1 large onion, finely chopped

2 stalks celery, finely chopped

3 cloves garlic, finely chopped

1 pound (500 g) boneless lamb, from shoulder or neck, cut into small cubes

12 ounces (350 g) pork loin, cut into small cubes

Salt and freshly ground black pepper

6 tomatoes, chopped, or 2 cups (400 g) canned tomatoes, with juice

1 tablespoon tomato paste (concentrate)

4 cups (1 liter) Chicken Stock (see pages 34–35)

1 carrot, halved

1 **bouquet garni (see note on page 392)**

1 **pound (500 g) Toulouse sausage or other garlic-flavored pork sausage, skinned and thickly sliced on the diagonal**

2 **tablespoons finely chopped fresh parsley**

2 **tablespoons finely chopped fresh thyme**

8 **tablespoons fresh bread crumbs + extra, as required**

Serves: 8–10
Preparation: 30 minutes
  + 12 hours to soak
Cooking: 4 hours
Level: 3

pan dries out too much • Uncover and stir in half the parsley and thyme. Simmer until the meat is tender and the sauce has thickened, about 1 hour more. • Preheat the oven to 425°F (220°C/gas 7). Stir in the remaining parsley and thyme. Sprinkle the bread crumbs over the top, pressing them down into the liquid with the back of the spoon to form a crust. Bake, uncovered, for about 20 minutes, or until the crust is golden brown. • Remove from the oven, partly break up the crust and give the cassoulet a good stir. It should be quite thick. If it is too liquid, stir in the crust and sprinkle with another layer of bread crumbs. • Bake at 450°F (235°C/gas 8) for about 15 minutes, until another crust has formed. The bread crumbs should absorb the liquid.

443

■ ■ ■ *There are many versions of this dish, which originally comes from the Languedoc region of southern France. The main ingredients of a traditional cassoulet are haricot beans, garlic-flavored pork sausage, mutton, salt pork, pork, and duck or goose. The dish can be adapted with more or less meat, but canned beans should never be used. The name cassoulet comes from the glazed earthenware pot in which the dish is cooked.*

SZEGED GOULASH

Heat the oil in a large saucepan over high heat. Add the pork and bacon and sauté until browned, 4–5 minutes. • Lower the heat to medium and add the onions, bell peppers, garlic, thyme, caraway seeds, and salt. Sauté until the vegetables begin to soften, 5–7 minutes. Add a few tablespoons of hot stock and stir in the tomato paste and sweet paprika. Simmer for 5 minutes. • Chop the sauerkraut and add to the pan with the apple and potatoes. Cook for 5 minutes, until nicely coated. • Pour 1 cup (250 ml) of the hot stock into the mixture. Cover and simmer over low heat for 1 1/4 hours. Stir after 30 minutes, adding more stock if the stew is dry or sticks to the pan. • Stir in the wine and 1 tablespoon of the sour cream. Cook for 15 minutes more. Season with salt and pepper. Add the hot paprika. • Blend the flour with the water and stir it in. Cook until the sauce has thickened. • Stir in the remaining sour cream and sprinkle with pickled chile. Serve hot.

■ ■ ■ *A hearty central European pork stew with sauerkraut. This stew is named after Szeged, a town in southern Hungary famous for the quality—and quantity—of the paprika grown there.*

1/4	cup (60 ml) sunflower oil
1	pound (500 g) lean pork, cut into small cubes
8	ounces (250 g) bacon or pancetta, chopped
3	large onions, thinly sliced
2	green bell peppers (capsicums), seeded and cut into thin strips
2	cloves garlic, finely chopped
1	tablespoon fresh thyme leaves
1	teaspoon crushed caraway seeds
1	teaspoon salt
	About 1 1/2 cups (375 ml) Beef Stock, heated (see pages 62–63)
1	tablespoon tomato paste (concentrate)
1	tablespoon sweet paprika
1	pound (500 g) sauerkraut, drained, rinsed under cold water, and drained again
1	apple, peeled, cored, and diced
2	medium potatoes, peeled and thickly sliced
1/4	cup (60 ml) dry red wine
2/3	cup (150 ml) sour cream
	Salt and freshly ground black pepper
1/2	teaspoon hot paprika
1	tablespoon all-purpose (plain) flour
3	tablespoons cold water
	Pickled chile, to serve

Serves: 4–6
Preparation: 15 minutes
Cooking: 2 hours
Level: 1

BIGOS (POLISH HUNTERS' STEW)

448

Season the flour generously with salt and pepper.
• Toss the venison, pork loin, and smoked pork chop
in the flour, shaking off the excess. • Heat 3
tablespoons of oil in a large saucepan over medium
heat. Add the bacon and sauté for 3 minutes. • Add
the onions and sauté until very soft and golden,
about 10 minutes. Transfer to a bowl and set aside.
• Add 2 tablespoons of oil to the pan and increase
the heat. Fry a single layer of meat over high heat
until well browned, 5–7 minutes. Transfer to the bowl
with the onions and bacon. Repeat the process,
adding the remaining 1 tablespoon of oil, if needed,
until all the meat is browned. • Return everything to
the pan and add the sauerkraut, tomatoes, bay
leaves, mushrooms, cloves, allspice, dill, and $1/2$
teaspoon of salt. Pour in the wine and apple juice.
Simmer for 2 minutes, stirring well. Pour in half the
stock. Stir well and bring to a boil. Cover and
simmer over low heat for $1^1/2$ hours. • Add the
cabbage, kielbasa, and remaining stock if there is
not enough moisture in the saucepan. Simmer until
the cabbage is cooked, about 30 minutes. Uncover
for the last 15 minutes, so the liquid reduces by half.
• Season with salt and pepper. Remove the bay
leaves. • Sprinkle with the parsley and serve hot.

■ ■ ■ *Bigos, or Polish hunters' stew, is made with pork
and venison. You can cook it with boned shoulder,
saddle, or leg of venison, or leg of wild boar.
Alternatively, use top round steak.*

3	tablespoons all-purpose (plain) flour
	Salt and freshly ground black pepper
1	pound (500 g) lean boneless venison, cut into small cubes
1	pound (500 g) pork loin or belly, cut into cubes
8	ounces (250 g) boneless smoked pork chop, cut into thin strips
6	tablespoons (90 ml) vegetable oil
8	ounces (250 g) bacon, cut into thin strips
2	onions, thinly sliced
2	pounds (1 kg) sauerkraut, drained, rinsed under cold water, drained again
4	tomatoes, peeled and finely chopped
2	bay leaves
8	ounces (250 g) mushrooms, quartered
5	cloves
8	allspice berries
$1/2$	teaspoon dill seeds
$1/4$	cup (60 ml) dry white wine
1	cup (250 ml) apple juice
2	cups (500 ml) Beef Stock (see pages 62–63)
1	pound (500 g) cabbage, finely shredded
8	ounces (200 g) kielbasa or wild boar sausages, thickly sliced
2	tablespoons finely chopped fresh parsley

Serves: 6–8
Preparation: 30 minutes
Cooking: $2^1/2$ hours
Level: 1

SCOTCH BEEF WITH DRIED FRUIT

450

Soak the prunes and apricots in cold water overnight. • Drain, reserving the soaking water, and set aside. • Season the beef with the salt and pepper. • Melt the butter in a large saucepan over medium-high heat. Brown the beef all over, 8–10 minutes. • Lower the heat to medium and add the onions, apple, brown sugar, cloves, $1/3$ cup (90 ml) of the whisky, $3/4$ cup (180 ml) water, and the bay leaf. Bring to a boil. Cover and simmer over low heat for $1^1/2$ hours. Check occasionally and turn the meat over. Add a little hot water and the remaining 2 tablespoons of whisky if the liquid has evaporated. • Test the meat at the end of the cooking time, and if it is not quite tender, cook for 30 minutes more. • Arrange the prunes and apricots around the beef, adding about $1/2$ cup (125 ml) of their soaking liquid to make sure that the meat and fruit are covered. Cook for 30 minutes more. Season with salt and pepper. • Slice the meat and transfer it to a serving dish. Place the fruit around the meat. Keep the meat and fruit in a warm oven while you prepare the sauce. • Blend the flour with a little water until smooth. Stir into the cooking juices to thicken into a sauce. Cook for 2 minutes, stirring constantly. Spoon the sauce over the meat and fruit and sprinkle with the parsley. • Serve hot.

8	ounces (250 g) pitted prunes
6	ounces (180 g) dried apricots
	Water
3	pound (1.5 kg) piece beef silverside or brisket
	Salt and freshly ground black pepper
2	tablespoons butter
2	medium onions, thinly sliced
1	large apple, thinly sliced
1	tablespoon dark brown sugar
1	teaspoon crushed cloves
½	cup (125 ml) whisky
1	bay leaf
1	tablespoon all-purpose (plain) flour
2	tablespoons finely chopped fresh parsley

Serves: 4–6
Preparation: 15 minutes + 12 hours to soak
Cooking: $2^1/2$ hours
Level: 2

SHREWSBURY STEW

Mix 1 tablespoon of the flour with the mustard powder, 1/4 teaspoon salt, and 1/4 teaspoon pepper in a medium bowl. Add the beef and toss to coat.
• Melt 3 tablespoons of butter in a large Dutch oven or saucepan over medium-low heat until very hot. Sauté the meat in small batches until browned, 7–8 minutes per batch. Transfer the meat to a plate.
• Melt the remaining 1 tablespoon of butter in the pot and add the rutabaga, onions, carrots, parsnips, and garlic, if using. Cook over low heat, turning often, until the vegetables begin to soften, about 10 minutes. Remove and set aside with the meat.
• Remove the pan from the heat and stir in the remaining 1 tablespoon of flour until all the juices have been absorbed. Return to the heat. • Mix in the tomato paste and 1 tablespoon of the whole-grain mustard. Gradually pour in the stock and cider. Stir with a balloon whisk until the sauce begins to thicken. Season with salt and pepper and add the thyme. • Return the meat and vegetables to the pan, stir well, and return to a simmer. Cover and simmer over low heat until the meat is tender, about 2 hours. Check occasionally and add a little more water if the sauce dries out too much during cooking. • Stir in the remaining 1 tablespoon of whole-grain mustard and the lemon juice. • Sprinkle with parsley and serve hot with the potatoes.

2   tablespoons all-purpose (plain) flour

4   teaspoons dry mustard powder

    Salt and freshly ground black pepper

2   pounds (1 kg) stew beef (preferably shin), cut into small cubes

4   tablespoons (60 g) butter or cooking juices from roasted beef

1   rutabaga (swede), peeled and cubed

2   large onions, quartered

2   medium carrots, diced

2   parsnips, peeled, halved, and quartered lengthwise

2   cloves garlic, finely chopped (optional)

1   tablespoon tomato paste (concentrate)

2   tablespoons whole-grain mustard

1¼ cups (300 ml) Beef Stock (see pages 62–63)

1¼ cups (300 ml) hard (dry) cider

1   teaspoon dried thyme, or 1 tablespoon fresh

    Water (optional)

    Freshly squeezed juice of ½ lemon

1   tablespoon finely chopped fresh parsley

    Freshly boiled potatoes, to serve

Serves: 6
Preparation: 20 minutes
Cooking: 2¼ hours
Level: 1

SWEET AND NUTTY VEAL CASSEROLE

Preheat the oven to 325°F (160°C/gas 3). • Put the butter in a Dutch oven or casserole dish. Add the veal and cover with the potatoes, carrots, apple, onion, garlic, curry powder, cumin, almonds, and coconut. Drizzle with the corn syrup. Pour the onion soup over the top. • Cover the casserole and bake for 2 hours. • Stir carefully and bake until the meat and vegetables are very tender, about 1 hour more. • Serve hot.

454

2   tablespoons butter

2   pounds (1 kg) veal, cut into small cubes

2   large potatoes, peeled and cut into small cubes

2   large carrots, cut in small cubes

1   large Granny Smith apple, peeled, cored and cut in small cubes

1   large onion, finely chopped

4   cloves garlic, finely chopped

1   tablespoon curry powder

$\frac{1}{2}$ teaspoon cumin seeds

$\frac{3}{4}$ cup (100 g) slivered almonds

$\frac{1}{2}$ cup (75 g) unsweetened shredded (desiccated) coconut

$\frac{1}{3}$ cup (90 ml) light corn (golden) syrup

2   cups (400 g) canned onion soup

Freshly cooked brown rice, to serve

■ ■ ■ *This unusual casserole is fairly hearty served on its own. If desired (or to stretch the number of servings to eight), serve over freshly cooked brown rice.*

Serves: 4–6
Preparation: 25 minutes
Cooking: 3 hours
Level: 1

FRENCH VEAL STEW

Place the veal, baby onions, studded onion, carrot, leek and bouquet garni in a large saucepan. Pour in the chicken stock and bring to a boil over high heat. Decrease the heat to low and gently simmer, skimming frequently, for 1–1¹/4 hours, until the veal is tender. • Strain the stock through a fine-mesh sieve, reserving the liquid. Remove the veal and baby onions and set aside. Discard the remaining vegetables and bouquet garni. • Melt the butter in a medium saucepan over medium heat. Add the flour and cook, stirring continuously with a wooden spoon, until the sauce begins to turn white, 1–2 minutes. Remove from the heat and gradually add 3¹/2 cups (875 ml) of the reserved cooking stock, whisking continuously, until a smooth sauce is formed. • Return to the heat and cook over low heat, stirring frequently, for 5 minutes, skimming the surface as needed. • Add the mushrooms and simmer for 10 more minutes. • Whisk the cream and egg yolks in a small bowl. • Add 1 cup (250 ml) of the hot sauce, stirring to combine. Pour the yolk mixture into the remaining sauce and stir to combine. Add the lemon juice and season with salt and pepper. • Return the veal to the pan and gently heat through. Do not boil as this will cause it to curdle. • Serve hot garnished with parsley.

■ ■ ■ *This is another classic French stew. It is known as* Blanquette de veau *in French.*

2	pounds (1 kg) veal shoulder or breast, cut into bite-size chunks
16	white baby onions
1	medium onion, studded with 2 cloves
1	medium carrot, halved
1	small leek, white part only, halved lengthwise
1	bouquet garni (see page 392)
5	cups (1.25 liters) Chicken Stock, heated (see pages 34–35)
2	tablespoons butter
¹/4	cup (30 g) all-purpose (plain) flour
12	button mushrooms, stalks removed
¹/2	cup (125 ml) light (single) cream
2	large egg yolks
	Freshly squeezed juice of ¹/2 lemon
	Salt and freshly ground black pepper
1	tablespoon finely chopped fresh parsley to garnish

Serves: 4–6
Preparation: 25 minutes
Cooking: About 2 hours
Level: 2

SHEPHERD'S PIE

Heat the oil in a large frying pan over medium heat. Add the onion and leek and sauté until soft and golden, 7–8 minutes. • Add 1 tablespoon of the butter if the oil does not cover the bottom of the pan. Stir in the garlic, carrot, and celery and sauté for 5 minutes. • Add the remaining tablespoon of butter and the mushrooms. Sauté for 4 minutes. • Add the meat, stirring it into the mixture. Cook over high heat until the meat browns, about 5 minutes. Stir with a wooden spoon or spatula to break up any lumps. Sprinkle with flour and mix in the tomato paste and Worcestershire sauce. • Cook for 3 minutes, stirring constantly. Pour in the stock. Add the bay leaf and thyme and bring to a boil. Cover and simmer over low heat for 15 minutes. Cook, uncovered, until the sauce thickens, 10–15 minutes. • Season with salt and plenty of pepper. • Preheat the oven to 375°F (190°C/gas 5). • Transfer the filling to a casserole or large deep baking dish and top with the mashed potatoes. • Bake for 20 minutes, or until golden. • Serve hot.

■ ■ ■ *Traditionally, shepherd's pie is made with the leftovers from a joint of lamb, while cottage pie is made with leftovers from beef. Both became popular in the 1870s with the introduction of grinding machines. Because most people do not cook large roasts anymore, the filling today is made by slowly cooking ground meat.*

2	tablespoons extra-virgin olive oil
1	onion, finely chopped
1	leek, trimmed and finely chopped
1–2	tablespoons butter
1	clove garlic, finely chopped
1	medium carrot, finely chopped
1	stalk celery, finely chopped
4	brown button mushrooms, thinly sliced
1	pound (500 g) ground (minced) lamb
1	tablespoon all-purpose (plain) flour
1	tablespoon tomato paste (concentrate)
1	tablespoon Worcestershire sauce
1	cup (250 ml) Beef Stock (see pages 62–63)
1	bay leaf
1	teaspoon finely chopped fresh thyme
	Salt and freshly ground black pepper
2	pounds (1 kg) potatoes, boiled and mashed with milk and butter

Serves: 4
Preparation: 30 minutes
Cooking: 75 minutes
Level: 1

ROAST LEG OF LAMB WITH VEGETABLES

Preheat the oven to 375°F (190°C/gas 5). • Lay the lamb out on a work surface and rub with the peppercorns, salt, and rosemary. Use a sharp knife to make holes in the meat and insert the garlic. Fold the meat over and tie with kitchen string. Let rest for 1 hour. • Place the lamb in a large roasting pan and rub with half the butter. Drizzle with the lemon juice. • Rub the potatoes, carrots, and onions with the remaining butter. Place them around the lamb in the roasting pan. • Roast for about 1$3/4$ hours, or until the lamb is cooked but still lightly pink. If you like lamb well done, bake for 2 hours or more. • Deglaze the pan with 1 tablespoon of boiling water and drizzle over the hot lamb.

1   leg of lamb, bone removed, about 5 pounds (2.5 kg)

1   teaspoon cracked black peppercorns

1   teaspoon salt

2   tablespoons fresh rosemary leaves

3   cloves garlic, halved

    Freshly squeezed juice of 1 small lemon

$3/4$ cup (200 g) butter, softened

4   medium potatoes, cut in bite-size chunks

2   medium carrots, cut in bite-size chunks

6   small onions, peeled and halved

Serves: 6
Preparation: 20 minutes
 + 1 hour to rest
Cooking: 2 hours
Level: 1

MECHOUI LAMB (MOROCCAN SLOW ROASTED SPICED LAMB)

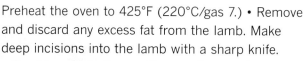

Preheat the oven to 425°F (220°C/gas 7.) • Remove and discard any excess fat from the lamb. Make deep incisions into the lamb with a sharp knife. • Combine the butter, garlic, paprika, cumin, coriander, salt, pepper, cayenne pepper, and cinnamon in a medium bowl. • Rub the butter over the lamb, pushing it into the incisions. • Place the lamb in a large baking tray and pour in the water. • Bake in the oven on the top shelf for 20 minutes. Move the lamb to the middle shelf, reduce the heat to 300°F (150°C/gas 2) and bake for 3 hours, or until the meat is tender and almost falling off the bone. • Baste with the pan juices frequently to keep the lamb moist and flavorsome. • Remove from the oven, cover with aluminum foil, and set aside to rest for 10 minutes. • Serve hot.

1	leg of lamb, about 6–7 pounds (3 kg)
½	cup (125 g) butter, softened
3	cloves garlic, finely chopped
3	teaspoons paprika
2	teaspoons ground cumin
2	teaspoons ground coriander
1	teaspoon salt
½	teaspoon freshly ground black pepper
½	teaspoon cayenne pepper
½	teaspoon ground cinnamon
1	cup (250 ml) water

Serves: 8
Preparation: 20 minutes
Cooking: 3 hours
Level: 2

STUFFED SHOULDER OF LAMB

464

Lamb: Place the lamb on a work surface and trim off most of the external fat. Trim off about 8 ounces (250 g) of meat. Spread out the shoulder so it lies flat, cut-side up. • Cook the salt pork in a large pot of boiling water for 10 minutes. Drain well. • Chop the 8 ounces of lamb in a food processor with the salt pork, shallots, garlic, and parsley. • Transfer to a bowl and stir in the egg. Season with salt, pepper, and thyme. • Spoon the stuffing mixture onto the shoulder of lamb, stuffing the mixture into any pockets and crevices left by the bones. Roll the roast around the stuffing to form a cylinder and tie in four or five places and around the edges with kitchen string. • Heat the oil in a large Dutch oven (saucepan) over medium heat. Add the lamb shoulder, and cook, turning occasionally until browned all over, about 20 minutes.

Sauce: When the meat is browned, add the onions and cook for 7–10 minutes. Pour in the wine and simmer until evaporated. Add the garlic, parsley, tomatoes, and bay leaves. Season with salt and pepper. Continue cooking for 5 minutes. Add the water and thyme. • Cover and simmer over low heat for about $1^1/2$ hours, or until the meat is very tender. • Cook the pasta in a large pot of salted boiling water until al dente. Drain well. • Serve the meat sliced with the pasta and meat sauce.

Lamb

- 3 pounds (1.5 g) boned lamb shoulder roast
- 8 ounces (250 g) salt pork or unsmoked bacon, cut into cubes
- 4 shallots
- 3 cloves garlic, peeled
  Small bunch parsley
- 1 large egg, lightly beaten
  Salt and freshly ground black pepper
- 2 teaspoons finely chopped fresh thyme
- 1/4 cup (60 ml) extra-virgin olive oil

Sauce

- 3 medium onions, finely chopped
- 1 cup (250 ml) dry white wine
- 5 cloves garlic, finely chopped
- 1 tablespoon finely chopped fresh parsley
- 8 firm-ripe tomatoes, peeled, seeded, and finely chopped
- 2 bay leaves
- 4 cups (1 liter) water
- 1 tablespoon finely chopped fresh thyme

- 1 pound (500 g) pasta to serve

Serves: 4–6
Preparation: 30 minutes
Cooking: $2^1/2$ hours
Level: 2

STUFFED VEAL

Cut a pocket into the piece of veal or beef. • Mix the ground veal, pork, lard, bread, Parmesan, Swiss chard, marjoram, pistachios, eggs, nutmeg, salt, and pepper in a large bowl. Stuff the meat with the mixture. Use a trussing needle and thread to stitch up the pocket. • Place in a large saucepan and cover with hot stock. Place over high heat and bring the stock to a boil. • Lower the heat and simmer gently for about 2 hours, or until the meat is very tender. • Cool the veal completely in the stock. Slice thinly and transfer to a serving plate.

■ ■ ■ *This recipe comes from Liguria, in northeastern Italy near the border with France. Aromatic and intricate, it is typical of the region. Serve with a bowl of pickled vegetables and mayonnaise.*

2 pounds (1 kg) boneless tenderloin veal or beef, in 1 piece

8 ounces (250 g) ground (minced) veal or beef

8 ounces (250 g) ground (minced) pork

4 ounces (125 g) lard or pancetta, very finely chopped

8 slices day-old bread, without crust, soaked in milk, and squeezed

3 tablespoons freshly grated Parmesan cheese

8 ounces (250 g) cooked Swiss chard (silverbeet), squeezed and finely chopped

2 tablespoons finely chopped fresh marjoram

¼ cup (25 g) pistachios, blanched and peeled

4 large eggs, lightly beaten

⅛ teaspoon freshly grated nutmeg

Salt and freshly ground white pepper

3 quarts (3 liters) Vegetable Stock (see page 94)

Serves: 6
Preparation: 30 minutes
Cooking: 2 hours
Level: 3

BOLLITO MISTO

Fill a large pot with about 6 quarts (6 liters) of cold water. Add the onions, celery, 1 of the carrots, peppercorns, and salt. Bring to a boil over medium-high heat. Add the beef, and when the water has returned to a boil, decrease the heat a little and cover. Simmer for 1 hour. • Add the veal, chicken, and tongue. Simmer for 1 hour, adding boiling water to cover the meats if necessary. Add the potatoes and remaining 8 carrots. Simmer until the meat and potatoes are very tender, about 1 hour. • Cook the pre-cooked cotechino sausage separately following the instructions on the package. • Drain and serve the meats and vegetables on a large heated serving platter.

2   medium onions, studded with 4–6 cloves

3   stalks celery, trimmed

9   large carrots, cut into chunks

20 black peppercorns

2   tablespoons coarse salt

4   pounds (2 kg) boneless beef, cut from brisket, bottom round, or rump roast

2   pounds (1 kg) boneless veal, cut from breast or shoulder

1   chicken, about 3 pounds (1.5 kg)

1   pound (500 g) calf's tongue

1   pre-cooked cotechino sausage, about 1½ pounds (750 g)

8   large potatoes, unpeeled, cut in half

◾ ◾ ◾ *In Italy, the meats and vegetables in this dish vary according to the region and the season. You may also vary them according to personal taste and what you have on hand. Cotechino sausage is now available both in Italy and abroad in a pre-cooked version sealed in a bag that usually only requires about 45 minutes boiling to finish cooking.*

Serves: 8–10
Preparation: 30 minutes
Cooking: 3 hours
Level: 2

VEGETABLES

GRILLED TOMATOES WITH GARLIC AND CHEESE SAUCE

472

Cheese Sauce: Mix the goat cheese, thyme, marjoram, chives, and scallion in a medium bowl until well mixed. Stir in the vinegar and wine.
• Set aside until ready to serve.
Tomatoes: Preheat a broiler (grill) to a high setting.
• Arrange the tomatoes on a large baking sheet cut-side up. Place 2–3 slices of garlic and a sprig of rosemary on each tomato half and drizzle with the oil. Season with salt and pepper. • Broil (grill) until the tomatoes have softened slightly, 5–10 minutes.
• Serve hot with the herb cheese sauce passed separately.

Cheese Sauce

1¼ cups (300 g) creamy fresh goat cheese, such as caprino or chèvre

1 tablespoon finely chopped fresh thyme

1 tablespoon finely chopped fresh marjoram

1 tablespoon snipped fresh chives

1 scallion (spring onion), white part only, thinly sliced

3 tablespoons white wine vinegar

3 tablespoons dry white wine

Tomatoes

12 small, ripe tomatoes, halved

4 large cloves garlic, thinly sliced

24 tiny sprigs fresh rosemary

¼ cup (60 ml) extra-virgin olive oil

Salt and freshly ground black pepper

Serves: 4–6
Preparation: 15 minutes
Cooking: 5–10 minutes
Level: 1

WILD MUSHROOM FRICASSEE

474

Halve or quarter the mushrooms so that they are all more or less the same size. • Heat the oil in a large frying pan over medium heat. Add the shallots and sauté until softened but not colored, 3–4 minutes. Stir in the garlic and add the butter. • Increase the heat to high and, when the butter has melted, add all the mushrooms to the pan. Gently stir the mushrooms, cover, and simmer over medium heat until they are beginning to soften, 5–6 minutes. • Add the salt, cider, and paprika. Stir gently and bring to a boil. Cover the pan and simmer over low heat for 5 more minutes. • Stir in the sun-dried tomatoes, 2 tablespoons of parsley, and the sour cream. Check the seasoning. • Bring back to a gentle boil and simmer for 2–3 minutes. • Transfer to a serving dish and sprinkle with the remaining 2 tablespoons of parsley. • Serve hot.

$1\frac{1}{2}$ pounds (750 g) mixed mushrooms (button, oyster, shiitake, chestnut, and/or chanterelle)

2 tablespoons extra-virgin olive oil

2 shallots, sliced

2 cloves garlic, crushed

2 tablespoons butter

$1\frac{1}{2}$ teaspoons salt

$2/3$ cup (150 ml) dry cider, sherry, or white wine

1 teaspoon smoked sweet paprika

2 ounces (50 g) sun-dried tomatoes, packed in oil, drained and chopped

4 tablespoons finely chopped fresh parsley

1 cup (250 ml) reduced-fat sour cream

Salt and freshly ground black pepper

Serves: 4
Preparation: 10–15 minutes
Cooking: 15–20 minutes
Level: 1

ASIAN VEGETABLES WITH OYSTER SAUCE

476

Place a large saucepan of water on high heat and bring to a boil. • Heat the oil in a large wok or frying pan over medium-high heat. Add the garlic and mushrooms and sauté until golden brown, about 5 minutes. • Pour in the oyster sauce and chicken stock and bring to a boil. Decrease the heat to low and simmer until slightly reduced, 2–3 minutes. • Meanwhile, cook the broccoli in the boiling water for 1 minute. Add the choi sum and bok choy and cook for 2 more minutes. • Add the cabbage and cook until just wilted, about 30 seconds. • Drain the vegetables well. • Add to the mushrooms in the pan and toss to combine and coat in the sauce. • Serve hot.

2   tablespoons peanut oil

2   cloves garlic, thinly sliced

1½ cups (150 g) sliced fresh mushrooms, such as oyster or shiitake

½   cup (125 ml) oyster sauce

¼   cup (60 ml) Chicken Stock (see pages 34–35)

1   bunch Asian broccoli

1   bunch baby choi sum

1   bunch baby bok choy

2   cups (100 g) Chinese cabbage, coarsely chopped

Serves: 4
Preparation: 15 minutes
Cooking: 10 minutes
Level: 1

CABBAGE KIMCHI

478

Cut the cabbage lengthwise into quarters. Remove and discard the core. Cut the quarters in half lengthwise and then crosswise into $1^1/2$ inch (4 cm) wide pieces. Set aside in a large bowl. • Peel the radish, halve lengthwise, and thinly slice crosswise. Add to the prepared cabbage. • Combine the water and salt in a medium bowl and pour over the vegetables. Toss to coat. • Cover with plastic wrap (cling film) and set aside to soak for at least 6 hours, or overnight. • Drain the vegetables. Rinse with cold water to remove excess salt. Squeeze out as much liquid as possible and transfer to a large bowl. • Combine the chives, garlic, chile paste, shrimp powder, ginger, and fish sauce in a medium bowl. Add to the cabbage mixture and toss well, wearing food handling gloves, (to prevent chile burn) to coat. • Transfer the spiced cabbage mixture to two 4-cup (1-liter) pickling jars. Cover with lids and set aside to ferment at room temperature for two days. • Place the jars in the refrigerator and leave to ferment for 7–10 days. • Serve as an accompaniment to fish and chicken dishes.

1	large Chinese cabbage, about 3 pounds (1.5 kg)
1	daikon (Asian radish)
2	cups (500 ml) water
$1/2$	cup (120 g) coarse sea salt
1	small bunch fresh chives, snipped
5	cloves garlic, finely chopped
4	tablespoons (60 ml) Korean chile paste
1	tablespoon dried shrimps, ground to a powder
1	(2-inch/5-cm) piece fresh ginger, finely grated
$1/4$	cup (60 ml) Thai fish sauce

Serves: 8–12
Preparation: 30 minutes
  + 6–12 hours to soak
  + 9–12 days to ferment
Level: 2

▩ ▩ ▩ *Cabbage kimchi is a Korean recipe for spicy fermented cabbage. By Chinese cabbage in this recipe we don't mean bok choy, but the paler cabbage also known as Napa cabbage.*

LEBANESE GARLIC MASH

Cook the potatoes in a large pot of salted boiling water until tender, 15–20 minutes. • Drain well, transfer to a large bowl, and mash until smooth. • Add the oil, lemon juice, garlic, and salt and stir until well blended. • Sprinkle with the mint and serve warm.

480

2	pounds (1 kg) potatoes, peeled and quartered
1/3	cup (90) ml extra-virgin olive oil
1/3	cup (90 ml) freshly squeezed lemon juice
3	cloves garlic, finely chopped
	Salt
3	tablespoons finely chopped fresh mint

Serves: 4–6
Preparation: 15 minutes
Cooking: 15–20 minutes
Level: 1

■ ■ ■ *These potatoes are especially good with roast, grilled, or braised fish or lamb.*

DOLMADES

Step 1: Soak the vine leaves in warm water for 10 minutes. • Drain and separate the leaves, setting aside the torn ones. • Heat 3 tablespoons of the oil in a medium saucepan over medium-low heat. Add the onion and sauté until softened, 3–4 minutes. • Add the rice and stir to coat. Add the water and bring to a boil. Decrease the heat to low, cover, and simmer until all the liquid is absorbed and the rice is almost cooked, 10–12 minutes. • Add the herbs and stir to combine. Season with salt and pepper. • Spread the rice out onto a baking sheet and set aside to cool slightly. • **Step 2:** Spread the leaves out flat, smooth-side down on a clean work surface with the stems facing you. Cut off the stems. • Place spoonfuls of filling mixture at the base of the leaves. Fold the sides in and roll up, but not too tightly, (to allow room for the rice to swell when cooked) into small logs. • **Step 3:** Line the base of a medium saucepan with the torn vine leaves and arrange the dolmades on top, seam-side down. Pour in the remaining oil and lemon juice. Cover with a heatproof plate to hold the dolmades down and prevent them from unrolling. • Place the saucepan over medium-high heat and bring to a boil. Decrease the heat to low and simmer gently until the rice is tender, about 30 minutes. • Remove from the heat and set aside to cool in the saucepan. • Refrigerate overnight. • Bring the dolmades back to room temperature and serve with the yogurt.

482

35	vine leaves in brine
1	cup (250 ml) + 3 tablespoons extra-virgin olive oil
1	medium onion, finely chopped
½	cup (100 g) long-grain rice
1	cup (250 ml) boiling water
4	tablespoons finely chopped fresh parsley
4	tablespoons finely chopped fresh dill
	Salt and freshly ground black pepper
⅓	cup (90 ml) freshly squeezed lemon juice
1	cup (250 g) plain yogurt to serve

Serves: 6
Preparation: 45 minutes
  + 12 hours to chill
Cooking: 1 hour
Level: 3

■ PREPARING DOLMADES

The best-known dolmades are vine leaves stuffed with rice and gently simmered over low heat until tender. But in many parts of the Balkans, the Middle East, and Central Asia, dolmades simply means stuffed vegetables. Stuffings can include meat, rice, potatoes and many other ingredients. They are often served with yogurt. This is a classic Greek recipe.

1. SOAK the vine leaves in warm water for 10 minutes. Drain and separate the leaves, setting aside the torn ones.

2. SPREAD the leaves out flat, smooth-side down on a clean work surface with the stems facing you. Cut off the stems. Place spoonfuls of filling mixture at the base of the leaves. Fold the sides in and roll up, but not too tightly, (to allow room for the rice to swell when cooked) into small logs.

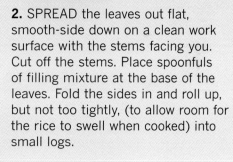

3. LINE the base of a medium saucepan with the torn vine leaves and arrange the dolmades on top, seam-side down. Pour in the remaining oil and lemon

juice. Cover with a heatproof plate to hold the dolmades down and prevent them from unrolling. Simmer over low heat until tender, about 30 minutes.

LEBANESE VEGETABLES

Heat the oil in a large saucepan over medium heat. Add the onion and garlic and sauté until lightly browned, about 5 minutes. • Add the beef and brown for 10 minutes. Season with salt and pepper. Sprinkle with cinnamon. • Add the potatoes and simmer for 10 minutes, stirring occasionally. • Add the zucchini and cook for 10 minutes more, stirring occasionally. • When the potatoes and zucchini are almost tender, break the eggs over the mixture, stirring to break the yolks. • Cook until the eggs are set, about 5 minutes. • Sprinkle with the parsley and serve hot.

486

1/4	cup (60 ml) extra-virgin olive oil
1	large onion, finely chopped
2	cloves garlic, finely chopped
8	ounces (250 g) ground (minced) beef
	Salt and freshly ground black pepper
1	teaspoon ground cinnamon
2	medium potatoes, peeled and cut into cubes
2	medium zucchini (courgettes), cut into cubes
4	large eggs
2	tablespoons finely chopped fresh parsley

Serves: 4
Preparation: 15 minutes
Cooking: 40 minutes
Level: 1

■ ■ ■ *These vegetables are easy to prepare and make a nutritious and filling meal. If liked, drizzle with a little freshly squeezed lemon juice just before serving.*

STUFFED GREEN BELL PEPPERS

Cook the rice in a large pot of salted boiling water for 5 minutes. Drain well. • Heat 2 tablespoons of the oil in a large frying pan over medium heat. Add the onions and sauté until lightly browned, about 5 minutes. Season with salt. • Add the pine nuts and rice. • Cook over medium heat, stirring often, for 10 minutes. • Add the currants, tomato, sugar, cinnamon, and paprika. Pour in the water and bring to a boil. • Cover and simmer until the water has been completely absorbed, 10–15 minutes. • Season with pepper. Remove from the heat and add the mint and dill. Cover and let stand for 10 minutes. • Fill the bell peppers with the filling and cover with the reserved tops. • Arrange the bell peppers in a casserole into which they fit snugly. • Drizzle with the remaining 4 tablespoons (60 ml) of oil and just enough hot water to cover the bottom of the pan. • Cover and simmer until tender, 45–50 minutes, adding more water if the sauce begins to dry. • Serve hot.

3/4 **cup (150 g) rice**

6 **tablespoons (90 ml) extra-virgin olive oil**

6 **onions, finely chopped**

Salt

2 **tablespoons pine nuts**

2 **tablespoons currants**

1 **tomato, finely chopped**

2 **tablespoons sugar**

1 **teaspoon cinnamon**

1 **teaspoon sweet paprika**

2/3 **cup (150 ml) hot water + extra as required**

Freshly ground black pepper

1 **tablespoon finely chopped fresh mint**

2 **tablespoons finely chopped fresh dill**

8 **green bell peppers (capsicums), seeded, tops reserved**

Serves: 4
Preparation: 10 minutes
Cooking: About 2 hours
Level: 1

ROMAN-STYLE SPINACH

490

Plump the raisins in cold water for 30 minutes. Drain well. • Heat the oil in a large frying pan over high heat. Add the garlic and pine nuts and sauté for 1 minute. • Add the spinach and raisins and sauté for 5 minutes. Season with salt and pepper. • Serve hot.

4 **tablespoons raisins**

3 **tablespoons extra-virgin olive oil**

2 **cloves garlic, finely chopped**

6 **tablespoons pine nuts**

3 **pounds (1.5 kg) tender young spinach leaves**

Salt and freshly ground black pepper

Serves: 6
Preparation: 20 minutes
+ 30 minutes to soak
Cooking: 6 minutes
Level: 1

▨ ▨ ▨ *Remember to rinse and drain the spinach at least five times to remove any gritty sand and dirt. Add the fresh spinach to the frying pan a handful at a time.*

POTATO STEW

Heat the oil in a large saucepan over high heat. Brown the bacon for 5 minutes with the olives, garlic, and bay leaf. • Scoop out the bacon, olives, garlic, and bay leaf with a slotted spoon and drain on paper towels, leaving the cooking juices in the pan. • Chop the potatoes into chunks if they are large, or leave whole if they are small. • Heat the pan with the cooking juices over medium heat. Add the potatoes and sauté for 5 minutes. • Bring the stock to a boil in a large saucepan then pour over the potatoes. Simmer until tender, 20–25 minutes. • Stir in the bacon mixture and serve hot or at room temperature.

1/4 cup (60 ml) extra-virgin olive oil

5 ounces (150 g) bacon, diced

1¹/2 cups (150 g) black olives

4 cloves garlic, peeled and left whole

1 bay leaf

2 pounds (1 kg) potatoes, peeled

4 cups (1 liter) Beef Stock (see page 62–63)

Serves: 4–6
Preparation: 15 minutes
Cooking: 30–40 minutes
Level: 1

ZUCCHINI AND TOMATOES

Place the tomatoes in a colander and sprinkle with salt. Let stand for 1 hour to drain off the excess water. • Heat the oil in a large frying pan over medium heat. Add the garlic, tomatoes, and zucchini and sauté until softened, 10–15 minutes. • Season with salt and pepper and sprinkle with the thyme. • Serve hot.

2	pounds (1 kg) firm-ripe tomatoes, quartered and seeded
	Salt
$1/4$	cup (60 ml) extra-virgin olive oil
1	clove garlic, finely chopped
6	zucchini (courgettes), cut into $1/2$-inch (1-cm) thick slices
	Freshly ground black pepper
1	tablespoon finely chopped fresh thyme

Serves: 6
Preparation: 15 minutes + 1 hour to drain
Cooking: 10–15 minutes
Level: 1

BEAN STEW
WITH CHORIZO

496

Cover beans with cold water and soak overnight. Drain and rinse. • Combine the beans with the water, chorizo, salt pork, onion, garlic, parsley, bay leaf, pepper, and cumin in a large pot. • Mix the oil and paprika until smooth in a small bowl then stir into the pot. • Bring to a boil, cover, and simmer until the beans are tender, about 2 hours. Season with salt. • Turn off the heat and let the stew stand for 30 minutes to thicken, then reheat. • Serve hot garnished with parsley.

2	cups (250 g) dried white kidney or cannellini beans
5	cups (1.25 liters) water
4	ounces (125 g) chorizo sausage or other mild sausage
4	ounces (125 g) salt pork or slab bacon, cut in 1 inch (2.5 cm) cubes
1	small onion, chopped
4	cloves garlic
2	tablespoons finely chopped parsley + extra to garnish
1	bay leaf
	Freshly ground black pepper
1/4	teaspoon ground cumin
1	tablespoon extra-virgin olive oil
1	teaspoon sweet paprika
	Salt

Serves: 4–6
Preparation: 15 minutes
+ about 12 hours to soak
and stand
Cooking: 2–3 hours
Level: 2

POTATOES WITH PEPPERS

Cook the potatoes in salted boiling water until tender, about 20 minutes. • Drain well, and cut into bite-sized pieces (or leave whole if small). • Heat the oil in a large frying pan over medium heat. Sauté the potatoes until lightly browned, about 5 minutes. • Pound the garlic, red pepper flakes, and cumin in a pestle and mortar until crushed. • Transfer to a small bowl and add the paprika and vinegar • Add the garlic mixture and bell pepper to the potatoes. Cook, stirring often, for 10 minutes. • Season with salt and serve hot.

498

$1^1/_2$ pounds (750 g) new potatoes

$^1/_3$ cup (90 ml extra-virgin olive oil

2 cloves garlic, chopped

$^1/_2$ teaspoon red pepper flakes

$^1/_2$ teaspoon cumin seeds

$^1/_4$ teaspoon hot paprika

2 tablespoons white wine vinegar

1 green bell pepper (capsicum), seeded and thinly sliced

Salt

Serves: 4–6
Preparation: 15 minutes
Cooking: 35 minutes
Level: 1

SWISS CHARD GRATIN

500

Prepare the Swiss chard by stripping the leaves off the stalks. Cook the leaves in a pot of salted boiling water for 4 minutes. Drain well and set aside. • Peel the stalks, removing the tough strands of fiber as much as possible. Cut into $1/2$-inch (1-cm) pieces. • Cook in a pot of salted boiling water until slightly softened, 5–7 minutes. Drain well and set aside. • Preheat the oven to 400°F (200°C/gas 6). • Melt the butter in a small saucepan over low heat. Stir in the flour. • Bring the milk to a boil and gradually pour into the flour mixture, beating constantly to make sure no lumps form. Continue cooking until the sauce has thickened. Season with salt, pepper, and nutmeg. • Finely chop the Swiss chard greens. Stir into the stalks and arrange in an ovenproof dish. Pour the white sauce over and sprinkle with the cheese. • Bake for 20–25 minutes, or until the cheese is nicely browned.

2 pounds (1 kg) Swiss chard (silverbeet)

2 tablespoons butter

2 tablespoons all-purpose (plain) flour

2 cups (500 ml) milk

Salt and freshly ground black pepper

$1/4$ teaspoon freshly grated nutmeg

$1/2$ cup (60 g) freshly grated firm cheese

Serves: 4–6
Preparation: 20–25 minutes
Cooking: 35–40 minutes
Level: 1

EGGPLANT PARMIGIANA

Put the eggplant in a colander and sprinkle with coarse sea salt. Let drain for 1 hour. • Shake off excess salt. Pat dry with paper towels. • Dip the eggplant in the flour until well coated, shaking off the excess. • Heat $1/3$ cup (90 ml) of oil in a large, frying pan over medium heat. Fry the eggplant in batches until tender. Add extra oil to the pan as required. • Drain on paper towels. Season with salt. • Heat 2 tablespoons of oil in a separate frying pan over medium heat. Sauté the onion and basil until softened, 3–4 minutes. • Stir in the tomatoes. Simmer over low heat for 30 minutes. • Preheat the oven to 375°F (190°C/gas 5). • Oil a large baking dish. • Arrange a layer of eggplant in the dish and sprinkle with Parmesan. Add a layer of mozzarella and eggs. Drizzle with tomato sauce and add another layer of eggplant. Repeat until all the ingredients are in the dish, finishing with a layer of Parmesan. • Bake for 30 minutes, or until lightly browned. • Serve hot.

6	medium eggplant (aubergines), with skin, cut in ½-inch (1-cm) slices
	Coarse sea salt or kosher salt
⅓	cup (50 g) all-purpose (plain) flour
1	cup (250 ml) extra-virgin olive oil
	Salt
1	large onion, finely chopped
2	tablespoons finely chopped fresh basil
1½	pounds (750 g) firm-ripe tomatoes, peeled and diced
1½	cups (200 g) freshly grated Parmesan cheese
8	ounces (250 g) mozzarella cheese, thinly sliced
3	hard-boiled eggs, sliced

Serves: 6
Preparation: 40 minutes
+ 1 hour to drain
Cooking: About 1½ hours
Level: 2

■ ■ ■ *This is a classic Italian vegetable dish. It is hearty enough to serve as a main course.*

STUFFED ZUCCHINI

Preheat the oven to 350°F (180°C/gas 4). • Set out an ovenproof baking dish. • Heat the oil in a medium frying pan over medium heat. Add the onion and sauté until lightly browned, about 5 minutes. • Add the garlic, pine nuts, raisins, and cinnamon. Season with salt and pepper. Simmer for 5 minutes. • Add the lamb and sauté until browned, about 10 minutes. • Blanch the zucchini in a large pot of salted boiling water until almost tender, about 5 minutes. Drain well. • Cut a lid out of the top of each zucchini and use a teaspoon to hollow out the flesh. • Add the zucchini flesh to the meat mixture and cook until all the liquid has been absorbed.
• Place the hollowed-out zucchini in the baking dish. Spoon enough filling into each one to fill.
• Season the tomatoes with salt and pepper. Pour into the baking dish with the zucchini. • Bake for 40–50 minutes, or until tender and well cooked.
• Place the zucchini on a serving dish and spoon the tomato sauce over the top. • Serve hot.

504

$^1/_4$ **cup (60 ml) extra-virgin olive oil**

1 **large onion, finely chopped**

2 **cloves garlic, finely chopped**

$^1/_2$ **cup (90 g) pine nuts**

$^1/_4$ **cup (25 g) raisins**

$^1/_2$ **teaspoon ground cinnamon**

Salt and freshly ground black pepper

1 **pound (500 g) ground (minced) lamb or beef**

6 **medium zucchini (courgettes)**

1 **pound (500 g) tomatoes, peeled and chopped**

Serves: 4
Preparation: 30 minutes
Cooking: About 1$^1/_4$ hours
Level: 1

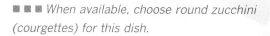 *When available, choose round zucchini (courgettes) for this dish.*

ROAST VEGETABLES

2 medium eggplant (aubergines), peeled and cut into cubes

Coarse sea salt or kosher salt

1 pound (500 g) potatoes, peeled and cut into cubes

1 pound (500 g) zucchini (courgettes), sliced

2 pounds (1 kg) firm-ripe tomatoes, cut into 1/2-inch (1-cm) slices

1 large red onion, sliced

1 cup (250 ml) extra-virgin olive oil

2 tablespoons finely chopped fresh parsley

2 tablespoons finely chopped fresh basil

Freshly ground black pepper

506

Sprinkle the eggplant with salt in a colander and let drain for 1 hour. • Preheat the oven to 350°F (180°C/gas 4). • Set out a large roasting pan. • Shake off excess salt from the eggplants. Pat dry with paper towels. • Mix the eggplants, potatoes, zucchini, tomatoes, onion, oil, parsley, and basil in the pan. Season with salt and pepper and mix well. • Bake for 55–65 minutes, or until the vegetables are tender. If the vegetables start to burn, cover with aluminum foil. • Serve hot.

■ ■ ■ *Sprinkling eggplant with salt before cooking draws out the moisture in a process known as "degorging." Larger, older eggplants have brown seeds that contain a bitter liquid. Salting removes some of this liquid and improves flavor and texture. It is not necessary to salt small, tender eggplants.*

Serves: 6
Preparation: 15 minutes + 1 hour to drain the eggplant
Cooking: 55–65 minutes
Level: 1

■ DEGORGING EGGPLANT

1. PUT the eggplant in a colander and sprinkle with coarse sea salt. Let drain for 1 hour.
2. SHAKE OFF excess salt. Pat dry with paper towels.

VEGETABLE SAMOSAS

Dough: Step 1: Sift the flour and salt into a medium bowl. Add the oil and then gradually add the water, stirring until a dough begins to form. • Knead the dough until smooth, about 10 minutes. • Lightly oil a medium bowl. Put the dough in it, cover with a clean kitchen towel, and set aside until required.

Filling: Melt the ghee in a large frying pan over medium heat. Add the onion, ginger, and garlic and sauté until softened, 3–4 minutes. • Add the mustard seeds, turmeric, cumin, and chile powder and sauté until the seeds begin to pop and the spices are fragrant, about 30 seconds. • Add the potato and peas and stir to coat. Season with salt and pepper. • **Step 2:** Divide the dough into 10 equal balls. • Roll one ball out to make an 8 inch (20 cm) disk. Cut the disk in half, brush the straight edge with water and shape into a cone. • **Step 3:** Put a tablespoonful of filling into the cone. Brush the round edge with water and fold over to encase the filling. Press along the round edge with the prongs of a fork to seal. Repeat the process with the remaining dough and filling. • Pour the oil into a deep-fryer or deep saucepan over medium heat and heat to 365°F (190°C). If you don't have a frying thermometer, test the oil temperature by dropping a small piece of bread into the hot oil. If the bread bubbles to the surface and begins to turn golden, the oil is ready. • **Step 4:** Fry the samosas a few at a time until golden brown, 3–5 minutes each batch. Remove using a slotted spoon and drain on paper towels. • Serve hot with mango chutney.

Dough

2	cups (300 g) all-purpose (plain) flour
½	teaspoon salt
3	tablespoons vegetable oil
¾	cup (180 ml) water

Filling

3	tablespoons ghee or vegetable oil
1	small onion, finely chopped
2	teaspoons finely grated fresh ginger
1	clove garlic, minced
½	teaspoon brown mustard seeds
2	teaspoons ground turmeric
2	teaspoons ground cumin
½	teaspoon chile powder
4	medium potatoes, boiled, peeled, and cut into very small cubes
1	cup (150 g) frozen peas
	Salt
	Mango chutney, to serve
4	cups (1 liter) vegetable oil for frying

Serves: 4
Preparation: 45 minutes
Cooking: 30 minutes
Level: 2

PREPARING SAMOSAS

Indian samosas are small, crisp flaky pastries stuffed with a variety of ingredients, from spicy vegetables to cheese, meat, and sweet fillings. They are usually served with chutney and eaten as a snack. Similar dishes are prepared in many parts of the Middle East and South Asia.

1. SIFT the flour and salt into a medium bowl. Add the oil, then gradually add the water, stirring until a dough forms. Knead until smooth, about 10 minutes.

2. DIVIDE the dough into 8 equal balls. Roll into 8 inch (20 cm) disks. Brush the edges with water and shape into cones.

3. PUT a tablespoonful of filling into each cone. Brush the round edges with water and fold over the filling. Seal the round edge with the prongs of a fork.

4. FRY the samosas a few at a time until golden brown, 3–5 minutes. Remove using a slotted spoon and drain on paper towels.

VEGETABLE PAKORAS

Raita Dipping Sauce: Combine the yogurt, cilantro, lemon juice, and cumin in a small bowl. Season with salt. Cover and refrigerate until required.

Batter: Sift the besan, baking soda, salt, cumin, and chile powder into a medium bowl. Gradually add the water, stirring to make a thick batter.

Vegetables: Pour the oil into a deep-fryer or deep saucepan over medium heat and heat to 365°F (190°C). If you don't have a frying thermometer, test the oil temperature by dropping a small piece of bread into the hot oil. If the bread bubbles to the surface and begins to turn golden, the oil is ready.
• Coat the vegetables in the batter a few at a time and fry in batches until golden-brown and cooked through, 4–5 minutes each batch. • Remove using a slotted spoon and drain on paper towels. Season with salt. • Serve hot with raita dipping sauce.

■ ■ ■ *Pakoras are vegetables (or fish, cheese, or meat) fried in a spiced chickpea batter. They are served as a snack in India, Pakistan, and Afghanistan. They are also known as bhajis.*

Raita Dipping Sauce
1   cup (250 g) plain yogurt
1   tablespoon finely chopped fresh cilantro (coriander)
2   teaspoons freshly squeezed lemon juice, strained
1/4   teaspoon ground cumin
  Salt

Batter
2   cups (300 g) besan (chickpea flour)
1/2   teaspoon baking soda (bicarbonate of soda)
1/2   teaspoon salt
1/2   teaspoon ground cumin
1/2   teaspoon chile powder
1 1/4   cups (300 ml) water

Vegetables
4   cups (1 liter) vegetable oil for frying
1   large potato, peeled and cut into thin slices
1   large onion, sliced into rings
1   red bell pepper (capsicum), seeded and sliced into lengths
1/2   small cauliflower, separated into small florets
  Salt

Serves: 4–6
Preparation: 15 minutes
Cooking: 15–20 minutes
Level: 1

TEMPURA VEGETABLES

Dipping Sauce: Place the dashi, soy sauce, mirin, and ginger in a small saucepan over medium heat and bring to a boil. • Set aside until required.

Vegetables: Step 1: Pour the oil into a deep-fryer or deep saucepan over medium heat and heat to 365°F (190°C). If you don't have a frying thermometer, test the oil temperature by dropping a small piece of bread into the hot oil. If the bread bubbles to the surface and begins to turn golden, the oil is ready. • Combine the egg yolk and water in a medium bowl. Sift the flour and cornstarch into the liquid, stirring with chopsticks until just combined. The batter is supposed to be a little lumpy. • **Step 2:** Coat the vegetables in the batter a few at a time. • Fry in batches until golden and cooked through, 4–5 minutes. • Remove with a slotted spoon and drain on paper towels. Repeat with the remaining vegetables. • Serve hot with the dipping sauce.

Dipping Sauce

- ³/₄ cup (180 ml) dashi stock
- 3 tablespoons soy sauce
- 2 tablespoons mirin
- 1 teaspoon minced ginger

Vegetables

- 4 cups (1 liter) vegetable oil for frying
- 1 large egg yolk
- 2 cups (500 ml) cold soda water
- 1½ cups (225 g) all-purpose (plain) flour
- ⅓ cup (50 g) cornstarch
- 1 small sweet potato, peeled and sliced ⅛ inch (3 mm) thick
- 1 carrot, sliced diagonally ⅛ inch (3 mm) thick
- 1 zucchini (courgette), sliced diagonally ¼ inch (5 mm) thick
- 1 small head broccoli, cut into small florets
- 2 small red bell peppers (capsicums), sliced

Serves: 4–6
Preparation: 20 minutes
Cooking: 15–20 minutes
Level: 2

▌ PREPARING TEMPURA VEGETABLES

1. COMBINE the egg yolk and water in a bowl. Sift in both flours, stirring with chopsticks. The batter should be a little lumpy.
2. COAT the vegetables in the batter a few at a time. Fry in batches until golden and cooked through, 4–5 minutes.

FALAFEL

1	pound (500 g) dried garbanzo beans (chickpeas), soaked overnight and drained
1	medium onion
3	cloves garlic, peeled
1	medium potato, peeled
1	bunch fresh parsley
1	teaspoon freshly ground coriander seeds
1	teaspoon freshly ground cumin
1	teaspoon dried oregano
2	tablespoons all-purpose (plain) flour
	Salt and freshly ground white pepper
2	teaspoons baking powder
4	cups (1 liter) vegetable oil for frying
	Pita bread, salad of sliced tomatoes, mixed salad greens, sliced red onion, and Greek yogurt to serve

Process the garbanzo beans, onion, garlic, potato, and parsley in a food processor until finely chopped. • Add the coriander, cumin, oregano, and flour, and process until well blended. • Season with salt and pepper. • Let rest for 2 hours. • Stir the baking powder into the mixture and shape into flattened patties. • Pour the oil into a deep-fryer or deep saucepan over medium heat and heat to 365°F (190°C). If you don't have a frying thermometer, test the oil temperature by dropping a small piece of bread into the hot oil. If the bread bubbles to the surface and begins to turn golden, the oil is ready. • Fry the patties in batches until golden brown, about 5 minutes each batch. • Drain well on paper towels. • Serve warm with pita bread, a salad of sliced tomatoes, mixed salad greens, sliced red onion, and Greek yogurt.

Serves: 8–12
Preparation: 20 minutes
+ 12 hours to soak
+ 2 hours to rest
Cooking: 30 minutes
Level: 2

■ ■ ■ *Falafel are small fritters made of dried garbanzo beans (chickpeas) or fava (broad) beans. They are popular throughout the Middle East where they are eaten as a snack or as part of a traditional meze (spread of appetizers).*

SALADS

FENNEL SALAD
WITH PINE NUTS

Toast the pine nuts in a small frying pan over medium heat until pale golden brown, 3-4 minutes. shake the pan often during cooking so that they don't burn. Set aside to cool a little. • Strip the tough, outer leaves from the fennel bulbs. Rinse and slice thinly lengthwise. Place on serving plates. Sprinkle with a little of the fennel tops to garnish. • Top with the Parmesan and pine nuts and season with the oil, lemon juice, salt, and pepper.

6 tablespoons pine nuts

4 small round fennel bulbs, with tops, to garnish

¼ cup (60 ml) extra-virgin olive oil

2 tablespoons freshly squeezed lemon juice

   Salt and freshly ground black pepper

4 ounces (120 g) Parmesan cheese, flaked

Serves: 4
Preparation: 10 minutes
Level: 1

BLUE CHEESE
AND PECAN SALAD

Salad: Preheat the oven to 350°F (180°C/gas 4).
• Cut the baguette in half lengthwise, then tear into small pieces. Bake until golden and crisp, about 5 minutes. • Place the arugula in 4 individual serving bowls. • Arrange the baguette and pears on top. Sprinkle with the pecans and cheese.

Dressing: Whisk the oil and lemon juice in a small bowl. Season with salt and pepper. • Drizzle a little of the dressing over each salad and serve.

Salad

½   baguette (French loaf)

1   bunch arugula (rocket)

2   large, ripe pears, halved then thinly sliced

1   cup (125 g) roasted pecans

4   ounces (125 g) blue cheese, cut or crumbled into chunks

Dressing

½   cup (125 ml) extra-virgin olive oil

2   tablespoons freshly squeezed lemon juice

    Salt and freshly ground black pepper

Serves: 4
Preparation: 10 minutes
Cooking: 5 minutes
Level: 1

FATTOUSH

Salad: Preheat the oven to 350°F (180°C/gas 4).
• Tear the bread into 2 inch (5 cm) pieces. • Place the bread on a large baking sheet, drizzle with the oil, and sprinkle with sumac. Toss to coat. • Bake for 5–10 minutes, until the bread is crisp and golden brown. • Combine the tomatoes, cucumber, radish, onion, parsley, mint, and scallions in a salad bowl and toss well. Tear the lettuce into small pieces and add to the salad. • Add the toasted bread to the salad.

Dressing: Whisk the oil, lemon juice, and garlic in a small bowl. Season with salt and pepper. • Drizzle over the salad and toss to combine. • Sprinkle with a little extra sumac and serve.

524

■ ■ ■ *Fattoush is a traditional Lebanese salad made with toasted pita bread, salad greens, tomatoes, and onions. Sumac is a Middle Eastern spice with a light lemon flavor. Buy it in Middle Eastern food stores. If you can't find it, just leave it out.*

Salad

2   Lebanese flatbreads or pita breads

¼   cup (60 ml) extra-virgin olive oil

1½ teaspoons sumac + extra to sprinkle

12 cherry tomatoes, halved

1   Lebanese or ordinary cucumber, peeled, halved lengthwise, seeded, and sliced

2   radishes, thinly sliced into rounds

½   small red onion, thinly sliced

½   cup (25 g) coarsely chopped fresh parsley

2   tablespoons coarsely chopped fresh mint

2   scallions (spring onions), thinly sliced

2   baby cos lettuces, outside leaves removed and discarded

Dressing

¼   cup (60 ml) extra-virgin olive oil

2   tablespoons freshly squeezed lemon juice

1   clove garlic, minced

    Salt and freshly ground black pepper

Serves: 4
Preparation: 15 minutes
Cooking: 5–10 minutes
Level: 1

APPLE, NUT, AND CELERY SALAD

Place the apples in a salad bowl. Drizzle with half the lemon juice to stop them from turning brown. • Add the celery, garlic, raisins, cumin, parsley, and nuts to the salad bowl. • Season with pepper and drizzle with the remaining lemon juice and the oil. • Toss well and serve.

2   large Granny Smith apples, cored and cut into bite-size pieces

¼   cup (60 ml) freshly squeezed lemon juice

6   stalks celery, trimmed and cut into bite-sized pieces

2   cloves garlic, finely chopped

½   cup (60 g) raisins

1   teaspoon cumin seeds

6   tablespoons finely chopped fresh parsley

1   cup (150 g) toasted salted nuts (peanuts, almonds, walnuts, cashews, etc.)

    Freshly ground black pepper

⅓   cup (90 ml) extra-virgin olive oil

Serves: 4
Preparation: 15 minutes
Level: 1

■ ■ ■ *Because the apples are not peeled in this salad, buy organic fruit so that you are sure they have not been treated with pesticides or other chemicals. Rinse thoroughly before use.*

POTATO AND TUNA SALAD

Cook the potatoes in their skins in a large pot of salted boiling water until tender, about 20 minutes. • Drain well and set aside until cool enough to handle. Slip off the skins and let cool completely. • Cut into bite-size pieces. • Place the onion in a large bowl with the water, vinegar, and 1 teaspoon salt. Let stand for 30 minutes. • Drain well. • Place the potatoes, tuna, cucumbers, olives, and onion in a large salad bowl. Season with salt and drizzle with the oil. • Toss gently and garnish with the tomato, egg, anchovies, bell pepper, and parsley. • Serve at once.

2 pounds (1 kg) waxy potatoes

1 medium onion, thinly sliced

¼ cup (60 ml) cold water

1 tablespoon white wine vinegar

Salt

1³/₄ cups (200 g) canned tuna in oil, drained

2 cucumbers, thinly sliced

1 cup (100 g) black and green olives

Salt

2 tablespoons extra-virgin olive oil

1 tomato, thinly sliced

2 hard-boiled eggs, quartered

8 salt-cured anchovy fillets

1 yellow bell pepper (capsicum), seeded, cored, and cut into thin strips

Fresh flat-leaf parsley leaves to garnish

Serves: 4
Preparation: 20 minutes + 30 minutes to cool and stand
Cooking: 20 minutes
Level: 1

MOROCCAN SALAD

Salad: Place a medium saucepan of water over high heat and bring to a boil. Score a cross in the base of the tomatoes. Blanch the tomatoes in the boiling water for 20 seconds then plunge into a bowl of iced water to stop the cooking process. • Peel the tomatoes, cut in half crosswise, and squeeze gently to remove the seeds. • Cut the cucumbers in half lengthwise and remove and discard the seeds.
• Finely dice the tomato, cucumber, bell pepper, and onion and place in a salad bowl.

Dressing: Whisk the oil, vinegar, and garlic in a small bowl. Season with salt and pepper. • Drizzle the dressing over the salad and toss to combine.
• Serve.

Salad

4	medium tomatoes
2	Lebanese or ordinary cucumbers
2	green bell peppers (capsicums)
1	small red onion

Dressing

5	tablespoons (75 ml) extra-virgin olive oil
1½	tablespoons red wine vinegar
1	clove garlic, minced
	Salt and freshly ground black pepper

Serves: 4
Preparation: 15 minutes
Level: 1

SALADE NIÇOISE

Salad: Place the tomatoes in a colander and sprinkle lightly with salt. Let stand for 1 hour to drain. • Arrange the salad greens in four to six salad bowls with the tomatoes around the edges. Put the bell pepper, tuna, celery, and shallots in the center. • Arrange the olives and anchovy fillets on top. Garnish with the egg wedges.

Vinaigrette: Whisk the oil, vinegar, mustard, salt, and pepper in a small bowl. • Drizzle over the salad and serve.

532

Salad

10 medium firm tomatoes, cut into 8 wedges

Salt

3   cups (150 g) mixed salad greens

1   red bell pepper (capsicum), seeded and cut into thin strips

8   ounces (250 g) canned tuna, drained

3   stalks celery, thinly sliced

3   shallots, finely chopped

12 black olives

6   salt-cured anchovy fillets

4   hard-boiled eggs, quartered

Vinaigrette

½   cup (125 ml) extra-virgin olive oil

2   tablespoons white wine vinegar

1   teaspoon Dijon mustard

Salt and freshly ground black pepper

■ ■ ■ *There are many variations on this classic salad. Feel free to experiment, but always keep the basic mix of tomato, tuna, eggs, and anchovies.*

Serves: 4–6
Preparation: 15 minutes
  + 1 hour to drain
Level: 1

CAESAR SALAD

534

Salad: Preheat the oven to 425°F (220°C/gas 7). Arrange the bread on a baking sheet. Drizzle with the oil and season with salt and pepper. Bake until crisp and golden brown, about 5 minutes. • Sauté the prosciutto in a large non-stick frying pan over medium heat until crisp and golden brown, about 5 minutes. Break into smaller pieces. • Place the lettuce in a salad bowl. Add the bread cubes, eggs, and Parmesan cheese. Top with the prosciutto and season generously with pepper.

Dressing: Combine the mayonnaise and anchovies in a small bowl. Mix with a fork, mashing the anchovies until they dissolve into the mayonnaise. • Whisk in the lemon juice, garlic, Worcestershire sauce, mustard, and vinegar. • Drizzle the dressing over the salad and serve immediately.

■ ■ ■ *This is the classic Caesar Salad, invented by Rosa Cardini, daughter of Caesar, an Italian immigrant in San Diego and owner of a busy restaurant just across the border in Tijuana. On July 4th in 1924 the restaurant was crowded and ingredients were running short. Rosa used what she had left and made the salad directly at customer's tables.*

Salad

2   thick slices bread, cut into cubes

2   tablespoons extra-virgin olive oil

  Salt and freshly ground black pepper

6   large thin slices prosciutto

1   head romaine (cos) lettuce

4   hard-boiled eggs, quartered

2   ounces (60 g) Parmesan cheese, in shavings

Dressing

1/2   cup (125 ml) mayonnaise

4   salt-cured anchovy fillets

  Freshly squeezed juice of 1 1/2 lemons

2   cloves garlic, finely chopped

  Dash of Worcestershire sauce

1   teaspoon Dijon mustard

1   tablespoon white wine vinegar

Serves: 4
Preparation: 15 minutes + 1 hour to drain
Cooking: 5 minutes
Level: 1

YAM NUA (THAI BEEF SALAD)

Salad: Preheat a barbecue or char-grill on high heat. • Brush the steak with peanut oil and grill until well browned and rare on the inside, about 2 minutes on each side. Set aside on a plate to rest and cool slightly, about 10 minutes. • Combine the cucumber, tomatoes, bean sprouts, mint, cilantro, and basil in a medium bowl.

Dressing: Whisk the lime juice, fish sauce, kecap manis, sesame oil, jaggery, chile, ginger, and garlic in a small bowl. • Thinly slice the beef and add to the salad. • Drizzle the dressing over the salad and toss to coat. • Separate the lettuce leaves, rinsing well under cold running water, to make lettuce cups. • Spoon the salad into the lettuce cups and serve.

536

1	pound (500 g) beef fillet or sirloin steak
1	tablespoon peanut oil
1	cucumber, halved lengthwise and thinly sliced diagonally
3	medium tomatoes, cut into wedges
1	cup (50 g) mung bean sprouts
¼	cup fresh mint leaves
¼	cup fresh cilantro (coriander) leaves
¼	cup Thai or ordinary basil leaves
1	small iceberg lettuce

Dressing

¼	cup (60 ml) freshly squeezed lime juice
3	tablespoons Thai fish sauce
2	tablespoons kecap manis (sweet dark soy sauce)
1	tablespoon sesame oil
1	tablespoon coarsely grated jaggery (palm sugar) or brown sugar
2	large red chiles, seeded and thinly sliced
1	($3/4$-inch/2-cm) piece fresh ginger, peeled and finely chopped
2	cloves garlic, finely chopped

Serves: 4
Preparation: 20 minutes
  + 10 minutes to rest
Cooking: 5 minutes
Level: 1

THAI GREEN PAPAYA SALAD

Place a large saucepan of water on high heat and bring to a boil. Blanch the beans for 1 minute then plunge into iced water to stop the cooking process. • Drain and transfer to a large bowl. • Finely shred the papaya. • Add the papaya, tomatoes, chile, and half of the peanuts to the beans. • Grind the shrimp to a powder in a mortar and pestle or small food processor. • Add the garlic and blend to make a paste. • Strain the tamarind, reserving the water and discarding the pulp. • Place the shrimp paste, tamarind water, fish sauce, lime juice, and jaggery in a small bowl and stir to combine. • Drizzle the dressing over the papaya and toss to combine. • Serve garnished with the remaining peanuts.

8	ounces (250 g) snake beans or green beans, cut into 1-inch (2.5-cm) lengths
2	large green papaya (pawpaw), peeled and seeded
8	ounces (250 g) cherry tomatoes, halved
2	small red chiles, seeded and thinly sliced
½	cup (80 g) toasted peanuts, coarsely chopped
1½	tablespoons dried shrimp
2	cloves garlic, finely chopped
1	teaspoon tamarind soaked in 3 tablespoons water
3	tablespoons Thai fish sauce
2	tablespoons freshly squeezed lime juice
1	tablespoon coarsely grated jaggery (palm sugar) or raw sugar

Serves: 4
Preparation: 30 minutes
Level: 2

GADO GADO (INDONESIAN SALAD WITH PEANUT SAUCE)

540

Peanut Sauce: Heat the oil in a small frying pan over medium-low heat. Add the shallot, garlic, and chiles and sauté until softened, 3–4 minutes. • Remove from the heat and set aside to cool slightly. • Place the peanuts and shallot mixture in a large mortar and pestle or food processor and grind or blend to make a smooth paste. • Add the coconut milk, lime juice and zest, soy sauce, and jaggery and blend to make a thick sauce. • Transfer the sauce to a small saucepan. Add the water and bring to a boil over medium heat. • Remove from the heat. Season with salt. Set aside.

Salad: Place the eggs in a small saucepan and cover with water. Bring to a boil over and cook for 8 minutes. Drain and cool in cold water. Peel and cut in quarters lengthwise. • Place a large pan of water on high heat and bring to a boil. Add the potatoes and cook until tender, 8–10 minutes. Remove using a slotted spoon and set aside. • Bring the water back to a boil and add the carrot and beans and cook for 1 minute. Add the cauliflower and cook until the vegetables are just tender, 2–3 minutes. • Remove the vegetables with a slotted spoon and refresh under cold water. Set aside. • Bring the water back to a boil, add the cabbage and cook until wilted, about 30 seconds. Drain and refresh under cold running water. Set aside. • Heat the oil in a medium frying pan over medium-high heat. Add the tofu and sauté until golden brown, about 5 minutes. • Drain on paper towels. • Arrange the vegetables, bean sprouts, tofu, and boiled egg on a large serving plate. Drizzle with the peanut sauce and scatter with fried shallots.

Peanut Sauce
2 tablespoons peanut oil
1 shallot, coarsely chopped
2 cloves garlic, coarsely chopped
2 small red chiles, halved lengthwise and seeded
1 cup (150 g) raw peanuts, lightly roasted
½ cup (125 ml) coconut milk
2 tablespoons freshly squeezed lime juice
½ teaspoon finely grated lime zest
1 tablespoon soy sauce
2 teaspoons coarsely grated jaggery (palm sugar) or brown sugar
½ cup (125 ml) water
Salt

Salad
4 large eggs
2 medium potatoes, cubed
1 carrot, thickly sliced diagonally
4 ounces (125 g) green beans
½ head cauliflower, cut into small florets
3 cups (150 g) coarsely chopped Chinese cabbage
3 tablespoons peanut oil
8 ounces (250 g) firm tofu, sliced
2 cups (100 g) bean sprouts
Fried shallots, to serve

Serves: 4
Preparation: 30 minutes
Cooking: 10–15 minutes
Level: 2

PASTA SALAD WITH MOZZARELLA AND TOMATOES

Cook the pasta in a large pot of salted boiling water until al dente. • Drain and rinse under cold running water until cold. Drain again and dry on a clean cloth. • Place in a salad bowl and toss with 2 tablespoons of oil. • Add the mozzarella, tomatoes, scallions, and celery to the bowl. • Whisk the remaining 4 tablespoons (60 ml) of oil with the lemon juice, salt, and plenty of pepper in a small bowl. Drizzle over the salad and toss well. • Sprinkle with the oregano and basil, toss again, and serve.

1   **pound (500 g) farfalle (bow-tie) pasta**

6   **tablespoons (90 ml) extra-virgin olive oil**

14 **ounces (400 g) baby mozzarellas (bocconcini)**

24 **cherry tomatoes, halved**

2   **scallions (spring onions), finely chopped**

1   **celery heart, thinly sliced**

   Freshly squeezed juice of 1 lemon

   Salt and freshly ground black pepper

½ **teaspoon dried oregano**

   Fresh basil to garnish

Serves: 4–6
Preparation: 20 minutes
Cooking: 15 minutes
Level: 1

CHICKEN WALDORF

544

Salad: Heat the oil in a grill pan over high heat. Season the chicken with salt and pepper. Add to the pan and grill until tender and cooked through, about 10 minutes. Set aside and keep warm.
• Place the apples in a large bowl and drizzle with the lemon juice. Add the watercress and walnuts and toss gently. • Cut the chicken into 1/2-inch (1-cm) thick slices and add to the salad.
Ranch Dressing: Sprinkle the garlic with the salt and chop finely together. • Mix the garlic and salt, bell pepper, scallion, shallot, parsley, cilantro, lemon juice, and black pepper together in a medium bowl. Add the yogurt, mayonnaise, and sour cream and whisk until smooth and creamy. • Drizzle the ranch dressing over the salad and serve.

■ ■ ■ *The Waldorf salad was invented at the very chic Waldorf Hotel in New York in the 1890s. It originally consisted of apples, celery, grapes, and walnuts dressed with mayonnaise, but has been enriched with many more ingredients over time.*

Salad

2   tablespoons extra-virgin olive oil

4   boneless skinless chicken breast halves

    Salt and freshly ground black pepper

2   red apples, cored and sliced

2   tablespoons freshly squeezed lemon juice

2   cups (100 g) watercress

1/3 cup (50 g) walnuts, toasted

Ranch Dressing

1   small clove garlic, coarsely chopped

1/4 teaspoon salt

1   tablespoon minced red bell pepper, (capsicum)

1   tablespoon minced scallion (spring onion), white and green parts

1/2 tablespoon minced shallot

1   teaspoon minced fresh parsley leaves

1/2 teaspoon minced fresh cilantro (coriander) leaves

1/2 teaspoon freshly squeezed lemon juice

    Pinch freshly ground black pepper

1/4 cup (60 ml) plain yogurt

1/4 cup (60 ml) mayonnaise

2   tablespoons sour cream

Serves: 4–6
Preparation: 20 minutes
Cooking: 15 minutes
Level: 1

GARBANZO BEAN SALAD WITH TZATZIKI DRESSING

Salad: Combine the garbanzo beans, tomatoes, and bell peppers in a bowl.

Tzatziki Dressing: Whisk the oil, vinegar, yogurt, mustard, garlic, sugar, salt, and pepper in a small bowl. • Drizzle the dressing over the salad and toss gently. • Divide the salad evenly among six individual salad bowls and serve.

Salad

4   cups (800 g) canned garbanzo beans (chickpeas), drained

2   firm, ripe tomatoes, diced

1   green bell pepper (capsicum), cut into thin strips

1   yellow bell pepper (capsicum), cut into thin strips

Tzatziki Dressing

¼   cup (60 ml) extra-virgin olive oil

2   tablespoons cider vinegar

½   cup (125 ml) low-fat yogurt

1   tablespoon Dijon mustard

1   clove garlic, finely chopped

1   teaspoon sugar

    Salt and freshly ground black pepper

Serves: 6
Preparation: 15 minutes
Level: 1

MINTED BARLEY SALAD

Salad: Cook the barley in salted boiling water until tender, about 30 minutes. • Drain in a colander and rinse under cold running water. Drain again and dry in a clean kitchen towel. • Place the barley in a medium salad bowl and add the parsley, mint, scallions, tomatoes, and bell pepper.
Dressing: Whisk the oil, lemon juice, salt, and pepper in a small bowl. Drizzle over the salad and toss well. • Chill for 30 minutes before serving.

Salad

1½ **cups (200 g) pearl barley**

3 **tablespoons finely chopped fresh parsley**

2 **tablespoons finely chopped fresh mint**

4 **scallions (spring onions), finely chopped**

4 **tomatoes, chopped**

1 **red or green bell pepper (capsicum) finely diced**

Dressing

¼ **cup (60 ml) extra-virgin olive oil**

2 **tablespoons freshly squeezed lemon juice**

½ **teaspoon salt**

Freshly ground black pepper

Serves: 4
Preparation: 15 minutes
  + 30 minutes to chill
Cooking: 30 minutes
Level: 1

GRILLED EGGPLANT AND BELL PEPPER SALAD

550

Salad: Slice off the four sides of the bell pepper and trim off the curved ends so that the pieces lie flat. • Brush the skin side with oil. • Broil (grill) under a hot broiler skin-side up until the skin has blackened and blistered. Place in a plastic bag and let stand for 15 minutes. • Cut the eggplant into $1/4$ inch (5-mm) thick slices. • Brush both sides of the eggplant with oil. Broil (grill) on both sides until browned and cooked through. Place the eggplant on four serving dishes. • Remove the skin from the bell peppers and cut into small squares. Sprinkle over the eggplant.

Dressing: Whisk the oil, lemon juice, garlic, paprika, cayenne pepper, salt, and parsley in a small bowl. Drizzle over the eggplants. • Let stand for 10 minutes before serving.

Salad

1   **red bell pepper (capsicum)**

4   **medium eggplants (aubergines)**

$1/4$ **cup (60 ml) extra-virgin olive oil**

Dressing

5   **tablespoons (75 ml) extra-virgin olive oil**

2   **tablespoons freshly squeezed lemon juice**

2   **cloves garlic, finely chopped**

$1/2$ **teaspoon sweet paprika**

$1/4$ **teaspoon cayenne pepper**

     Salt

2   **tablespoons coarsely chopped fresh parsley**

Serves: 4
Preparation: 15 minutes
   + 25 minutes to stand
Cooking: 25 minutes
Level: 2

ROAST BEETS AND HAZELNUT SALAD

If the beets have their greens attached, remove them and set aside. • Preheat the oven to 400°F (200°C/gas 6) • Place the beets in a large bowl and drizzle with the oil. Toss well. Place the beets in a baking dish. Cover with foil or a lid and roast for 30–45 minutes (depending on size) until tender. • Remove the beets from the oven and set aside until cool enough to handle. Peel the skin away and discard. Slice the beets lengthwise and season with salt and pepper. • Heat 1 tablespoon of butter in a large frying pan over medium-high heat. Add the beet greens and toss until wilted, 1–2 minutes. Remove and set aside. • Add the balsamic vinegar to the pan and bring to a boil. Whisk in the remaining butter. Add beets to the pan and toss until the balsamic vinegar mixture has reduced and the beets are covered in a shiny sheen. • Transfer the beets to a bowl and top with the wilted leaves. Sprinkle with the dill and roasted hazelnuts. Season with extra pepper if liked, and serve.

552

18 small beets (beetroots), with peel, green stems attached if possible

3 tablespoons extra-virgin olive oil

Salt and freshly ground black pepper

2 tablespoons butter

2 tablespoons balsamic vinegar

3 tablespoons fresh dill, snipped

½ cup (70 g) hazelnuts, roasted and chopped

Serves: 4–6
Preparation: 20 minutes
Cooking: 30–45 minutes
Level: 1

EGGPLANT ZAALOOK (MOROCCAN COOKED EGGPLANT SALAD)

Cut the eggplant into $1^1/2$ inch (4 cm) dice. • Heat the oil in a large frying pan over medium-low heat. Add the garlic, paprika, and cumin and sauté until softened and fragrant, 3–4 minutes • Add the eggplant and cook over low heat for 15 minutes. • Meanwhile, place a medium saucepan of water over high heat and bring to a boil. Score a cross in the base of the tomatoes. Blanch the tomatoes in the boiling water for 20 seconds then plunge into a bowl of iced water to stop the cooking process. • Peel the tomatoes, cut in half crosswise, and remove and discard the seeds. Coarsely chop the flesh. • Add the tomatoes to the eggplant and simmer until softened, 20–30 minutes. • Add the lemon juice, parsley, and cilantro and roughly mash together to make a chunky purée. Season with salt and pepper. • Serve warm or at room temperature.

3 large eggplant (aubergines)

$1/3$ cup (90 ml) extra-virgin olive oil

2 cloves garlic, minced

$1^1/2$ teaspoons hot paprika

1 teaspoon cumin

3 medium tomatoes

3 tablespoons freshly squeezed lemon juice

3 tablespoons finely chopped fresh parsley

3 tablespoons finely chopped fresh cilantro (coriander)

Salt and freshly ground black pepper

Serves: 4
Preparation: 15 minutes
Cooking: 40–50 minutes
Level: 1

DESSERTS

LOKUM (TURKISH DELIGHT)

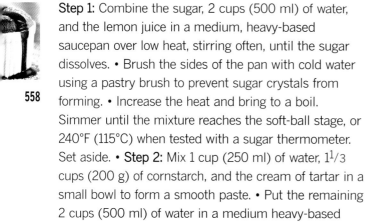

558

Step 1: Combine the sugar, 2 cups (500 ml) of water, and the lemon juice in a medium, heavy-based saucepan over low heat, stirring often, until the sugar dissolves. • Brush the sides of the pan with cold water using a pastry brush to prevent sugar crystals from forming. • Increase the heat and bring to a boil. Simmer until the mixture reaches the soft-ball stage, or 240°F (115°C) when tested with a sugar thermometer. Set aside. • **Step 2:** Mix 1 cup (250 ml) of water, $1^1/3$ cups (200 g) of cornstarch, and the cream of tartar in a small bowl to form a smooth paste. • Put the remaining 2 cups (500 ml) of water in a medium heavy-based saucepan and bring to a boil. • Pour the paste into the boiling water, whisking to combine. **Step 3:** Cook, stirring constantly, until very thick, 3–4 minutes. • Gradually stir the sugar syrup into the thickened mixture. • Decrease the heat to low and cook, stirring frequently, until thick, syrupy, and a pale golden color, 35–40 minutes. • **Step 4:** Turn off the heat and stir in the rose water and food coloring. • Line a 7 x 11-inch (18 x 28 cm) cake pan with parchment paper and lightly grease with oil. • **Step 5:** Spoon the mixture into the pan and spread with a lightly oiled spatula to create a smooth surface. Cover with lightly oiled parchment paper and let set overnight. • **Step 6:** When set, cut into 36 squares with an oiled knife. • Sift the confectioners' sugar and remaining 4 tablespoons of cornstarch into a medium bowl. Add the squares a few at a time and toss to coat. • Store in an airtight container, with parchment paper between each layer to prevent sticking.

4	cups (800 g) sugar
5	cups (1.25 liters) water
2	teaspoons freshly squeezed lemon juice, strained
$1^1/3$	cups (200 g) + 4 tablespoons cornstarch (cornflour)
$1^1/2$	teaspoons cream of tartar
2	tablespoons rose water
	Few drops red food coloring
	Vegetable oil to grease
$1/3$	cup (50 g) confectioners' (icing) sugar

Makes: 36 pieces
Preparation: 45 minutes
   + 12 hours to set
Cooking: About 1 hour
Level: 3

PREPARING LOKUM

Lokum, or Turkish Delight, as it is known in most western countries, is a popular sweet all over the Middle East. According to legend, it was invented by Hadji Bekir, confectioner to the sultan at the royal court in Constantinople at the end of the 18th century. There are many flavors, and some versions contain chopped nuts or puréed apricots. Ours is a classic recipe.

1. COMBINE the sugar, 2 cups (500 ml) of water, and lemon juice over low heat. Brush the sides of the pan to prevent sugar crystals from forming.

2. MIX 1 cup (250 ml) of water, $1^1/3$ cups (200 g) of cornstarch, and cream of tartar. • Bring 2 cups (500 ml) of water to a boil and whisk in the paste.

3. COOK, stirring constantly, until very thick, 3–4 minutes. Gradually stir in the sugar syrup and simmer for 35–40 minutes.

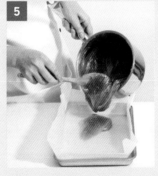

4. TURN OFF the heat and stir in the rose water and food coloring.

5. SPOON the mixture into the pan and spread with an oiled spatula. Cover with oiled parchment paper and let set overnight.

6. CUT into 36 squares with an oiled knife. Roll in the confectioners' sugar and cornstarch.

TRUFFLES

562

Place the chocolate in a large bowl. • Bring the cream to boiling point in a saucepan over medium heat. • Pour over the chocolate and stir until the chocolate has melted and the mixture is smooth and well blended. Set aside to cool. • Stir in the rum extract. • Refrigerate until the mixture is thick, 3–4 hours. • Sift the cocoa into a dessert plate and dust your hands with it. • Shape the chocolate mixture into truffles about the size of a large marble. • Roll one-third of the truffles in the coconut, one-third in the almonds, and one-third in the cocoa. • Store in the refrigerator for up to two days.

8   **ounces (250 g) dark chocolate**

1   **cup (250 ml) heavy (double) cream**

2   **tablespoons dark rum extract (essence)**

1/2 **cup (75 g) unsweetened cocoa powder to dust**

Shredded (desiccated) coconut, to decorate

Finely chopped almonds to decorate

Makes: About 30 truffles
Preparation: 20 minutes
   + 3–4 hours to chill
Cooking: 5 minutes
Level: 1

■ ■ ■ *Truffles are easy to prepare and are a wonderful, slightly extravagant way to finish a meal. Serve with cups of expresso coffee.*

CRÈME CARAMEL WITH FRESH FRUIT SALAD

564

Crème Caramel: Preheat the oven to 350°F (180°C/gas 4). • Oil a 6-cup (1.5-liter) pudding mold or ovenproof bowl. • Heat the milk in a medium saucepan over low heat. • Add $1/2$ cup (100 g) of sugar and stir until dissolved. Add the vanilla and bring to a boil. Remove from the heat and discard the vanilla pod. • Whisk the eggs lightly in a bowl then whisk in the hot milk mixture. • Put the remaining $1/2$ cup (100 g) of sugar in a small saucepan over medium-low heat and cook until caramelized, 5–10 minutes. • Pour the caramel into the prepared mold. • Pour the custard into the mold over the caramel. • Place the mold in a roasting pan and fill the pan with enough water to come half way up the sides. Bake for about 1 hour, until just set in the center. • Let cool completely. Chill in the refrigerator for at least 3 hours.
Fresh Fruit Salad: Combine the strawberries, peaches, banana, and lemon juice in a bowl. Stir in the brown sugar and rum. • Heat the preserves in a small saucepan over low heat. • Turn the crème caramel out onto a serving dish. Serve with the fruit salad drizzled with the preserves.

Crème Caramel

4	cups (1 liter) milk
1	cup (200 g) sugar
1	vanilla pod
6	large eggs

Fresh Fruit Salad

2	cups (300 g) strawberries, sliced
4	canned peach halves, drained and cut into small cubes
1	large ripe banana, peeled and slices
	Freshly squeezed juice of 1 lemon
2	tablespoons brown sugar
2	tablespoons rum
$1/3$	cup (100 g) black currant preserves (jam)

Serves: 4–6
Preparation: 30 minutes
  + 3 hours to chill
Cooking: $1^1/4$ hours
Level: 2

■ ■ ■ *Another simple, classic dessert. We have suggested that you serve the crème caramel with fresh fruit salad, but it can also be served by itself. If preferred, cook the custard in 4–6 ramekins.*

CHOCOLATE MOUSSE

Combine the chocolate and butter in a double boiler over barely simmering water, stirring occasionally, until melted and smooth. • Beat the sugar and egg yolks with an electric mixer on high speed until thick. • With mixer on low, or by hand, gradually add the chocolate and coffee, beating until combined. • Beat the egg whites with an electric mixer on medium speed until soft peaks form. • In a separate bowl whip the cream until soft peaks form. • Fold the egg whites and cream into the chocolate mixture. • Spoon the mousse into serving dishes, cover, and refrigerate for 4 hours. • Serve topped with whipped cream and chocolate curls.

6   ounces (180 g) top quality dark chocolate, coarsely chopped

$1/4$ cup (60 g) butter, cubed

$1/2$ cup (100 g) superfine (caster) sugar

3   large eggs, separated

$1/4$ cup (60 ml) very strong black coffee

$1/3$ cup (90 ml) heavy (double) cream + extra whipped to serve

Chocolate curls to serve

Serves: 4
Preparation: 20 minutes + 4 hours to chill
Cooking: 10 minutes
Level: 1

■ ■ ■ *This classic French dessert is simple to prepare and always a winner. Top with a few fresh raspberries, if liked.*

BLUE MERINGUE

Meringue: Preheat the oven to 225°F (110°C/gas 1/2). • Line two baking sheets with parchment paper. • **Step 1:** Put the egg whites and salt in a clean bowl. Begin by whisking gently, gradually increasing speed as the whites gain in volume. If beating with an electric mixer, begin on low and work up to medium speed. • **Step 2:** When the egg whites stand in soft peaks add the cream of tartar and begin adding the sugar a few tablespoons at a time. It should take 2–3 minutes to beat in all the sugar. Do not overbeat. If beating with an electric mixer, increase speed to high. • **Step 3:** Fill a piping bag about half full with the meringue and twist the top closed to stop the meringue from spilling out. Pipe out meringues onto the baking sheets, spacing well. • **Step 4:** Disks of meringue can be made in the same way. Fill the piping bag with meringue and pipe in a spiral pattern, beginning in the center to make disks about 9 inches (23 cm) in diameter. • **Step 5:** Bake for about 1 hour, until the meringues peel away easily from the paper and feel firm to the touch on the bottoms.

Filling: Beat the cream, confectioners' sugar, and vanilla in a medium bowl until thick. Add enough blue coloring to make an ice-blue cream. • Stick the meringues together in pairs with the cream and decorate with the candied violets. • Alternatively, spread three-quarters of the cream on one disk of meringue and top with the other disk. Spread with the remaining cream and decorate with the violets.

Meringues

4	large egg whites
1/8	teaspoon salt
1¼	cups (250 g) superfine (caster) sugar
1/2	teaspoon cream of tartar

Filling

1	cup (250 ml) heavy (double) cream
1	tablespoon confectioners' (icing) sugar
1/2	teaspoon vanilla extract (essence)
	Few drops blue food coloring
	Candied violets to decorate

Serves: 6–8
Preparation: 30 minutes
Cooking: 1 hour
Level: 1

You can either make small meringues and stick them together with the colored filling or make two large disks of meringue and fill with the cream. For perfect meringue, always make sure that the eggs whites contain no traces of yolk and add the sugar very gradually, beating it so that it dissolves into the whites before baking.

1. PUT the egg whites and salt in a clean bowl. Begin by whisking gently, gradually increasing speed as the whites gain in volume.

2. WHEN the egg whites stand in soft peaks add the cream of tartar and begin adding the sugar a few tablespoons at a time. Do not overbeat.

3. FILL a piping bag about half full with the meringue and twist the top closed to stop the meringue from spilling out. Pipe out meringues onto the baking sheets, spacing well.

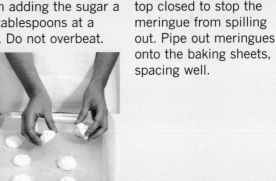

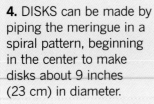

4. DISKS can be made by piping the meringue in a spiral pattern, beginning in the center to make disks about 9 inches (23 cm) in diameter.

5. BAKE for about 1 hour, until the meringues peel away easily from the paper and feel firm to the touch on the bottoms.

MINI BOMBE ALASKA

572

Strawberry Ice Cream: Combine the cream and vanilla bean and seeds in a medium saucepan over medium-low heat and bring to a boil. Remove from the heat and set aside. • Beat the egg yolks and sugar in a medium heatproof bowl with an electric mixer on high speed until pale and creamy. • Slowly stir one-third of the hot cream into the egg mixture. Stir in the rest. • Place the bowl over a saucepan of barely simmering water and cook, stirring constantly, until the custard coats the back of a spoon. Remove from the heat, discarding the vanilla bean. • Purée the strawberries and liqueur in a blender and strain through a fine-mesh sieve. Stir into the custard and refrigerate until cooled, about 30 minutes. • Pour the mixture into an ice-cream maker and churn according to the manufacturer's instructions.

Meringue Topping and Base: Preheat the oven to 425°F (220°C/gas 7). • Line a baking sheet with parchment paper. • Beat the egg whites in a medium bowl with an electric mixer on medium speed until soft peaks form. Gradually beat in the sugar until stiff peaks form. • Melt the preserves in a small saucepan over low heat. Brush generously on one side of the ladyfingers. Sandwich two fingers together using a little meringue mixture as glue, and place side by side on the prepared sheet. Continue until you have six sponge finger bases. • Place a scoop of ice cream on each base. Cover completely with a large dollop of the meringue. Create decorative peaks using a spatula or the back of a spoon. • Immediately bake for 4–5 minutes, or until golden. • Serve immediately.

Strawberry Ice Cream

2 cups (500 ml) heavy (double) cream

1/2 vanilla bean, split lengthwise and seeds scraped

5 large egg yolks

1/2 cup (100 g) superfine (caster) sugar

3 cups (500 g) fresh strawberries

1 tablespoon strawberry liqueur

Meringue Topping and Base

3 large egg whites

1/2 cup (100 g) superfine (caster) sugar

1/2 cup (100 g) strawberry preserves (jam)

12 small ladyfingers (sponge fingers)

Serves: 6
Preparation: 45 minutes
   + 30 minutes to cool
   + time to churn
Cooking: 15 minutes
Level: 2

FRESH FRUIT SALAD WITH MERINGUE

574

Fresh Fruit Salad: Cut the pineapple in half vertically. Scoop out the flesh, reserving the juice and shells. Remove the hard core and chop the flesh into bite-sized pieces. • Place in a bowl with the juice. • Segment the orange and add to the bowl. • Add all the remaining fruit to the bowl. • Mix in the lime juice, kirsch, and vanilla sugar. • Spoon the fruit salad into the pineapple shells, piling it up in the middle.

Meringue Topping: Preheat the oven to 425°F (220°C/gas 7). • Beat the egg whites with an electric mixer in a large clean bowl until soft peaks form. Gradually beat the sugar into the meringue until glossy and standing in stiff peaks. • Spoon the meringue over the fruit salad, making sure the edges are sealed. • Place the pineapple halves on a baking sheet and bake for 5–8 minutes, until the meringue is golden. • Serve within and hour of baking the meringue.

Fresh Fruit Salad

1   large fresh pineapple, with leaves

1   orange, peeled

1   banana, peeled and sliced

1   kiwifruit, peeled and sliced

1   large peach or 2 apricots, peeled, pitted, and thinly sliced

1   mango, peeled, pitted, and chopped into small pieces

1   cup (150 g) fresh strawberries, hulled

1   small bunch of seedless grapes (about 5 ounces/ 150 g), halved

1   tablespoon freshly squeezed lime juice

2   tablespoons kirsch or white rum

1   teaspoon vanilla sugar

Meringue Topping

3   large egg whites

$3/4$ cup (150 g) superfine (caster) sugar

Serves: 4–6
Preparation: 30 minutes
Cooking: 5–8 minutes
Level: 1

GREEN APPLE SORBET WITH CALVADOS

Combine the sugar, $^3/4$ cup (200 ml) of the water, and glucose in a saucepan over medium heat and bring to a boil. Remove from the heat and let cool. • Peel and core the apples, then slice thinly. Put in a bowl of cold water with the lemon juice. • Drain the apples and chop in a food processor until smooth. • Measure 1 cup (250 g) of the apple purée and stir it into the cooled sugar syrup. Stir in the remaining $^1/4$ cup (60 ml) of water and the food coloring, if using. • Transfer to an ice-cream maker and churn according to the manufacturer's instructions. • Serve the sorbet in 4–6 small glasses. • Drizzle with Calvados and serve.

$^3/4$ **cup (150 g) sugar**

1 **cup (250 ml) water**

2 **tablespoons (30 g) glucose or light corn (golden) syrup**

2–3 **drops green food coloring (optional)**

2 **Granny Smith apples**

Freshly squeezed juice of 1 lemon

Calvados at room temperature

Serves: 4
Preparation: 15 minutes
    + time to churn
Cooking: 10 minutes
Level: 1

■ ■ ■ *Calvados is an apple brandy produced in Normandy. Replace with another apple brandy or liqueur if preferred.*

GREEN TEA ICE CREAM

Combine the water and tea powder in a small bowl and set aside. • Combine the milk and cream in a medium saucepan over medium-high heat and bring to a boil. • Meanwhile, beat the egg yolks and sugar in a medium bowl with an electric mixer on high speed until pale and thick. • Pour in the tea mixture and stir to combine. • Gradually pour the hot milk mixture into the yolks, whisking to combine. • Return to the saucepan and cook, stirring continuously, over low heat until the mixture begins to thicken, 8–10 minutes. Do not over heat or the mixture will curdle. • Rest the pan in a sink full of iced water, stirring occasionally, until the mixture has cooled. • Strain through a fine-mesh sieve. • Pour the mixture into an ice cream machine and churn according to the manufacturer's instructions. • If you do not have an ice-cream maker, pour the mixture into a freezer-proof container and freeze for 1 hour. • Stir with a fork to break up the ice particles and return to the freezer. Repeat this process 3–4 times, until the ice cream is thick, creamy, and frozen.

2 tablespoons boiling water

1 tablespoon green tea powder

1 cup (250 ml) milk

1 cup (250 ml) heavy (double) cream

2 large egg yolks

1/4 cup (50 g) superfine (caster) sugar

Serves: 4
Preparation: 15 minutes
  + time to churn
Cooking: 10 minutes
Level: 2

FRUITY TIRAMISÙ

580

Set out a deep glass bowl, about 8–10 inches (20–25 cm) in diameter. • Scoop out the passion fruit seeds and pulp and push through a fine-mesh sieve. Reserve the passion fruit purée. • Immerse the nectarines or peaches in boiling water, leave for 2–3 minutes. Drain, cut in half, pit, and peel. Finely chop the flesh and add to the purée. • Sweeten the coffee with the vanilla sugar and 2 tablespoons of Marsala. Pour into a shallow dish. • In a separate bowl, whisk the mascarpone with the superfine sugar and vanilla. Whisk in the remaining 6 tablespoons (90 ml) Marsala and the orange juice. • Dip half the cookies into the coffee mixture and use them to line the bottom of the glass bowl. • Spread with half the mascarpone mixture and sprinkle with grated chocolate. Spoon the fruit over the chocolate. • Place the remaining cookies in the dish to soak up the coffee mixture, and arrange on top of the fruit. Dust with 1 tablespoon of cocoa. Spread the remaining mascarpone over the cookies, dust with the remaining 1 tablespoon of cocoa powder, and sprinkle with the chocolate shavings and orange zest. • Refrigerate for at least 4 hours before serving.

4   ounces (125 g) dark (70% cacao) chocolate, coarsely grated + extra shavings to decorate

4   ripe passion fruits or granadillas, cut in half

2   ripe nectarines or peaches

$1\frac{1}{4}$ cups (300 ml) brewed strong coffee

2   tablespoons vanilla sugar

8   tablespoons (125 ml) Marsala wine or medium-dry sherry

2   cups (500 g) mascarpone cheese

2   tablespoons superfine (caster) sugar

2   teaspoons vanilla extract (essence)

2   tablespoons freshly squeezed orange juice, strained

8   ounces (250 g) almond cookies or biscotti

2   tablespoons unsweetened cocoa powder

1   tablespoon finely grated zest from an organic orange to decorate

Serves: 4–6
Preparation: 40 minutes
   + 4 hours to chill
Level: 2

PEARS IN RED WINE

Preheat the oven to 350°F (180°C/gas 4). • Peel the pears carefully, leaving them whole with the stem still attached. • Transfer to a deep casserole into which they fit snugly, standing upright, stem-side up. Sprinkle with half the sugar. Pour in the wine and add the cloves, lemon zest, and cinnamon. • Bake for about 1 hour, or until tender. The time will vary depending on how firm the pears are. Test by inserting a thin skewer deep into one to see if it is tender. They should be an attractive russet color. • Lift the pears carefully out of the wine and place upright in a serving dish or individual glass dishes. • Reduce the cooking liquid over medium heat until it has thickened to a pouring syrup. Discard the cloves, lemon zest, and cinnamon and pour the syrup over the pears. • Serve at room temperature.

4 large firm cooking pears

$1^1/4$ cups (250 g) sugar

3 cups (750 ml) full-bodied, dry red wine

3 cloves

2 pieces lemon zest

1 ($^3/4$-inch/2-cm) cinnamon stick

Serves: 4
Preparation: 10 minutes
Cooking: About $1^1/4$ hours
Level: 1

BAKED AMARETTI APPLES

584

Preheat the oven to 350°F (180°C/gas 4). • Remove the cores from the apples using an apple corer. Score the skin around the circumference, so that it splits neatly when it cooks. • Combine the brown sugar, butter, amaretti cookies, almonds, and cloves in a small bowl, using your fingers to mix together. • Stuff the apples with the amaretti filling and place in a small baking pan into which they will fit snugly. • Heat the apple juice and honey in a small saucepan over medium heat until the honey has melted, about 3 minutes. • Pour the apple juice mixture over and around the apples. • Bake for 50 minutes, or until the apples are soft and cooked through. • To serve, place the apples on individual serving plates, drizzle with a little of the syrup, and place a dollop of crème fraîche on the side.

4	tart apples, such as Granny Smith
4	teaspoons light brown sugar
4	teaspoons unsalted butter, softened
6	amaretti cookies, crushed
2	tablespoons flaked almonds
1/2	teaspoon ground cloves
1	cup (250 ml) apple juice
2	tablespoons honey
1/2	cup (125 ml) crème fraîche or whipped cream

Serves: 4
Preparation: 10 minutes
Cooking: 50–55 minutes
Level: 1

CHERRY CLAFOUTIS

Put the cherries in a bowl with 2 tablespoons of the kirsch. Let soak for 1 hour. • Combine the flour and sugar in a medium bowl. Beat in the egg yolks, milk, and 3 tablespoons of the melted butter until smooth. • Drain the cherries, adding the kirsch juice to the batter. • In a clean bowl, whisk the egg whites until stiff. Fold into the batter. • Preheat the oven to 375°F (190°C/gas 5). • Brush the remaining butter over the bottom and sides of a 9-inch (23-cm) pie pan or an ovenproof dish with a pastry brush. • Put the cherries in the prepared pan and shake the pan to distribute them evenly. Pour in the batter and shake again, so everything is level. • Bake for 25–30 minutes, until golden, puffed, and set in the center. • Remove from the oven and drizzle with the remaining 2 tablespoons kirsch. Let cool for 15 minutes. • Dust generously with confectioners' sugar before serving straight from the dish.

1	pound (500 g) black cherries, stems removed and pitted
4	tablespoons (60 ml) kirsch or dark rum to soak
1/2	cup (75 g) all-purpose (plain) flour
1/3	cup (75 g) superfine (caster) sugar
2	large eggs, separated
1 1/4	cups (300 ml) milk
4	tablespoons (60 g) unsalted butter, melted
	Confectioners' (icing) sugar to dust

Serves: 4
Preparation: 20 minutes
    + 1 hour to soak + 15
    minutes to cool
Cooking: 25–30 minutes
Level: 1

■ ■ ■ *This cherry pudding originally comes from the Limousin region of France, where it is made with unpitted sour cherries. Although pitting is tedious, we suggest that you do so. If using canned or bottled cherries, drain well before using.*

PINEAPPLE SOUFFLÉS

Soufflés: Preheat the oven to 325°F (170°C/gas 3).
• Oil six 1-cup (250-ml) ramekins. • Cook the
pineapple in a saucepan over high heat until all the
juice has evaporated, 1–2 minutes. • Transfer to a
food processor and chop until smooth. • Combine
the milk, cream, and lemon zest in a saucepan over
medium heat and bring to a boil. • Beat 1 whole egg
and 2 egg yolks with the flour and sugar in a
saucepan. • Very slowly add the boiling milk
mixture, stirring constantly. • Cook over low heat,
stirring constantly, until thickened, 5–7 minutes.
• Remove from the heat and stir in the butter. Let
cool. • Stir in the pineapple purée. • Beat the 6
egg whites in a large bowl until stiff. Fold into the
pineapple mixture. • Spoon the mixture into the
ramekins. • Bake until well risen and lightly
browned, about 20 minutes.

Sauce: Combine three-quarters of the pineapple
with the sugar in a food processor and chop until
smooth. • Stir in the crème de cassis and the
reserved pineapple. • Dust the soufflés with
confectioners' sugar and serve hot with the
pineapple sauce.

588

Soufflés

1¼ cups (250 g) crushed canned pineapple, drained
1 cup (250 ml) milk
¼ cup (60 ml) heavy (double) cream
Finely grated zest of ¼ lemon
3 large eggs, separated + 4 large egg whites
½ cup (75 g) all-purpose (plain) flour
½ cup (100 g) sugar
2 tablespoons butter

Sauce

1¼ cups (250 g) crushed canned pineapple, drained
¼ cup (50 g) sugar
1 tablespoon crème de cassis
2 tablespoons confectioners' (icing) sugar

Serves: 6
Preparation: 20 minutes
Cooking: 45 minutes
Level: 3

CHOCOLATE SOUFFLÉS

590

Chocolate Sauce: Melt the chocolate and butter in a double boiler over barely simmering water. • Bring the milk to a boil in a small saucepan. Remove from the heat and gradually beat into the melted chocolate. Set aside.

Soufflé: Preheat the oven to 450°F (230°C/gas 8). • Butter six individual $3/4$-cup (180-ml) soufflé molds. • Sift the flour into a small bowl. • Bring the milk to a boil in a small saucepan. • Place the chocolate in a saucepan over medium heat and pour in $3/4$ cup (180 ml) milk, beating until smooth. Do not let it boil. • Pour in the remaining milk and bring to a boil for 30 seconds. Remove from the heat and set aside. • Beat 4 egg yolks with the sugar in a large bowl with an electric mixer at high speed until pale and thick. With mixer at low speed, gradually beat in the flour, followed by the chocolate mixture. • Return to the saucepan and bring to a boil over medium heat for 1 minute. Transfer to a large bowl and let cool. • Beat the remaining 4 egg yolks into the chocolate mixture. • With mixer at high speed, beat the egg whites with the salt in a large bowl until stiff peaks form. • Use a large rubber spatula to fold the egg whites into the chocolate mixture. • Pour the batter into the prepared molds. • Bake for 8–10 minutes, or until risen. • Dust with confectioners' sugar. • Serve with the chocolate sauce spooned over the top.

Chocolate Sauce

5   ounces (150 g) dark chocolate, coarsely chopped

1   tablespoon butter

$1/3$ cup (90 ml) milk

Soufflé

$1/2$ cup (75 g) all-purpose (plain) flour

$1 2/3$ cups (400 ml) milk

5   ounces (150 g) dark chocolate, coarsely chopped

8   large eggs, separated

$1/2$ cup (100 g) sugar

$1/8$ teaspoon salt

Confectioners' (icing) sugar to dust

Serves: 4–6
Preparation: 45 minutes
Cooking: 1 hour
Level: 3

ROMAN CREAM CAKES

592

Dissolve the yeast in $1/2$ cup (125 ml) of the warm water. Let stand until foamy, about 10 minutes.
• Sift 1 cup (150 g) of flour into a large bowl and make a well in the center. Pour in the yeast mixture and enough warm water to form a firm dough.
• Place the dough in a clean bowl. Cover with a clean cloth and let rise in a warm place until doubled in bulk, about 45 minutes. • While the dough is rising, lightly beat together 3 eggs and the egg yolks, oil, sugar, lemon zest, and vanilla in a medium bowl. • Sift the remaining 2 cups (300 g) flour onto a work surface and make a well in the center. Knead in the egg mixture. Continue kneading as you gradually add the remaining water to form a soft dough. • Knead in the dough that has doubled in bulk. • Shape into 2-inch (5-cm) long oval loaves. Arrange on greased baking sheets and cover with a kitchen towel. Let rest in a warm place until doubled in bulk, about 45 minutes. • Preheat the oven to 350°F (180°C/gas 4). • Beat the remaining egg and brush over the loaves. • Bake for 15–20 minutes, or until golden brown. • Beat the cream in a medium bowl until stiff. Fit a pastry bag with a $1/2$-inch (1-cm) star tip and fill with the cream. • Slice the cooled loaves horizontally and pipe in the cream. Dust generously with confectioners' sugar.

$1/2$ ounce (15 g) fresh compressed yeast or 1 ($1/4$-ounce/7-g) package active dry yeast

$1^1/3$ cups (300 ml) lukewarm water

3 cups (450 g) all-purpose (plain) flour

4 large eggs + 2 large egg yolks

3 tablespoons extra-virgin olive oil or other vegetable oil

$3/4$ cup (150 g) sugar

Finely grated zest of 1 lemon

1 teaspoon vanilla extract (essence)

1 cup (250 ml) heavy (double) cream

Confectioners' (icing) sugar to dust

Serves: 8–12
Preparation: 50 minutes + $1^1/2$ hours to rise
Cooking: 15–20 minutes
Level: 2

■ ■ ■ *These little buns are known as "maritozzi" and are a typical Roman treat.*

BERRY MILLEFEUILLE

594

Pastry: Preheat the oven to 400°F (200°C/gas 6).
• Line a large baking sheet with parchment paper.
• Roll out the pastry on a lightly floured surface, cut into two rectangles measuring about 9 x 4 inches (23 x 10 cm), and place on the baking sheet. Prick each pastry rectangle all over with a fork. • Bake for 10–12 minutes, until puffed and golden. Transfer at once to racks and sprinkle evenly with confectioners' sugar. Leave to cool. • When cold, cut the pastry rectangles in half lengthwise with a serrated knife.
Filling: Combine the raspberries and strawberries in a bowl. Add the vinegar and superfine sugar. Stir and set aside for 20 minutes. • Beat the cream in a medium bowl until thickened. Fold in the mascarpone. Stir in the fruit. Refrigerate this mixture for at least 1 hour. • Assemble the pastries about an hour before serving. • Place a pastry sheet on a serving plate or board and spread with one-third of the filling. Top with another sheet and a layer of filling and press down gently. Repeat the process, finishing with the last pastry sheet on top. • Dust with confectioners' sugar. Cut into slices with a serrated knife and serve.

■■■*Millefeuille, better known in North America as a Napoleon, is made up of layers of puff pastry, usually filled with vanilla pastry cream. A classic French dessert, its original name can be translated as "thousand layer cake." An excellent, very crisp Napoleon can also be made using phyllo pastry instead of puff pastry.*

Pastry

1   sheet (about 8 ounces/250 g) puff pastry, thawed if frozen

1–2 tablespoons confectioners' (icing) sugar

Filling

1   cup (150 g) fresh raspberries

1   cup (150 g) fresh strawberries, sliced

1   teaspoon balsamic vinegar

2   tablespoons superfine (caster) sugar

1/2   cup (125 ml) heavy (double) cream

8   ounces (250 g) mascarpone cheese

Serves: 6–8
Preparation: 50 minutes
  + 80 minutes to chill
Cooking: 10–12 minutes
Level: 2

MOROCCAN FILLED PASTRY SNAKE

596

Pastry: Combine the ground almonds, confectioners' sugar, and cinnamon in a medium bowl. Add the orange flower water and stir to combine. • Divide the filling into three equal portions and shape into logs, slightly shorter than the width of a sheet of filo pastry. • Preheat the oven to 350°F (180°C/gas 4). • Line a large baking sheet with parchment paper. • Lay three sheets of filo pastry on top of each other, brushing with melted butter between each layer. Keep the remaining filo covered with a damp clean kitchen towel to prevent it from drying out. **Step 1:** Place a log of filling across the long edge of the prepared pastry and loosely roll up (leaving room for the filling to expand when cooking) to enclose. Repeat the process with the remaining filling and filo sheets. • **Step 2:** Place one of the pastry logs on the prepared baking sheet, seam-side down. Curve to form a tight spiral, pinching the center end closed. Wrap the remaining logs, one at a time around the spiral, joining the ends together, to create a coiled snake-shaped pastry. • Brush the top with the remaining melted butter and egg yolk. • Bake for 30 minutes, until crisp and golden brown. **Honey Syrup:** Heat the honey and orange flower water in a small saucepan. • **Step 3:** Remove the M'hencha from the oven and brush with honey syrup. Set aside to cool slightly. • Serve warm or at room temperature.

Pastry

1¹/₃ cups (150 g) ground almonds

³/₄ cup (125 g) confectioners' (icing) sugar

1 teaspoon ground cinnamon

3 tablespoons orange flower water

9 sheets filo pastry

¹/₄ cup (60 g) butter, melted

1 large egg yolk

Honey Syrup

3 tablespoons honey, warmed

1 tablespoon orange flower water

Serves: 12
Preparation: 30 minutes
Cooking: 30 minutes
Level: 2

PREPARING MOROCCAN FILLED PASTRY SNAKE

This delicious sweet pastry is known as M'hencha (snake) in Morocco where it is served on all special occasions. In a popular variation the almonds are replaced with same amount of pistachos.

1. PLACE a log of filling across the long edge of the pastry and loosely roll up (leaving room for the filling to expand when cooking) to enclose.

2. PLACE one of the pastry logs on the prepared baking sheet, seam-side down. Curve to form a tight spiral, pinching the center end closed. Wrap the remaining logs, one at a time around the spiral, joining the ends together, to create a coiled snake.

3. BRUSH the cooked pastry with the honey syrup while still warm. Serve warm or at room temperature.

GOOD FRIDAY FRITTERS

Bring the milk, 3 tablespoons of sugar, and aniseeds to a boil in a medium saucepan. Stir in the vanilla. • Sift the flour into a large bowl. • Stir in the lemon zest and cinnamon and make a well in the center. • Pour in the boiling milk mixture and stir until smooth. • Add the eggs, one at a time, whisking until just blended after each addition. • Stir in the apples. • Heat the oil in a large frying pan to very hot. • Fry tablespoons of the batter in batches until golden brown all over, about 5 minutes each batch. • Drain well on paper towels. • Dust with the remaining sugar and aniseeds and serve warm.

600

$1^3/4$ **cups (430 ml) milk**

$1/2$ **cup (100 g) sugar**

1 **teaspoon ground aniseeds + extra to dust**

$1/2$ **teaspoon vanilla extract (essence)**

$1^1/2$ **cups (225 g) all-purpose (plain) flour**

Finely grated zest of 1 organic lemon

$1/2$ **teaspoon ground cinnamon**

4 **large eggs**

4 **apples, peeled, cored, and finely chopped**

2 **cups (500 ml) olive oil, for frying**

Serves: 4–6
Preparation: 15 minutes
Cooking: 20 minutes
Level: 2

■ ■ ■ *These fritters come from Italy where they are traditionally served on Good Friday.*

GHULAB JAMAN (INDIAN DUMPLINGS)

602

Syrup: Combine the water, sugar, cardamom, cloves, and rosewater in a large saucepan. Bring to a boil over medium-high heat, stirring occasionally, until the sugar dissolves. • Decrease the heat to medium-low and simmer until syrupy, about 15 minutes. Remove from the heat and set aside to cool.

Dumplings: Sift the milk powder, flour, and baking powder into a bowl. Add the sesame oil and milk and knead to form a soft dough. Shape the dough into twenty-four walnut-size balls. • Pour the oil into a deep-fryer or deep saucepan over medium heat and heat to 365°F (190°C). If you don't have a frying thermometer, test the oil temperature by dropping a small piece of bread into the hot oil. If the bread bubbles to the surface and begins to turn golden, the oil is ready. • Fry the dumplings in batches until golden brown, about 5 minutes each batch. Remove with a slotted spoon and drain on paper towels. • Transfer the dumplings to the prepared syrup and set aside to soak for 4 hours. • Serve warm or at room temperature with the syrup.

Sugar Syrup

5   cups (1.25 liters) water
5   cups (1 kg) sugar
4   cardamom pods, bruised
1/2 teaspoon whole cloves
1   tablespoon rosewater

Dumplings

3   cups (450 g) milk powder
1   cup (150 g) all-purpose (plain) flour
1   teaspoon baking powder
1/3 cup (90 ml) sesame oil
3/4 cup (180 ml) milk
4   cups (1 liter) vegetable oil for frying

Serves: 12
Preparation: 30 minutes
  + 4 hours to soak
Cooking: 30 minutes
Level: 2

CHURROS WITH HOT CHOCOLATE SAUCE

Hot Chocolate Sauce: Combine the milk and cinnamon in a medium saucepan and bring to a boil. • Decrease the heat to low, add the chocolate, and stir until melted. • Combine the cornstarch and water in a small bowl and stir to make a paste. Add the paste to the hot chocolate milk and heat, stirring constantly, until thickened enough to coat the back of the spoon, about 10 minutes. • Remove from the heat and strain through a fine-mesh sieve, discarding the solids. • Cover the chocolate milk with a piece of parchment paper to prevent a skin from forming. Set aside.

Churros: Combine the water and butter in a small saucepan and bring to a boil. Decrease the heat to medium. • Add the flour, stirring constantly until the dough begins to come away from the sides of the pan, 3–4 minutes. • Transfer to an electric mixer. Gradually add the egg, at little at a time, ensuring it is fully incorporated before adding more, until the dough is glossy and elastic. Set aside to cool for 10 minutes. • Pour the oil into a deep-fryer or deep saucepan over medium heat and heat to 365°F (190°C). If you don't have a frying thermometer, test the oil temperature by dropping a small piece of bread into the hot oil. If the bread bubbles to the surface and begins to turn golden, the oil is ready. • Sprinkle the sugar and cinnamon on a large plate ready to coat the hot churros. • Transfer the dough to a pastry bag fitted with a large star nozzle. • Pipe 4-inch (10-cm) lengths into the oil and fry until golden. • Remove with a slotted spoon and toss in the sugar and cinnamon to coat. • Serve hot with the chocolate sauce.

Hot Chocolate Sauce

4	cups (1 liter) milk
1	(1-inch/2.5-cm) cinnamon stick
8	ounces (250 g) top quality dark chocolate, coarsely chopped
2	tablespoons cornstarch (cornflour)
2	tablespoons water

Churros

1	cup (250 ml) water
1/3	cup (90 g) butter
1	cup (150 g) all-purpose (plain) flour
2	small eggs, lightly beaten
4	cups (1 liter) vegetable oil for frying
1/3	cup (70 g) superfine (caster) sugar
1	tablespoon ground cinnamon

Serves: 6
Preparation: 30 minutes
  + 10 minutes to cool
Cooking: 30 minutes
Level: 2

CAKES, TARTS, AND PIES

608

BASIC BUTTER CAKE

Preheat the oven to 350°F (180°C/gas 4). • Line two 8- or 9-inch (20- or 23-cm) round cake pans with parchment paper. Butter the paper. • Sift the flour, baking powder, and salt into a large bowl. • **Step 1:** Beat the butter, sugar, and vanilla in a large bowl with an electric mixer at medium speed until creamy. • Add the egg yolks one at a time, beating until just blended after each addition. • **Step 2:** With mixer at low speed, gradually beat in the mixed dry ingredients, alternating with the milk. • **Step 3:** In another bowl, using a clean beater, beat the egg whites until stiff but not dry. • Use a large rubber spatula to fold them into the batter. • Spoon the batter into the prepared pans. • Bake for 45–55 minutes, or until a toothpick inserted into the center comes out clean. • Cool the cake in the pan for 10 minutes. Turn out onto a rack. Carefully remove the paper and let cool completely.

■■■*A well-made butter cake has a moist, fine-grained crumb and an even texture. Success depends on incorporating enough air bubbles into the batter. Begin by creaming the butter and sugar in a large bowl. Make sure that the butter is not cold; it should be softened, not straight from the refrigerator. The eggs and milk (or other liquid) should also be at room temperature. Sometimes the eggs are added whole, other times the whites are beaten separately and folded in at the end. Folding is not stirring; you should lift the batter gently upward and fold it over the whites so that the mixture does not deflate.*

3	cups (450 g) all-purpose (plain) flour
1	tablespoon baking powder
½	teaspoon salt
1	cup (250 g) butter, softened
2	cups (400 g) sugar
2	teaspoons vanilla extract (essence)
4	large eggs, separated
1	cup (250 ml) milk

Serves: 10–12
Preparation: 15 minutes
Cooking: 45–55 minutes
Level: 1

PREPARING BASIC BUTTER CAKE

A basic butter cake has a moist, sweet crumb and is very versatile. You can flavor the batter with extracts and aromas, slice the cooked cake and fill it with cream, preserves, or fruit, glaze or frost it, or simply enjoy a plain slice with a cup of tea of coffee. Butter cakes are not hard to make; here is our favorite, never-fail recipe.

1. BEAT the butter and sugar in the bowl of an electric mixer on medium speed until pale and creamy. Add the egg yolks one at a time, beating until just combined after each addition.

2. WITH MIXER at low speed, gradually beat in the mixed dry ingredients, alternating with the milk. Make sure that the milk (or other liquid, depending on the recipe) is at room temperature. Adding the mixed dry ingredients and the liquid alternately helps prevent the batter from curdling and keeps it light and creamy.

3. BEAT the egg whites until stiff but not dry. Use a large rubber spatula to fold into the batter.

LAMINGTONS

Cake: Preheat the oven to 375°F (190°C/gas 5). • Line an 8-inch (20 cm) square baking pan with parchment paper. • Beat the egg whites in a with an electric mixer until soft peaks form. • Beat the yolks, sugar, and vanilla in a separate bowl until pale and thick. • Fold 1 large spoonful of whites into the yolk mixture. Fold in the remaining whites. • Sift the cornstarch, flour, and baking powder into a medium bowl. • Gradually fold the flour mixture into the egg mixture. • Pour the cake mixture into the prepared pan. • Bake for 30 minutes, until a skewer comes out clean. • Let sit in the pan for 5 minutes. Turn out onto a rack to cool completely.

Frosting: Bring the water and butter to a boil in a small saucepan. • Sift the confectioners' sugar and cocoa into a bowl. Stir in the water mixture to make a thin frosting.

Step 1: Split the cake into two layers. Spread raspberry preserves on the bottom layer and top with the other layer. Measure and cut into 16 squares. • **Step 2:** Dip into the frosting and toss in the coconut.

Cake

6	large eggs, separated
1	cup (200 g) superfine (caster) sugar
1	teaspoon vanilla extract (essence)
$^2/_3$	cup (100 g) cornstarch (cornflour)
2	tablespoons all-purpose (plain) flour
2	teaspoons baking powder
$^2/_3$	cup (250 g) raspberry preserves (jam), warmed

Frosting

$^1/_2$	cup (125 ml) water
$^1/_4$	cup (60 g) butter
3	cups (450 g) confectioners' (icing) sugar
$^1/_3$	cup (50 g) cocoa powder
$1^1/_2$	cups (185 g) shredded (desiccated) coconut

Makes: 16 lamingtons
Preparation: 20 minutes
Cooking: 30 minutes
Level: 2

◼ PREPARING LAMINGTONS

1. SPREAD raspberry preserves over the bottom layer and top with the other layer. Measure for cutting.
2. HOLD each piece of cake with 2 forks, and dip into the frosting. Toss in the coconut until well coated.

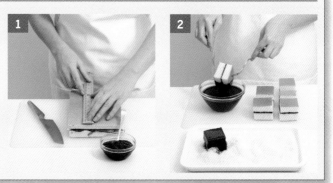

TARTE TATIN

612

Preheat the oven to 350°F (180°C/gas 4). • Heat the sugar and water in a small saucepan over low heat until caramelized. • Spoon the caramel into a 9-inch (23-cm) round cake pan. • Sprinkle with 1 tablespoon of brown sugar and dot with the butter. • Arrange the apples in the prepared pan and sprinkle with the remaining brown sugar. • Roll the pastry out into a 9-inch (23-cm) round on a lightly floured surface. Cover the apples with the pastry, sealing the edges. • Bake for 40–45 minutes, or until golden brown. • Invert the cake onto a serving plate and let cool. • Serve warm or at room temperature.

½ cup (100 g) sugar

1 tablespoon cold water

1¼ cups (250 g) firmly packed dark brown sugar

½ cup (125 g) butter, cut up

6 apples, peeled, cored and quartered

1 recipe Sweet Tart Pastry (see pages 644–646)

Serves: 6–8
Preparation: 25 minutes
Cooking: 40–45 minutes
Level: 2

THREE MILK CAKE

Cake: Preheat the oven to 350°F (180°C/gas 4). • Line a 10-inch (25-cm) springform pan with parchment paper. • Sift the flour, baking powder, and salt into a small bowl. • Beat the egg yolks, 3/4 cup (150 g) of sugar, and vanilla with an electric mixer until pale and thick. • Add the flour mixture and milk alternately, stirring until combined. • Beat the egg whites in a medium bowl until soft peaks begin to form. Gradually add the remaining 1/4 cup (50 g) sugar, beating until thick and glossy. • Fold a large spoonful of the whites into the yolk mixture. Fold in the remaining whites. • Pour the mixture into the prepared pan. • Bake for 35–40 minutes, until the cake springs back with gently pressed and a skewer comes out clean. • Let cool in the pan for 15 minutes.

Milk Syrup: Place all the syrup ingredients in a medium bowl and whisk to combine. • Poke holes in the top of the cake with a skewer. Gradually pour the syrup over the cake, waiting for each addition to be absorbed before adding the next. • Dust the cake generously with confectioners' sugar and serve with whipped cream, if desired.

■ ■ ■ *This cake comes from Mexico and Central America and is known in Spanish as* Pastel de tres leche *(Three milk cake).*

Cake

1¼ cups (180 g) all-purpose (plain) flour

1½ teaspoons baking powder

Pinch of salt

5 large eggs, separated

1 cup (200 g) superfine (caster) sugar

1 teaspoon vanilla extract (essence)

¼ cup (60 ml) milk

Confectioners' (icing) sugar to dust

Whipped cream to serve (optional)

Milk Syrup

2 cups (400 ml) canned sweetened condensed milk

1½ cups (375 ml) canned evaporated milk

¾ cup (180 ml) light (single) cream

1 tablespoon dark rum

1 teaspoon vanilla extract (essence)

Serves: 12
Preparation: 25 minutes
Cooking: 35–40 minutes
Level: 1

LINZERTORTE

Preheat the oven to 350°F (180°C/gas 4). • Line the base of a 9-inch (23-cm) springform pan with parchment paper. Lightly grease the sides. • Spread the hazelnuts in a baking dish and toast until golden brown, about 10 minutes. Place in a clean kitchen towel and rub off the skins. • Place the hazelnuts and almonds in a food processor and chop until finely ground. Set aside. • Sift the flour, cinnamon, baking powder, and salt into a medium bowl. • Beat the butter and sugar in a large bowl with an electric mixer on medium speed until pale and creamy. Beat in the egg yolk. • With mixer on low, beat in the nut mixture and mixed dried ingredients. • Divide the dough in half. Press one half into the base and about $3/4$ inch (2 cm) up the sides of the prepared pan. • Roll the remaining dough into a 12-inch (30-cm) disk on a piece of parchment paper. Place on a baking sheet. Chill the dough until firm, about 30 minutes. • Spread the raspberry preserves over the pastry in the pan. Use a fluted pastry wheel to cut the remaining pastry into $3/4$-inch (2-cm) wide strips. Place over the preserves in a lattice pattern. • Put the cake in the freezer for 30 minutes. • Preheat the oven to 350°F (180°C/gas 4). • Bake the cake until golden brown, 35–40 minutes. • Place on a wire rack and let cool for 15 minutes. Loosen the pan sides and carefully remove the base. Let cool completely. • Dust with confectioners' sugar just before serving.

$1/2$ cup (60 g) hazelnuts

1 cup (150 g) blanched almonds

$1^1/3$ cups (200 g) all-purpose (plain) flour

1 teaspoon ground cinnamon

$1/2$ teaspoon baking powder

$1/4$ teaspoon salt

$3/4$ cup (180 g) butter

1 cup (200 g) sugar

1 large egg yolk

$1^1/3$ cups (350 g) raspberry preserves (jam)

Confectioners' (icing) sugar to dust

Serves: 8
Preparation: 30 minutes
+ 1 hour to chill and freeze
Cooking: 35–40 minutes
Level: 2

CHOCOLATE CHIP CAKE

Cake: Preheat the oven to 350°F (180°C/gas 4).
• Line a deep 8-inch (20-cm) springform pan with parchment paper. Lightly grease the sides. • Sift the flour, cocoa, baking soda, baking powder, and salt into a medium bowl. • Beat the butter and sugar in a large bowl with an electric mixer on medium-high speed until creamy. Beat in the coffee granules and vanilla. • Add the eggs one at a time, beating until just blended after each addition. • With mixer on low, beat in the mixed dry ingredients, alternating with the milk and chocolate chips. • Spoon the batter into the prepared pan. • Bake for 45–50 minutes, until risen and a toothpick inserted into the center comes out clean. • Cool in the pan for 15 minutes. Turn out onto a rack and let cool.
Frosting: Melt the butter and chocolate in a double boiler over barely simmering water. • When smooth and glossy set aside to cool. • Spread over the top and sides of the cake.

Cake

1⅓ cups (200 g) all-purpose (plain) flour

½ cup (75 g) unsweetened cocoa powder

1 teaspoon baking soda (bicarbonate of soda

½ teaspoon baking powder

¼ teaspoon salt

½ cup (125 g) butter, softened

1 cup (200 g) firmly packed light brown sugar

1 tablespoon freeze-dried instant coffee granules

1 teaspoon vanilla extract (essence)

2 large eggs

¾ cup (185 ml) milk

½ cup (90 g) dark chocolate chips

Chocolate Frosting

½ cup (125 g) butter

4 ounces (125 g) dark chocolate, chopped

Serves: 8–10
Preparation: 30 minutes
   + time to cool
Cooking: 45–50 minutes
Level: 2

STRAWBERRY CREAM GATEAU

Génoise: Preheat the oven to 375°F (190°C/gas 5). • Butter a 9-inch (23-cm) springform pan. Line with parchment paper. • **Step 1:** Sift the flour and cornstarch into a bowl. • **Step 2:** Beat the eggs and sugar in a large heatproof bowl. • Fit the bowl into a saucepan of barely simmering water. Whisk until the sugar has dissolved and the mixture is hot. Remove from the heat and beat until tripled in volume. • **Step 3:** Fold in the dry ingredients. • **Step 4:** Place 2 cups of batter in a bowl and fold in the butter and vanilla. Fold this mixture back into the batter. Spoon into the prepared pans. • Bake for 30–40 minutes, until risen and golden brown. • Cool in the pan for 5 minutes. Remove the pan sides and paper and let cool.

Strawberry Filling: Soak the strawberries in the liqueur for 1 hour. • Stirring constantly, heat the egg yolks, wine, and sugar in a heatproof bowl over barely simmering water until the mixture coats a metal spoon. • Sprinkle the gelatin over the lemon juice. Stir into the egg yolk mixture until dissolved. • Put the pan in a bowl of ice water and stir until cooled. Refrigerate, stirring occasionally, until chilled. • Stir one-third of the whipped cream into the yolk mixture. Drain the strawberries, reserving the juice, and stir into the yolk mixture. • Split the cake horizontally. Butter a 9-inch (23-cm) springform pan. Place one layer in the pan. Drizzle with half the strawberry juice. Spread with the egg mixture and top with the remaining cake layer. Drizzle with the remaining juice. Chill for 6 hours.

• Loosen and remove the pan sides. Spread with the remaining cream. Top with almonds and strawberries.

Génoise

²/₃ cup (100 g) cake flour

²/₃ cup (100 g) cornstarch (cornflour)

6 large eggs

³/₄ cup (150 g) superfine (caster) sugar

¹/₃ cup (90 g) butter, melted and cooled slightly

1 teaspoon vanilla extract (essence)

Strawberry Filling

2 pounds (1 kg) strawberries, halved (reserve 12 whole to decorate)

¹/₂ cup (125 ml) orange liqueur

8 large egg yolks

1¹/₄ cups (300 ml) dry white wine

1 cup (200 g) sugar

2 tablespoons unflavored gelatin

3 tablespoons freshly squeezed lemon juice

1¹/₂ cups (375 ml) heavy (double) cream, whipped

¹/₂ cup sliced almonds, toasted

Serves: 8–10
Preparation: 1 hour + 7 hours to soak and chill
Cooking: 20–40 minutes
Level: 2

PREPARING A GÉNOISE

A Génoise is a classic French sponge cake. It is the basis of many cakes and desserts, including our delicious Strawberry Cream Gateau. This recipe can be baked in one or two 9-inch (23-cm) pans. For many-layered cakes, the two cakes can be sliced into two layers each. If baking in two pans, decrease the baking time to 20–30 minutes.

1. SIFT the flour and cornstarch into a medium bowl.

2. BEAT the eggs and sugar in a large bowl over barely simmering water. Remove from heat and beat until tripled in volume and very thick.

3. USE a large rubber spatula to gradually fold the dry ingredients into the batter.

4. PLACE 2 cups of batter in a small bowl and fold in the melted butter and vanilla. Fold into the batter. Spoon into the baking pans.

CHOCOLATE ROLL WITH LEMON FILLING

Chocolate Roll: Preheat the oven to 350°F (180°C/ gas 4). • Line the bottom and sides of a 13 x 9-inch (33 x 23-cm) jelly-roll pan with parchment paper. Oil the paper lightly. • Beat the eggs, sugar, and vanilla in a bowl with an electric mixer fitted with a whisk until pale and thick. • Sift the rice flour and cocoa together and fold into the egg mixture. • Fold in the melted butter. • Spoon the batter into the pan. • Bake for about 20 minutes, or until springy when pressed in the center. • Leave the cake in the pan for 5 minutes to cool. • Dust a clean kitchen towel with confectioners' sugar. Turn the cake out onto the towel. Roll up the cake, using the towel as a guide. Leave, seam-side down, until cool. **Filling:** Beat the cream cheese until smooth. Add the confectioners' sugar, lemon juice, and lemon curd, beating well. • Spread the lemon curd cream over the cake and roll up. • Transfer to a serving plate, dust with confectioners' sugar, and sprinkle with the grated chocolate. • Chill for 30 minutes before serving.

Chocolate Roll

4 large eggs

3/4 cup (150 g) superfine (caster) sugar

1 teaspoon vanilla extract (essence)

1/3 cup (50 g) unsweetened cocoa powder

2 tablespoons rice flour

1/4 cup (60 g) butter, melted

2 tablespoons grated dark chocolate

Confectioners' (icing) sugar, for dusting

Filling

1 (8-ounces/250-g) package cream cheese, softened

2/3 cup (100 g) confectioners' (icing) sugar, sifted

2 tablespoons freshly squeezed lemon juice

1/4 cup (60 g) lemon curd

Serves: 6–8
Preparation: 30 minutes
  + 2 1/2 hours to cool
  and chill
Cooking: 12–15 minutes
Level: 3

WHITE CHOCOLATE AND ALMOND CHEESECAKE

Crust: Preheat the oven to 300°F (150°C/gas 2).
• Butter a 9-inch (23-cm) springform pan.
• Combine the cookie crumbs with the melted butter and press the mixture into the bottom of the pan. Refrigerate while you prepare the filling.

Filling: Beat the cream cheese and sugar in a large bowl with an electric mixer on low speed until smooth. • Add the eggs, vanilla, and amaretto, and beat until well combined. • Melt the chocolate in a double boiler over barely simmering water, stirring often. • Leave to cool for a few minutes, then add to the cream cheese mixture. • Stir in the ground almonds and lemon zest. • Pour the filling over the cookie crust in the pan and sprinkle the top with the flaked almonds. • Bake for 1^1/2 hours, or until slightly firm on top. • Turn off the oven and leave the cheesecake inside to cool and set for 2 hours.
• Chill in the pan in the refrigerator for 2 hours.

Raspberry Coulis: Process the raspberries and confectioners' sugar in a food processor or blender until smooth, about 30 seconds. • Alternately, mash the raspberries and confectioners' sugar with a fork.
• Serve the cheesecake with the coulis and cream.

Crust

1^1/4 cups (150 g) finely crushed amaretti cookie crumbs

3 tablespoons unsalted butter, melted

Filling

2 pounds (1 kg) cream cheese, softened

^{1}/4 cup (50 g) sugar

4 large eggs

Seeds from 2 vanilla pods, or 2 teaspoons vanilla extract (essence)

1 tablespoon amaretto (almond liqueur)

12 ounces (350 g) white chocolate, broken into pieces

^{3}/4 cup (75 g) blanched almonds, toasted and finely ground

1 teaspoon finely grated lemon zest

3 tablespoons flaked almonds

Raspberry Coulis

2 cups (300 g) fresh raspberries

^{1}/3 cup (50 g) confectioners' (icing) sugar

Whipped cream to serve

Serves: 6–8
Preparation: 30 minutes
   + 1–2 hours to cool
   + 2 hours to chill
Cooking: 1^1/2 hours
Level: 2

MARBLED CHOCOLATE CHEESECAKE

628

Crust: Combine the crumbs, ground hazelnuts, and butter in a bowl. Press into the bottom of a 10-inch (25-cm) springform pan. Refrigerate for 30 minutes. **Filling:** Combine the gelatin and water in a small heatproof bowl over a saucepan of barely simmering water, stirring occasionally until dissolved. • Melt the chocolate in a double boiler over barely simmering water, stirring occasionally, until smooth. Set aside to cool. • Beat the cream cheese and sugar in a medium bowl with an electric mixer on medium speed until smooth and creamy. • Add the gelatin and beat until combined. • Divide the mixture evenly between two bowls. Add the melted chocolate to one bowl and stir to combine. Add the hazelnuts and frangelico to the other and stir to combine. • Whip the cream in a small bowl until soft peaks form. Divide in half and fold into the chocolate and hazelnut mixtures. • Pour the fillings alternately into the prepared base and create a swirl pattern using a skewer or the end of a small knife. Refrigerate until set, at least 6 hours.

Crust

- 1²/₃ cups (220 g) plain chocolate wafer (biscuit) crumbs
- 1/3 cup (30 g) ground hazelnuts
- 1/3 cup (125 g) butter, melted

Filling

- 2 teaspoons unflavored powdered gelatin
- 2 tablespoons water
- 5 ounces (150 g) dark chocolate
- 2 (8-ounce) packages (500 g) cream cheese, softened
- 1/3 cup (50 g) confectioners' (icing) sugar
- 2 tablespoons hazelnuts, lightly toasted and finely chopped
- 2 tablespoons hazelnut liqueur, such as Frangelico
- 1 cup (250 ml) light (single) cream

Serves: 10–12
Preparation: 30 minutes + 6¹/2 hours to chill
Level: 1

BLACK FOREST ICE CREAM CAKE

Cake Base: Preheat the oven to 350°F (180°C/gas 4). • Lightly grease a 9-inch (23 cm) springform pan and line the base with parchment paper. • Beat the butter, sugar, and vanilla in a medium bowl with an electric mixer on medium speed until pale and creamy. Beat in the egg until just blended. • Sift the flour, cocoa, and baking powder into a small bowl. With mixer on low, add the flour mixture and sour cream alternately to the batter. • Spoon the batter into the prepared pan. • Bake for 25–30 minutes, until a skewer comes out clean when inserted into the center. • Let cool in the pan for 10 minutes, then turn out onto a wire rack and let cool completely.
Filling: Soften the ice cream at room temperature, about 15 minutes. Stir in the kirsch. • Line the sides of a clean 9-inch (23-cm) springform pan with parchment paper and tighten the sides. • Place the cooled sponge base back in the pan. Sprinkle with the cherries. • Spoon the ice-cream over the cherries and smooth the top. • Cover with plastic wrap (cling film) and freeze for 4 hours.
Topping: Beat the cream and confectioners' sugar in a medium bowl with an electric mixer until soft peaks form. • Remove the cake from the pan and spread the cream over the top and sides. Decorate with the chocolate shavings and freeze until solid, at least 4 more hours.

Cake Base

1/3 cup (90 g) butter, softened

3/4 cup (150 g) superfine (caster) sugar

1/3 teaspoon vanilla extract (essence)

1 large egg

3/4 cup (125 g) all-purpose (plain) flour

1/3 cup (50 g) unsweetened cocoa powder

1 teaspoon baking powder

1/2 cup (125 ml) sour cream

Filling

4 cups (500 g) chocolate ice cream

2 tablespoons kirsch or cherry liqueur

2 cups (400 g) canned pitted black cherries, drained

Topping

1 1/2 cups (375 ml) heavy (double) cream

2 tablespoon confectioners' (icing) sugar

3 ounces (90 g) dark chocolate, shaved, to decorate

Serves: 10–12
Preparation: 1 hour
  + 8 hours to freeze
Cooking: 25–30 minutes
Level: 2

STRAWBERRY ICE CREAM CAKE

632

Strawberry Ice Cream: Purée 1 pound (500 g) of the strawberries in a blender with $^1/_4$ cup (50 g) of the sugar and the water until smooth. Press the purée through a fine-mesh sieve to remove the seeds. • Combine the milk, cream, and remaining $1^1/_4$ cups (250 g) of sugar in a saucepan over medium-low heat. Stir until the sugar has completely dissolved then bring to a boil. • Remove from the heat and let cool completely. • Add the strawberry purée and mix well. Transfer to your ice cream machine and freeze following the manufacturer's instructions. • Leave the ice cream to soften at room temperature until softened and spreadable, 10–15 minutes. • Slice the top off one of the butter cakes to make a flat surface. Cut each cake in half horizontally. Reserve the only remaining rounded layer for the top of the cake. Set aside. • Butter an 8-inch (20-cm) springform pan. Place one layer of cake in the pan and spread evenly with one-third of the ice cream. Top with another layer of cake and repeat cover with softened ice cream. Repeat with the third layer of cake and top with the remaining ice cream. Top with the domed layer of cake. • Freeze overnight. • Remove 15 minutes prior to serving. Decorate with the whole strawberries, dust with confectioners' sugar, and serve.

■ ■ ■ *If pushed for time, use store-bought ice cream of your preferred flavor.*

Strawberry Ice Cream

$1^1/_2$ **pounds (750 g) fresh strawberries**

$1^1/_2$ **cups (300 g) sugar**

2 **tablespoons water**

2 **cups (500 ml) milk**

1 **cup (250 ml) heavy (double) cream**

1 **recipe Basic Butter Cake, baked in two 8-inch (20-cm) pans (see pages 608–609)**

To Decorate

1 **cup (150 g) fresh strawberries**

Confectioners' (icing) sugar to dust

Serves: 8–10
Preparation: 15 minutes
  + 12 hours to freeze
Level: 3

GALETTE DES ROIS

Preheat the oven to 400°F (200°C/ gas 6). Lightly grease a baking sheet. • Unroll half the pastry and cut out a 10-inch (25-cm) circle. Place on the prepared baking sheet. • Beat the butter and sugar in a medium bowl with an electric mixer on medium-high speed until pale and creamy. • Add the ground almonds, egg yolks, brandy, and almond extract, beating until just blended. • Hide the bean in the filling and spread on the pastry round leaving a $3/4$-inch (1-cm) border all around. • Lightly brush the border with some of the remaining egg. • Unroll the remaining pastry, cut out an 11-inch (28-cm) circle, and place on top of the filling. Press to seal and trim to size. • Using a sharp knife, score the pastry in a swirl pattern, starting from the center and working outward. Do not cut through to the filling. • Glaze the top of the pastry with the remaining egg, taking care not to brush the edges as this will stop the pastry from rising. • Bake for 30–35 minutes, until well puffed and golden brown. Serve warm or at room temperature.

1	pound (500 g) ready rolled puff pastry, thawed if frozen
$1/2$	cup (125 g) butter, softened
$1/3$	cup (70 g) superfine (caster) sugar
$3/4$	cup (75 g) ground almonds
3	large egg yolks, lightly beaten + 1 large egg, lightly beaten, to glaze
1	tablespoon kirsch (clear cherry brandy) or other brandy
$1/2$	teaspoon almond extract (essence)
1	dried bean

Serves: 8–10
Preparation: 30 minutes
Cooking: 30–35 minutes
Level: 2

■ ■ ■ *Galette de Rois is a traditional French cake baked or bought from bakeries around Epiphany (6 January). The cake has a hidden dried bean. The person who receives the bean in their slice of cake becomes king for the day and must offer the next cake.*

SAINT HONORÉ

Base: Preheat the oven to 400°F (200°C/gas 6).
• Combine the flour and sugar in a medium bowl. Cut in the butter until the mixture resembles coarse crumbs. Stir in the egg yolk until a smooth dough forms. • Roll the dough out on a lightly floured work surface into a 10-inch (25-cm) round. Prick all over with a fork and place on a baking sheet. Brush a little beaten egg around the edge.

Choux Pastry: Line a baking sheet with parchment paper. • Place the water, butter, sugar, and salt in a medium pan over medium-low heat. When the mixture boils, remove from the heat and add the flour all at once. Use a wooden spoon to stir vigorously until a smooth paste forms. • Return to medium heat and stir constantly until the mixture pulls away from the pan sides. Remove from the heat and let cool for 5 minutes. • Add 5 eggs, one at a time, beating until just blended after each addition. The batter should be shiny and stiff enough to hold its shape if dropped onto a baking sheet. • Fit a pastry bag with a plain 3/4-inch (2-cm) tip and half fill with pastry. Pipe the pastry around the edge of the base. • Brush some beaten egg over the top. • Bake for 20–25 minutes, or until golden. Cool the pastry completely on a rack. • Line a baking sheet with parchment paper. Fill a pastry bag with the remaining choux pastry. Pipe heaps the size of small walnuts on the prepared sheet.

636

Base

1¹⁄₃ cups (200 g) all-purpose flour

1 tablespoon sugar

¹⁄₃ cup (90 g) + 1 tablespoon cold butter

1 large egg yolk + 1 large egg, lightly beaten

Choux Pastry

2 cups (500 ml) water

²⁄₃ cup (180 g) butter, cut up

1 tablespoon sugar

¹⁄₄ teaspoon salt

1²⁄₃ cups (250 g) all-purpose (plain) flour

6 large eggs, 1 lightly beaten

Filling

2 cups (500 ml) milk

4 large egg yolks

³⁄₄ cup (150 g) sugar

¹⁄₂ cup (75 g) all-purpose (plain) flour

1 tablespoon dark rum

1 teaspoon vanilla extract (essence)

Frosting

1   **cup (150 g) confectioners' (icing) sugar**

2   **tablespoons boiling water**

1   **tablespoon unsweetened cocoa powder**

Caramel Glaze

1   **cup (200 g) sugar**

2   **tablespoons water**

Serves: 10–12
Preparation: About 2 hours
Cooking: 35–45 minutes
Level: 3

Brush with the remaining beaten egg. • Bake for 15–20 minutes, or until golden. Cool on racks.

Filling: Warm the milk in a saucepan over low heat. • Beat the egg yolks and sugar in a large bowl with an electric mixer at high speed until pale and thick. • Use a large rubber spatula to fold in the flour. • Gradually stir in the hot milk. • Transfer the mixture to a medium saucepan. Bring to a boil, stirring constantly. • Remove from the heat and stir in the rum and vanilla. Set aside to cool completely. • Spread the cooled filling into the pastry base, smoothing the top with a knife or spatula.

Frosting: Mix the confectioners' sugar and enough boiling water in a small bowl to make a smooth frosting. • Spoon half the frosting over the filling. Trace intersecting lines (criss-cross pattern) on the frosting with a small knife. Stir the cocoa into the remaining frosting. Spoon the frosting into a pastry bag. Use the lines as a guide to pipe thin lines over the cake.

Caramel Glaze: Warm the sugar and water in a saucepan over medium heat until the sugar has dissolved. Continue cooking, without stirring, until pale gold in color. Remove from the heat. • Dip the tops of the choux puffs in the caramel to glaze. • Dip the bases of the puffs in the caramel and stick on the crown, pressing down lightly.

YULE LOG

Cake: Preheat the oven to 350°F (180°C/gas 4). Line a jelly-roll pan with parchment paper. • Sift the flour, cocoa, and cinnamon into a small bowl. • Beat the eggs and $1/2$ cup (100 g) of superfine sugar in a large bowl with an electric mixer on medium speed until thick, creamy, and tripled in volume. • Add the vanilla and beat to combine. • Gently fold in the flour mixture in two batches. • Fold in the melted butter until just incorporated. Spoon the batter into the prepared pan. • Bake for 15–20 minutes, until the sponge springs back when pressed. • Lay a clean kitchen towel on a work surface and dust with extra superfine sugar. • Remove the sponge from the oven and turn out onto the towel. Roll up lengthwise and place on a wire rack, seam-side down, to cool.

Filling: Beat the cream in a small bowl until soft peaks form. Add the chestnut purée and stir to combine. • Unroll the sponge, peel away the paper, and spread with the filling, leaving a $3/4$-inch (2-cm) border. Sprinkle with the hazelnuts, re-roll the cake, and trim the ends. • Place on a large serving plate. Diagonally cut 4 inches (10 cm) off the end and place it along the log to resemble a branch. • Chill in the refrigerator.

Chocolate Buttercream: Melt the chocolate in a double boiler over barely simmering water. Set aside. • Beat the butter and vanilla in a large bowl until pale and creamy. • Pour in the cooled chocolate, beating until blended. Gradually add the confectioners' sugar, beating until blended. • Spread the buttercream over the Yule log. Using the prongs of a fork, create a bark pattern. If liked, decorate with holly leaves.

Cake

- $1/2$ cup (75 g) all-purpose (plain) flour
- 2 tablespoons unsweetened cocoa powder
- 1 teaspoon ground cinnamon
- 4 large eggs
- $1/2$ cup (100 g) superfine (caster) sugar + extra to sprinkle
- 1 teaspoon vanilla extract (essence)
- 2 tablespoons butter, melted and cooled

Filling

- $1/2$ cup (125 ml) heavy (double) cream
- 1 (8-ounce/250-g) can sweetened chestnut purée
- $1/4$ cup (40 g) hazelnuts, lightly toasted and finely chopped

Chocolate Buttercream

- 3 ounces (90 g) dark chocolate
- 1 cup (250 g) butter, softened
- $1/2$ teaspoon vanilla extract (essence)
- 2 cups (300 g) confectioners' (icing) sugar

  Holly leaves, to decorate (optional)

Serves: 8
Preparation: 45 minutes
Cooking: 15–20 minutes
Level: 3

INDIVIDUAL CHRISTMAS CAKES

Cakes: Stir the candied fruit, grape juice, and brown sugar in a large bowl. Cover and set aside for 8 hours. • Preheat the oven to 300°F (150°C/gas 2). Butter a 12-cup muffin pan and line with paper cups. • Sift the flour, baking powder, baking soda, cinnamon, nutmeg, and salt into a large bowl. • Use a large rubber spatula to stir the egg whites, oil, milk, and 2 tablespoons of brandy into the fruit mixture. Stir in the dry ingredients. • Spoon the batter evenly into the cups. • Bake for 75–80 minutes, or until a toothpick inserted into the center comes out clean. • Drizzle the hot cakes with the remaining 2 tablespoons of brandy. • Cool the cakes completely in the pan. Turn out onto racks to decorate.

Holly Decorations: Dust a work surface lightly with confectioners' sugar. Knead the marzipan until soft. Roll out to $1/8$ inch (3 mm) thick. • Use a leaf-shaped cutter to stamp out 24 small holly shapes. • Lightly brush green coloring over each leaf. Dry the leaves on waxed paper. Shape the remaining marzipan into 24 tiny berriess. Brush with red food coloring.

Frosting: Warm the preserves in a saucepan over low heat. Brush each cake with a thin layer of preserves. • Knead the marzipan until soft. Divide into 12 equal pieces. Roll out one piece at a time to $1/8$ inch (3 mm) thick. Fit the marzipan over each cake. • Mix the confectioners' sugar and water to make a smooth paste. Dot the leaves and berries with a little frosting and arrange on each cake to look like holly decorations.

Cakes

4	cups (200 g) chopped mixed candied fruit
$1^{1/2}$	cups (375 ml) white grape juice
$3/4$	cup (150 g) firmly packed dark brown sugar
$2^{1/2}$	cups (375 g) all-purpose (plain) flour
$1^{1/2}$	teaspoons baking powder
1	teaspoon baking soda (bicarbonate of soda)
1	teaspoon ground cinnamon
1	teaspoon ground nutmeg
$1/2$	teaspoon salt
2	large egg whites, lightly beaten
$1/4$	cup (60 ml) vegetable oil
$1/3$	cup (90 ml) milk
4	tablespoons (60 ml) brandy

Holly Decorations

2	ounces (60 g) marzipan
$1/2$	teaspoon green food coloring
$1/2$	teaspoon red food coloring

Frosting

$1/3$	cup (100 g) apricot preserves (jam)
8	ounces (250 g) marzipan
1	tablespoon confectioners' (icing) sugar
1	teaspoon water

Serves: 12
Preparation: 1 hour + 8 hours to soak
Cooking: 75–80 minutes
Level: 2

▪ PREPARING SWEET TART PASTRY

The instructions on these pages show you how to prepare a slightly sweet tart pastry (pâte sucrée), how to transfer it to the pan without breaking, and how to pre-bake the crust (a technique known as "baking blind"). We have suggested two ways to mix the dough: in a food processor or by hand. The food processor method is easier and will make an excellent crust, although it is

1. BY MACHINE: Combine the flour, sugar, and salt in a food processor with a metal blade. Add the butter and pulse until it resembles coarse crumbs.

2. WITH the machine running, add the egg and cream. Pulse until the mixture just comes together.

3. BY HAND: Stir the flour, sugar, and salt. Cut or rub in the butter until the mixture resembles coarse bread crumbs.

4. WHISK the egg and cream in a small bowl. Stir into the butter and flour mixture with a wooden spoon.

5. TURN the dough out onto a sheet of plastic wrap. Press into a 6-inch (18-cm) disk and wrap. Chill for 30 minutes.

6. LIGHTLY grease or spray an 11-inch (28-cm) tart pan with a removeable bottom.

important not to overprocess the dough. For the skilled baker, the hand method will produce the lightest and flakiest crust. When the dough is mixed and you are shaping it into a disk for chilling, check that there are tiny flakes of butter visible beneath the surface of the dough; this means that it is not overmixed or over-processed and will be flaky. We suggest that you use all-purpose (plain) flour. Some cooks use a mixture of all-purpose and pastry flour to create a more tender crust. Do not use cake flour or bread flour. For pastry ingredients, see page 646.

7. UNWRAP the dough and place on a cool work surface (marble is ideal). Flour the dough lightly on both sides.

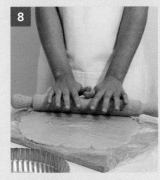

8. ROLL the dough out between two sheets of plastic wrap until $1/8$ inch (3 mm) thick and about 13 inches (33 cm) in diameter.

9. REMOVE the top layer of plastic. Dust the rolling pin with flour and roll the pastry around it, removing the other layer of plastic as you work.

10. UNROLL the pastry over the pan. Ease it into the sides of the pan. Fold the excess dough back to create a rim.

11. PREHEAT the oven to 400°F (200°C/gas 6). Line the crust with foil. Fill with pie weights or dried beans. Bake for 5 minutes. Remove the beans and foil.

12. LOWER the oven temperature to 375°F (190°C/gas 5). Bake for 5–10 minutes more, until firm and golden brown.

FRESH BERRY TART

Prepare the sweet tart pastry and bake the tart shell as explained on pages 644–645. Set aside while you prepare the filling.

Vanilla Pastry Cream: Whisk the eggs and cornstarch in a small bowl until smooth. Gradually whisk in $1/4$ cup (60 ml) of milk. • Place the sugar in a medium saucepan. Stir in the remaining $1^3/4$ cups (440 ml) of milk. • Place the pan over medium heat and bring to a boil, stirring occasionally. Remove from the heat. • Add 2–3 tablespoons of the hot milk mixture to the cornstarch mixture, whisking until smooth. • Whisk all the cornstarch mixture into the hot milk. Return to medium heat and bring to a boil, whisking rapidly. The mixture will thicken quickly. • Remove from the heat and whisk in the vanilla, salt, and butter. • Pour the mixture into a medium bowl and cover the surface with a piece of plastic wrap (cling film). Let cool to room temperature.

To Finish: Beat the cream until thickened. Fold into the cooled pastry cream. • Spoon the pastry cream into the cooled tart crust and top with the fruit.

Sweet Tart Pastry

$1^2/3$ cups (250 g) all-purpose (plain) flour

$1/3$ cup (65 g) superfine (caster) sugar

$1/4$ teaspoon salt

$2/3$ cup (150 g) cold unsalted butter, cut in cubes

1 large egg

2 tablespoons heavy (double) cream

Vanilla Pastry Cream

2 large eggs

3 tablespoons cornstarch (cornflour)

2 cups (500 ml) milk

$1/2$ cup (100 g) sugar

1 teaspoon vanilla extract (essence)

$1/8$ teaspoon salt

1 tablespoon unsalted butter

To Finish

1 cup (250 ml) heavy (double) cream

3 cups (450 g) mixed fresh berries, halved, if large

Serves: 6–8
Preparation: 30 minutes
  + 1 hour to cool
Cooking: 10 minutes
Level: 2

LEMON MERINGUE PIE

Prepare the pastry and bake the tart shell as explained on pages 644–646. Set aside while you prepare the filling.

Filling: Preheat the oven to 375°F (190°C/gas 5). • Combine $1/4$ cup (50 g) of sugar with the lemon juice and zest and juice in a small saucepan over medium heat and stir until the sugar has dissolved. • Whisk the egg yolks in a heatproof bowl and gradually add the hot lemon mixture. • Strain through a fine-mesh sieve and return to the heatproof bowl. Place over a saucepan of simmering water and cook, stirring continuously, until the mixture thickens to coat the back of a wooden spoon. Do not allow the mixture to boil. • Remove from the heat and stir in the butter cubes, one at a time, until fully combined. • Pour the hot mixture into the prepared tart shell and set aside.

Topping: Beat the egg whites and vanilla with an electric mixer on medium speed until soft peaks form. • Gradually add the remaining $1/4$ cup (50 g) of sugar a little at a time, beating until the meringue becomes thick and glossy. • Spoon the meringue topping over the lemon filling, using a spatula to create wave-like peaks. • Bake for 10 minutes, or until light golden. Remove from the oven and cool to room temperature. • Serve with the whipped cream.

1   recipe Sweet Tart
    Pastry (see pages
    644–646)

Filling and Topping

$1/2$ cup (100 g) superfine
    (caster) sugar

5   tablespoons freshly
    squeezed lemon juice,
    strained

1   teaspoon finely grated
    organic lemon zest

3   large eggs, separated

$1/4$ cup (60 g) cold
    unsalted butter, cubed

$1/4$ teaspoon vanilla
    extract (essence)

$3/4$ cup (180 ml) heavy
    (double) cream,
    whipped

Serves: 8
Preparation: 30 minutes
    + 1 hour to cool
Cooking: 10 minutes
Level: 2

TART AU CHOCOLAT

650

Prepare the pastry and bake the tart shell as explained on pages 644–646. Set aside while you prepare the filling.

Filling: Pour the cream into a heavy saucepan and bring slowly to a boil. As soon as the first bubbles appear, remove from the heat and stir in the chocolate. • Add the Cointreau and stir until all the chocolate has melted. Whisk until smooth, then let cool for 15 minutes. • Pour into the pastry shell and leave to set for at least 2 hours. • Decorate the top of the tart with a few raspberries. Serve wedges of pie with the extra raspberries on the side.

1   recipe Sweet Tart Pastry (see pages 644–646)

Filling

1²/₃ cups (400 ml) heavy (double) cream

12   ounces (350 g) dark chocolate (70% cacao), coarsely chopped

1   tablespoon Cointreau or brandy

1   cup (250 g) fresh raspberries to serve

Serves: 8
Preparation: 40 minutes
    + 45 minutes to cool
    + 2 hours to chill
Level: 2

PREPARING FLAKY PASTRY

The instructions on these pages show you how to prepare a flaky pastry (pâte brisée), how to transfer it to the pan without breaking, as well as how to prepare a lattice-topped pie. We have suggested two ways to mix the dough: in a food processor or by hand. The food processor method is easier and will make an excellent crust, although it is important not to

1. BY MACHINE: Put the flour and salt in a food processor. Add the butter and pulse until the mixture resembles coarse crumbs.

2. ADD 6 tablespoons (90 ml) of water and pulse 5–6 times. Pinch the mixture together; if it does not hold together add more water.

3. COMBINE the flour and salt in a bowl. Cut or rub in the butter until the mixture resembles coarse crumbs.

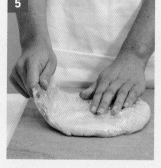

4. ADD 6 tablespoons (90 ml) of water and stir with a rubber spatula. Add enough extra water to form a stiff dough.

5. PRESS the dough into a disk and wrap in plastic wrap (cling film). Chill in the refrigerator for at least 1 hour.

6. DIVIDE the dough in half. Roll out one piece into a 13-inch (33-cm) disk. Re-wrap the other piece and chill.

overprocess the dough. For the skilled baker, the hand method will produce the lightest and flakiest crust. We suggest that you use pastry flour or all-purpose (plain) flour. Do not use cake flour or bread flour. When baking a double-crust pie, remember that the filling will produce steam which must escape otherwise the top of the pie will puff up or the filling will burst the edges and seep out. To prevent this, cut vents into the top of the pie with a sharp knife or skewer so that the steam can escape. For pastry ingredients, see page 654.

7. ROLL the pastry around the rolling pin and drape over the pan. Trim the top edge by running the rolling pin over it. Chill for 30 minutes.

8. PREPARE the filling and spoon it into the chilled crust. Roll out the remaining dough and place over the filling, tucking in the edges.

9. FOR a lattice-topped pie, roll the remaining dough into an oval about 10 x 12 inches (28 x 30 cm). Cut into 3/4-inch (2-cm) strips.

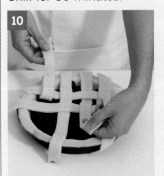

10. PLACE half the strips over the filling in one direction. Fold back every other strip a little past the center. Place a strip crosswise on top.

11. UNFOLD the strips. Fold back the strips that were not folded back before. Lay a second strip crosswise on top.

12. CONTINUE until all the strips are on the pie. Trim to 1/2 inch (1 cm) overhang. Moisten with water and tuck in under the crust.

BLUEBERRY PIE

654

Prepare the flaky pastry as explained on pages 652–653. Set aside while you prepare the filling. **Filling:** Combine the sugar, cornstarch, lemon zest, lemon juice, and salt in a large bowl. Add the blueberries and toss well to coat. Pour the filling into the chilled crust. • Prepare the lattice topping following the instructions on page 653. • Preheat the oven to 400°F (200°C/gas 6) at least 20 minutes before you are ready to bake. • Bake the pie until the crust is golden brown and the filling is bubbling between the strips of pastry. • Serve warm or at room temperature.

Flaky Pastry

$2^2/3$ cups (400 g) pastry
flour or all-purpose
(plain) flour

$^1/4$ teaspoon salt

1 cup (250 g) cold
unsalted butter,
cut in cubes

6–8 tablespoons (90–120
ml) iced water

Filling

$^1/2$ cup (100 g) sugar

2 tablespoons cornstarch
(cornflour)

2 tablespoons freshly
squeezed lemon juice

$^1/4$ teaspoon salt

4 cups (600 g) fresh
blueberries

Serves: 8
Preparation: 40 minutes
+ 45 minutes to cool
+ $1^1/2$ hours to chill
Level: 2

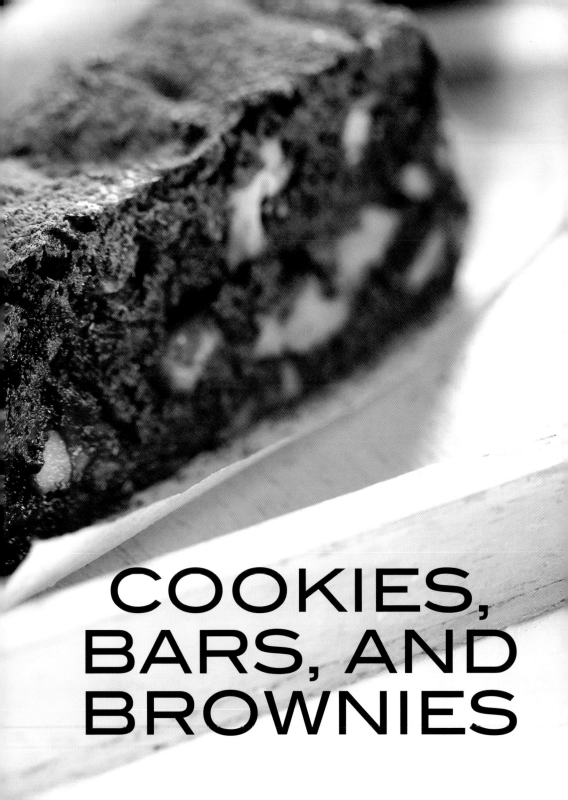

COOKIES, BARS, AND BROWNIES

OATMEAL AND RAISIN COOKIES

Preheat the oven to 350°F (180°C/gas 4). • Combine the flour, baking powder, nutmeg, and salt in a medium bowl. • **Step 1:** Line two large cookie sheets with parchment paper. • **Step 2:** Beat the butter and sugar either by hand or with an electric mixer on medium speed until pale and creamy. • Add the eggs one at a time, beating until just combined. • Stir in the mixed dry ingredients by hand until just combined. Stir in the rolled oats and raisins by hand. • **Step 3:** Scoop heaped tablespoons of cookie dough and roll into balls. Place on the prepared cookie sheets spacing about 2 inches (5 cm) apart. Flatten the cookies slightly with the tines of a fork dipped in cold water. • Bake for 18–22 minutes, until pale golden brown. Rotate the cookie sheets halfway through the cooking time for even baking. • **Step 4:** Cool the cookies on the sheets until slightly firm, about 3 minutes. • Use a metal spatula to transfer to wire racks to cool completely.

1²/₃ cups (250 g) all-purpose (plain) flour

½ teaspoon baking powder

¼ teaspoon ground nutmeg

¼ teaspoon salt

1 cup (250 g) unsalted butter softened

1 cup (200 g) sugar

2 large eggs

3 cups (270 g) old-fashioned rolled oats

1½ cups (140 g) raisins

Makes: About 30 cookies
Preparation: 15 minutes
Cooking: 18–22 minutes
Level: 1

■ PREPARING DROP COOKIES

These are basic drop cookies, the easiest and quickest type of cookie to make at home. Follow these steps for perfect results. Do not overbake these cookies—they should be just slightly chewy. Most cookies are made with all-purpose (plain) flour. Today's flour doesn't require sifting for perfect cookies (but you may sift the flour and other dry ingredients together, if preferred).

1. LINE two large cookie sheets with parchment paper.

2. BEAT the butter and sugar by hand or electric mixer on medium speed until creamy. Add the eggs one at a time,. Stir in the dry ingredients, rolled oats and raisins by hand.

3. FLATTEN the cookies slightly with the tines of a fork dipped in cold water.

4. COOL on the baking sheets until slightly firm, about 3 minutes. Use a metal spatula to transfer to wire racks to cool completely.

CHEWY GINGER COOKIES

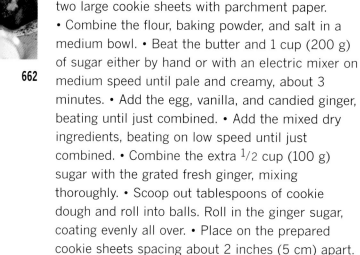

Preheat the oven to 375°F (190°C/gas 5). • Line two large cookie sheets with parchment paper. • Combine the flour, baking powder, and salt in a medium bowl. • Beat the butter and 1 cup (200 g) of sugar either by hand or with an electric mixer on medium speed until pale and creamy, about 3 minutes. • Add the egg, vanilla, and candied ginger, beating until just combined. • Add the mixed dry ingredients, beating on low speed until just combined. • Combine the extra 1/2 cup (100 g) sugar with the grated fresh ginger, mixing thoroughly. • Scoop out tablespoons of cookie dough and roll into balls. Roll in the ginger sugar, coating evenly all over. • Place on the prepared cookie sheets spacing about 2 inches (5 cm) apart. Flatten the cookies slightly with the tines of a fork dipped in the ginger sugar. • Bake for 15–18 minutes, until golden brown and just set in the centers. Rotate the cookie sheets halfway through the cooking time for even baking. • Cool the cookies on the sheets until slightly firm, about 3 minutes. Use a metal spatula to transfer to wire racks to cool completely.

2	cups (300 g) all-purpose (plain) flour
1	teaspoon baking powder
1/4	teaspoon salt
1	cup (250 g) unsalted butter, softened
1	cup (200 g) sugar + 1/2 cup (100 g) for rolling
1	large egg
1 1/2	teaspoons vanilla extract (essence)
3	tablespoons finely chopped candied (glacé) ginger
2	teaspoons finely grated fresh ginger

Makes: About 30 cookies
Preparation: 15 minutes
Cooking: 15–18 minutes
Level: 1

SNICKERDOODLES

664

Preheat the oven to 400°F (200°C/gas 6). • Line two large cookie sheets with parchment paper. • Combine the flour, cream of tartar, baking soda, and salt in a medium bowl. • Beat the butter and 1 1/2 cups (300 g) sugar either by hand or with an electric mixer on medium speed until pale and creamy. • Add the eggs one at a time, beating until just combined. • Add the mixed dry ingredients, beating on low speed until just combined. • Combine the extra 4 tablespoons sugar with the cinnamon, mixing thoroughly. • Scoop out tablespoons of cookie dough and roll into balls. Roll in the cinnamon sugar, coating evenly all over. • Place on the prepared cookie sheets spacing about 2 inches (5 cm) apart. • Bake for 10–12 minutes, until light golden and just set in the centers. Rotate the cookie sheets halfway through the cooking time for even baking. • Cool the cookies on the sheets until slightly firm, about 3 minutes. Use a metal spatula to transfer to wire racks to cool completely.

2 1/3 cups (350 g) all-purpose (plain) flour

2 teaspoons cream of tartar

1 teaspoon baking soda (bicarbonate of soda)

1/4 teaspoon salt

1 cup (250 g) unsalted butter, softened

1 1/2 cups (300 g) sugar + 1/2 cup (100 g) extra, for rolling

2 large eggs

2 tablespoons ground cinnamon

Makes: About 30 cookies
Preparation: 15 minutes
Cooking: 10–12 minutes
Level: 1

▩ ▩ ▩ *Snickerdoodles are a classic, old-fashioned New England cookie. No one quite knows the origin of the name (although there are many theories), but the cookies are believed to be of German or Dutch origin.*

CRISP CHOCOLATE CHIP COOKIES

666

Preheat the oven to 375°F (190°C/gas 5). • Line three large cookie sheets with parchment paper. • Combine the flour, baking soda, and salt in a medium bowl. • Beat the melted butter, both sugars, and corn syrup either by hand or with an electric mixer on medium speed until creamy. • Add the egg yolk, milk, and vanilla, beating until just combined. • Add the mixed dry ingredients, beating on low speed until just combined. Stir in the chocolate chips by hand. • Scoop out scant tablespoons of cookie dough and roll into balls. Place on the prepared cookie sheets spacing about 2 inches (5 cm) apart.• Bake for 10–12 minutes, until deep golden brown. Rotate the cookie sheets halfway through the cooking time for even baking. • Cool the cookies on the sheets until slightly firm, about 3 minutes. Use a metal spatula to transfer to wire racks to cool completely.

1²⁄₃ cups (250 g) all-purpose (plain) flour

1 teaspoon baking soda (bicarbonate of soda)

¹⁄₄ teaspoon salt

¹⁄₂ cup (125 g) unsalted butter, melted and cooled

¹⁄₂ cup (100 g) sugar

¹⁄₂ cup (100 g) firmly packed light brown sugar

2 tablespoons light corn (golden) syrup

1 large egg yolk

3 tablespoons milk

1 tablespoon vanilla extract (essence)

1 cup (180 g) dark chocolate chips

Makes: About 40 cookies
Preparation: 15 minutes
Cooking: 10–12 minutes
Level: 1

CHEWY DOUBLE-CHOCOLATE COOKIES

Combine the flour, cocoa, baking powder, and salt in a medium bowl. • Melt the chocolate in a double-boiler over barely simmering water. Set aside. • Beat the eggs and vanilla in a small bowl. Set aside. • Beat the butter and both sugars either by hand or with an electric mixer on medium speed until creamy. • Gradually beat in the egg mixture and then the chocolate. • Gradually add the mixed dry ingredients, beating on low speed until just combined. • Cover the bowl with plastic wrap (cling film) and let stand at room temperature for 20 minutes. • Preheat the oven to 350°F (180°C/gas 4). • Line three large cookie sheets with parchment paper. Scoop out heaped tablespoons of cookie dough and roll into balls. Place on the prepared cookie sheets spacing about 2 inches (5 cm) apart. • Bake for 10–12 minutes, until the edges have just begun to set but the centers are still soft. Rotate the cookie sheets halfway through the cooking time for even baking. • Cool the cookies on the sheets until slightly firm, about 10 minutes. • Slide the parchment paper with the cookies onto a wire rack to cool completely. Remove the cooled cookies from the parchment paper using a metal spatula.

2 cups (300 g) all-purpose (plain) flour

1/2 cup (75 g) unsweetened cocoa powder

2 teaspoons baking powder

1/2 teaspoon salt

1 pound (500 g) dark chocolate, chopped

4 large eggs

2 teaspoons vanilla extract (essence)

2/3 cup (150 g) unsalted butter, softened

11/2 cups (300 g) firmly packed light brown sugar

1/2 cup (100 g) sugar

Makes: About 36 cookies
Preparation: 15 minutes
  + 20 minutes to stand
Cooking: 10–12 minutes
Level: 1

PEANUT BUTTER COOKIES

Preheat the oven to 350°F (180°C/gas 4). • Line three large cookie sheets with parchment paper. • Combine the flour, baking soda, baking powder, and salt in a medium bowl. • Beat the butter, both sugars, and vanilla either by hand or with an electric mixer on medium speed until creamy. • Beat in the peanut butter. • Add the eggs one at a time, beating until just combined. • Stir in the mixed dry ingredients by hand until just combined. Stir in the peanuts by hand. • Scoop heaped tablespoons of cookie dough and roll into balls. Place on the prepared cookie sheets spacing about 2 inches (5 cm) apart. Flatten the cookies slightly with the tines of a fork dipped in cold water. • Bake for 10–12 minutes, until puffed and light golden brown. Rotate the cookie sheets halfway through the cooking time for even baking. • Cool the cookies on the sheets until slightly firm, about 3 minutes. Use a metal spatula to transfer to wire racks to cool completely.

2¹⁄₃ cups (350 g) all-purpose (plain) flour

½ teaspoon baking soda (bicarbonate of soda)

½ teaspoon baking powder

½ teaspoon salt

1 cup (250 g) unsalted butter, softened

1 cup (200 g) firmly packed light brown sugar

1 cup (200 g) sugar

2 teaspoons vanilla extract (essence)

1 cup (250 g) crunchy peanut butter

2 large eggs

1 cup (180 g) dry-roasted peanuts, coarsely chopped

Makes: About 42 cookies
Preparation: 15 minutes
Cooking: 10–12 minutes
Level: 1

CANESTRELLI

672

Combine the flour and salt in a large bowl. Use your fingertips to rub in the butter until the mixture resembles coarse crumbs. • Stir in the sugar. • Make a well in the center and add the eggs and vanilla. Mix to make a soft dough. Cover the bowl with a clean kitchen towel and let rest for 1 hour. Preheat the oven to 350°F (180°C/gas 4). • Line four cookie sheets with parchment paper. • Roll out the dough on a lightly floured surface to $1/2$ inch (1 cm) thick. Cut out the cookies using different-shaped cookie cutters: stars, flowers, and half-moons. • Use a spatula to transfer them to the prepared cookie sheets. Brush with the lightly beaten egg white. • Bake for 20 minutes, or until golden brown. Rotate the cookie sheets halfway through the cooking time for even baking. • Let cool on the baking sheets for 3 minutes, then transfer to wire racks to cool completely. • Dust with a thick coating of confectioners' sugar just before serving.

$3^{1}/3$ cups (500 g) all-purpose (plain) flour

1 teaspoon salt

$1^{2}/3$ cups (400 g) unsalted butter, softened

1 cup (200 g) sugar

3 large eggs + 1 large egg white, lightly beaten

2 teaspoons vanilla extract (essence)

1 cup (150 g) confectioners' (icing) sugar, to dust

Makes: About 50 cookies
Preparation: 15 minutes
   + 1 hour to rest
Cooking: 20 minutes
Level: 1

▨ ▨ ▨ *Canestrelli are Italian cookies from the Liguria region, in the northwest. Dust generously with confectioners' sugar and serve with coffee.*

WHITE CHOCOLATE FLORENTINES

Preheat the oven to 325°F (170°C/gas 3). • Line four cookie sheets with parchment paper. • Heat the cream with the vanilla pod, butter, and sugar in a medium saucepan over medium heat, stirring constantly, until the sugar has dissolved. Bring to a boil and remove from the heat immediately. Discard the vanilla pod and let cool. • Mix the almonds, hazelnuts, candied peel, cherries, angelica, and flour in a large bowl. • Stir in the cooled cream mixture and mix well. • Drop heaped teaspoons of the mixture 4 inches (10 cm) apart onto the prepared cookie sheets, spreading them to make 2 inch (5 cm) circles. Do not place more than five cookies on one sheet. • Bake, one sheet at a time, for 10–12 minutes, or until golden around the edges. Rotate the cookie sheets halfway through the cooking time for even baking. • Cool on the sheets until the cookies firm slightly. Transfer to racks and let cool completely. • Melt the white chocolate in a double boiler over barely simmering water. • Lay the cold florentines flat-side upward on a sheet of parchment paper, and brush the chocolate over them with a pastry brush. For a thick coating, paint the cookies several times. Let set before serving.

½ cup (125 ml) heavy (double) cream

¼ vanilla pod

2 tablespoons butter

½ cup (100 g) sugar

½ cup (50 g) coarsely chopped almonds

¼ cup (30 g) coarsely chopped hazelnuts

1 cup (100 g) finely chopped mixed candied peel

¼ cup (25 g) finely sliced red candied (glacé) cherries

1 tablespoons finely chopped candied (glacé) angelica

2 tablespoons all-purpose (plain) flour

8 ounces (250 g) white chocolate, coarsely chopped

Makes: 18–20 cookies
Preparation: 45 minutes
Cooking: 10–12 minutes
Level: 3

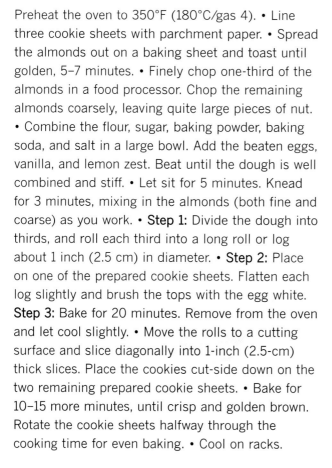

PRATO BISCOTTI

Preheat the oven to 350°F (180°C/gas 4). • Line three cookie sheets with parchment paper. • Spread the almonds out on a baking sheet and toast until golden, 5–7 minutes. • Finely chop one-third of the almonds in a food processor. Chop the remaining almonds coarsely, leaving quite large pieces of nut. • Combine the flour, sugar, baking powder, baking soda, and salt in a large bowl. Add the beaten eggs, vanilla, and lemon zest. Beat until the dough is well combined and stiff. • Let sit for 5 minutes. Knead for 3 minutes, mixing in the almonds (both fine and coarse) as you work. • **Step 1:** Divide the dough into thirds, and roll each third into a long roll or log about 1 inch (2.5 cm) in diameter. • **Step 2:** Place on one of the prepared cookie sheets. Flatten each log slightly and brush the tops with the egg white. **Step 3:** Bake for 20 minutes. Remove from the oven and let cool slightly. • Move the rolls to a cutting surface and slice diagonally into 1-inch (2.5-cm) thick slices. Place the cookies cut-side down on the two remaining prepared cookie sheets. • Bake for 10–15 more minutes, until crisp and golden brown. Rotate the cookie sheets halfway through the cooking time for even baking. • Cool on racks.

1½ cups (200 g) whole unblanched almonds

2 cups (300 g) all-purpose (plain) flour

½ cup (100 g) sugar

½ teaspoon baking powder

½ teaspoon baking soda (bicarbonate of soda)

¼ teaspoon salt

3 large eggs, lightly beaten

1 teaspoon vanilla extract (essence)

1 teaspoon finely grated lemon zest

1 large egg white, lightly beaten

Makes: About 24 cookies
Preparation: 40 minutes
Cooking: 35–40 minutes
Level: 2

◾ PREPARING BISCOTTI

Biscotti are delicious and chewy Italian cookies. They get their name, and their chewiness, from being cooked twice: *bi* (meaning twice) and *cotti* (cooked). Prato cookies come from the city of Prato, which is right next door to Florence. They are traditionally served with a glass of *vin santo* (holy wine) for dunking.

1. DIVIDE the dough into thirds, and roll each third into a long roll or log about 1 inch (2.5 cm) in diameter.

2. PLACE on one of the prepared cookie sheets. Flatten each log slightly and brush the tops with the egg white.

3. BAKE for 20 minutes. Remove from the oven and let cool slightly. Move the rolls to a cutting surface and slice diagonally 1-inch (2.5-cm) thick. Place the cookies on the two remaining prepared cookie sheets to finish baking.

DOUBLE CHOCOLATE BISCOTTI

Preheat the oven to 325°F (170°C/gas 3). • Line three cookie sheets with parchment paper. • Combine the flour, cocoa, baking powder, and salt in a medium bowl. • Beat the butter and sugar in a large bowl with an electric mixer at high speed until creamy. • Add the vanilla and eggs, beating until just blended. • Mix in the dry ingredients, walnuts, and chocolate to form a stiff dough. • Divide the dough in half. • Form the dough into two 12-inch (30-cm) logs and place 3 inches (8 cm) apart on one prepared cookie sheet, flattening the tops. • Bake for 20 minutes, or until firm to the touch. • Transfer to a cutting board to cool for 15 minutes. • Cut on the diagonal into 1-inch (2.5-cm) thick slices. • Arrange the slices cut-side down on the remaining two prepared cookie sheets and bake for 10–15 minutes more, until crisp. Rotate the cookie sheets halfway through the cooking time for even baking. • Cool on racks.

2½ cups (375 g) all-purpose (plain) flour

¾ cup (125 g) unsweetened cocoa powder

2 teaspoons baking powder

¼ teaspoons salt

½ cup (125 g) butter, softened

1½ cups (250 g) sugar

½ teaspoons vanilla extract (essence)

3 large eggs

1 cup (100 g) coarsely chopped walnuts

1 cup (180 g) dark chocolate chips

Makes: About 36 cookies
Preparation: 40 minutes
Cooking: 30–35 minutes
Level: 2

LADY KISSES

Cookies: Preheat the oven to 300°F (150°C/gas 2). • Line two cookie sheets with parchment paper. • Beat the butter and sugar in a large bowl with an electric mixer at high speed until pale and creamy. • Use a large rubber spatula to fold in the hazelnuts, flour, and salt. Shape into balls the size of walnuts. • Place on the prepared cookie sheets spacing about 2 inches (5 cm) apart. • Bake for 25–30 minutes, or until lightly browned. Rotate the cookie sheets halfway through the cooking time for even baking. • Cool completely on a rack.

Filling: Melt the chocolate in a double boiler over barely simmering water. Remove from the heat. • Heat the cream in a small saucepan until warm. Stir the warm cream into the melted chocolate and continue mixing until cooled. • Spread the filling onto half the cookies. Join the halves together.

Cookies

7	tablespoons (105 g) butter, softened
$3/4$	cup (150 g) superfine (caster) sugar
$1^{1}/4$	cups (150 g) hazelnuts, toasted and finely ground
$3/4$	cup (125 g) all-purpose (plain) flour
$1/4$	teaspoon salt

Filling

8	ounces (180 g) dark chocolate
$2/3$	cup (150 ml) heavy (double) cream

Makes: About 20 cookies
Preparation: 20 minutes
Cooking: 40–45 minutes
Level: 1

■ ■ ■ *These Italian cookies are known as* Baci di dame *in their homeland. The hazelnuts go beautifully with the dark chocolate, but you can also make them with a white chocolate filling.*

FRENCH MACAROONS

Vanilla Macaroons: Line two large cookie sheets with parchment paper. • Combine the confectioners' sugar and ground almonds in a food processor and blend to make a fine powder. • Pass the almond mixture twice through a fine-mesh sieve. Discard any large particles. • Place 3 ounces (90 g) of the egg whites and salt in a medium bowl and beat with an electric mixer on medium speed until soft peaks begin to form. • Gradually add the superfine sugar until it is all incorporated and the mixture is thick and glossy. • Add the almond mixture and stir to combine. Stir in the remaining egg white. • Spoon the mixture into a piping bag fitted with a $1/2$-inch (1-cm) piping nozzle. Pipe 1-inch (2.5-cm) disks onto the prepared baking sheets. Set aside until a thin crust begins to form on top of the disks, 4–5 hours. Gently touch the surface of the disks with your finger and when the mixture does not stick they are ready. • Meanwhile, preheat the oven to 275°F (140°C/gas 1.) • Bake for 10–15 minutes, until firm, but not colored. Remove from the oven and set aside to cool.

Vanilla Ganache: Place the cream, chocolate, and vanilla bean paste in a small heatproof bowl and melt over a saucepan of barely simmering water, stirring frequently, until smooth. • Chill in the refrigerator for 20 minutes, stirring occasionally until cooled and thickened. • Spread or pipe the ganache onto half of the macaroons and sandwich together.

Vanilla Macaroons

- $3/4$ cup (125 g) confectioners' (icing) sugar
- 1 cup (100 g) ground almonds
- 1-2 ($3^{1}/2$ ounces/100 g) egg whites, left at room temperature for 24 hours
- $1/4$ teaspoon salt
- $1/3$ cup (70 g) superfine (caster) sugar

Vanilla Ganache

- $1/2$ cup (125 ml) light (single) cream
- 4 ounces (120 g) white chocolate, coarsely chopped
- $1/4$ teaspoon vanilla bean paste

Makes: About 40 macaroons
Preparation: 30 minutes + 4–5 hours to rest
Cooking: 10–15 minutes
Level: 3

Pistachio Macaroons: Replace the ground almonds with the same amount of ground pistachios.
For the ganache: omit the vanilla bean paste and add 2 teaspoons of finely ground pistachios and a few drops of green food coloring.

Chocolate Macaroons: Replace the ground almonds with 3 ounces (90 g) of ground hazelnuts and 2 tablespoons unsweetened cocoa powder.
For the ganache: replace the white chocolate with dark chocolate and omit the vanilla bean paste.

■ ■ ■ *French macaroons make an attractive and superb-tasting dessert and are great with tea or coffee. They can be flavored and colored to make a rainbow array of cookies. Here you will find the recipes for classic vanilla, pistachio, and chocolate macaroons.*

CHINESE ALMOND COOKIES

Preheat the oven to 350°F (180°C/gas 4). • Line two baking sheets with parchment paper. • Combine the flour, baking powder, and baking soda in a medium bowl. • Beat the butter and sugar in a medium bowl with an electric mixer at high speed until pale and creamy. • Add the egg and almond extract and beat until incorporated. • With mixer on low, gradually add the mixed dry ingredients, beating until just combined. • Shape the dough into 30 balls.
• Arrange the balls on the prepared baking sheets, spacing them 1 inch (2.5 cm) apart. Press your thumb in the center of each cookie to make an indent and place an almond in the hollow. • Bake for 10–15 minutes, until golden brown. Rotate the cookie sheets halfway through the cooking time for even baking. • Cool on the sheets until the cookies firm slightly. Transfer to racks and let cool completely.

2½ cups (450 g) all-purpose (plain) flour

½ teaspoon baking powder

½ teaspoon baking soda (bicarbonate of soda)

6 ounces (180 g) butter, softened

¾ cup (150 g) superfine (caster) sugar

1 large egg, lightly beaten

1 teaspoon almond extract (essence)

30 whole blanched almonds to decorate

Makes: 30 cookies
Preparation: 15 minutes
Cooking: 10–15 minutes
Level: 1

■ ■ ■ *These simple butter cookies are a classic in Chinese American baking. They are served at Chinese New Year and are believed to bring riches and good luck. Serve them with tea or coffee at any time.*

POLVORONES

Preheat the oven to 350°F (180°C/gas 4).• Line two cookie sheets with parchment paper. • Sift the flour and cinnamon into a medium bowl. • Chop the almonds in a food processor to make fine crumbs. Add to the flour and stir to combine. • Beat the butter and sugar in a medium bowl with an electric mixer at high speed until pale and creamy. • With mixer on low, gradually add the flour mixture, beating until just combined. • Shape the dough into 25 balls. • Place the balls on the prepared baking sheets, spacing them 1-inch (2.5 cm) apart. Gently press the balls to flatten slightly. • Bake for 20–25 minutes, until golden brown. Rotate the cookie sheets halfway through the cooking time for even baking. • Cool on the sheets until the cookies firm slightly. Transfer to racks and let cool completely. • Dust generously with confectioners' sugar just before serving.

2 cups (300 g) all-purpose (plain) flour

1 teaspoon ground cinnamon

1 cup (150 g) blanched almonds, lightly toasted

8 ounces (250 g) butter, softened

½ cup (100 g) superfine (caster) sugar

1 cup (150 g) confectioners' (icing) sugar to dust

Makes: 25 cookies
Preparation: 15 minutes
Cooking: 20–25 minutes
Level: 1

■ ■ ■ *These rich and crumbly butter and cinnamon cookies come from Mexico. They go by many names, including Mexican Sugar Cookies and Mexican Wedding Cakes. Polverones are also made in Spain and are especially popular at Christmas time.*

HEDGEHOG SLICE

Slice: Line an 8-inch (20 cm) square cake pan with aluminum foil, leaving plenty of foil overhanging the edges. • Stir the condensed milk and butter in a small saucepan over low heat until the butter melts. • Remove from the heat and add the vanilla. Sift in the cocoa, stirring to combine. • Combine the crushed cookies, walnuts, and coconut in a medium bowl. • Stir into the condensed milk mixture until well combined. • Spread the mixture in the prepared pan, smoothing the top with the back of a spoon to create a smooth surface. • Cover and refrigerate until firm, at least 4 hours.

Frosting: Sift the confectioners' sugar and cocoa into a small bowl. • Combine the water and butter in a small bowl. • Gradually pour the water mixture into the frosting, stirring until smooth. • Spread over the slice and refrigerate for 15 minutes to set. • Remove from the refrigerator and lift out onto a chopping board using the overhanging foil. • Dip a sharp knife into boiling water and cut the hedgehog slice into 24 squares.

▓ ▓ ▓ Hedgehog slice comes from Australia. It can be stored in an airtight container for up to a week.

Slice

1   cup (250 ml) sweetened condensed milk

¼   cup (60 g) butter

1   teaspoon vanilla extract (essence)

3   tablespoons unsweetened cocoa powder

2   cups (250 g) coarsely crushed plain sweet cookies (biscuits)

½   cup (60 g) walnuts, coarsely chopped

3   tablespoons shredded (desiccated) coconut

Frosting

1   cup (150 g) confectioners' (icing) sugar

2   tablespoons unsweetened cocoa powder

2   tablespoons boiling water

2   teaspoons butter

Makes: 24 pieces
Preparation: 15 minutes + 4 hours to set
Cooking: 5 minutes
Level: 1

GINGER CRUNCH

Ginger Crunch: Preheat the oven to 350°F (180°C/gas 4). • Line a rectangular 13 x 9 inch (32 x 23 cm) baking pan with aluminum foil, leaving plenty of foil overhanging the edges. • Beat the butter and sugar in a medium bowl with an electric mixer on high speed until pale and creamy. • With mixer on low speed, beat in the flour, ginger, and baking powder and until a dough begins to form. • Turn out onto a clean work surface and knead to fully combine. • Press the dough into the prepared baking pan, smoothing with the back of a spoon to create an even surface. • Bake for 15–20 minutes, until golden brown. • Set aside on a rack.

Frosting: Combine the confectioners' sugar and ginger in a small saucepan. Add the corn syrup and butter and warm over low heat, stirring occasionally, until the butter and syrup have melted together to form a frosting. • Pour over the warm base, tilting the pan slightly to spread evenly. • Cover and set aside in a cool place until set, about 4 hours. • Lift out onto a clean chopping board using the overhanging foil. • Dip a sharp knife into boiling water and cut the ginger crunch into 24 squares.

Ginger Crunch

- ⅔ cup (150 g) butter, softened
- ½ cup (100 g) superfine (caster) sugar
- 2 cups (300 g) all-purpose (plain) flour
- 2 teaspoons ground ginger
- 1 teaspoon baking powder

Frosting

- 2 cups (300 g) confectioners' (icing) sugar
- 2 tablespoons ground ginger
- 4 tablespoons light corn (golden) syrup
- ½ cup (125 g) butter, cubed

Makes: 24 pieces
Preparation: 20 minutes
Cooking: 15–20 minutes
Level: 1

▨ ▨ ▨ Ginger Crunch is a recipe from New Zealand. It can be stored in an airtight container for up to a week.

CHOCOLATE AND WALNUT FUDGE BROWNIE

Preheat the oven to 350°F (180°C/gas 4). • Line a 7 x 9 inch (18 x 23 cm) baking pan with parchment paper. • Stir the chocolate, butter, and cream in a double boiler over barely simmering water until smooth. • Beat the brown sugar, eggs, and vanilla with an electric mixer on medium speed until thick. • Gradually add the chocolate mixture, stirring to combine. • Stir in the flour, baking powder, and salt. Add the walnuts and stir to combine. • Spoon the mixture into the prepared pan. Smooth with the back of a spoon to create an even surface. • Bake for 25–35 minutes, or until firm to the touch. When tested with skewer the center should be moist but not raw. Do not overbake. • Remove from the oven and set aside to cool in the pan. • Remove the brownie from the pan and place on a clean chopping board. Cut into sixteen pieces and dust with cocoa powder. • Serve, with whipped cream, if desired.

12 ounces (350 g) top quality dark chocolate, coarsely chopped

½ cup (125 g) butter, cubed

¼ cup (60 ml) heavy (double) cream

1½ cups (300 g) firmly packed brown sugar

3 large eggs

1 teaspoons vanilla extract (essence)

¾ cup (110 g) all-purpose (plain) flour

½ teaspoon baking powder

¼ teaspoon salt

¾ cup (90 g) walnuts, coarsely chopped

Unsweetened cocoa powder to dust

Whipped cream to serve (optional)

Makes: 16 brownies
Preparation: 15 minutes
Cooking: 25–35 minutes
Level: 1

BLONDIES

Preheat the oven to 350°F (180°C/gas 4). • Line a 7 x 9-inch (18 x 23-cm) baking pan with parchment paper. • Stir the chocolate and butter in a double boiler over barely simmering water until smooth. Combine the flour, baking powder, cinnamon, and salt in a medium bowl. • Beat the sugar, eggs, and vanilla in a large bowl with an electric mixer on medium-high speed until pale and thick. • With mixer on low, gradually add the chocolate, beating to combine. Beat in the mixed dry ingredients. • Spoon the mixture into the prepared pan and spread out evenly. • Bake for 25–35 minutes, or until firm to the touch. When tested with skewer the center should be moist but not raw. Do not overbake. • Remove from the oven and set aside to cool in the pan. • Remove the brownie from the pan and place on a clean chopping board. Cut into 16 pieces and dust with confectioners' sugar.

8 ounces (250 g) white chocolate, coarsely chopped

½ cup (125 g) butter, cubed

1¼ cups (180 g) all-purpose (plain) flour

½ teaspoon baking powder

½ teaspoon ground cinnamon

¼ teaspoon salt

½ cup (100 g) firmly packed light brown sugar

4 large eggs, lightly beaten

1 teaspoon vanilla extract (essence)

Confectioners' (icing) sugar to dust

Makes: 16 brownies
Preparation: 15 minutes
Cooking: 25–35 minutes
Level: 1

Index

Breads

Cakes and Pies

Cookies, Brownies and Bars

VEGETABLES